The M&A Failure Trap

*Why Most Mergers and Acquisitions
Fail and How the Few Succeed*

BARUCH LEV
FENG GU

WILEY

Published by John Wiley & Sons, Inc., Hoboken, New Jersey.
Published simultaneously in Canada.

For general information on our other products and services or for technical support, please contact our Customer Care Department within the United States at (800) 762-2974, outside the United States at (317) 572-3993 or fax (317) 572-4002.

Wiley also publishes its books in a variety of electronic formats. Some content that appears in print may not be available in electronic formats. For more information about Wiley products, visit our web site at www.wiley.com.

Library of Congress Cataloging-in-Publication Data

Names: Lev, Baruch, author. | Gu, Feng, 1968- author.
Title: The M&A failure trap : why most mergers and acquisitions fail and how the few succeed / Baruch Lev and Feng Gu.
Description: Hoboken, New Jersey : Wiley, [2025] | Series: Wiley finance series | Includes bibliographical references and index.
Identifiers: LCCN 2024031604 (print) | LCCN 2024031605 (ebook) | ISBN 9781394204762 (hardback) | ISBN 9781394204786 (adobe pdf) | ISBN 9781394204779 (epub)
Subjects: LCSH: Consolidation and merger of corporations. | Success in business.
Classification: LCC HD2746.5 .L47 2024 (print) | LCC HD2746.5 (ebook) | DDC 658.1/6—dc23/eng/20240809
LC record available at https://lccn.loc.gov/2024031604
LC ebook record available at https://lccn.loc.gov/2024031605

Cover Design: Wiley
Cover Image: Just_Super/Getty Images
Author Photos: Courtesy of author
SKY10085720_092324

Contents

You surely have heard about mergers and acquisitions
(M&As) – the largest and most consequential investments companies make, but you probably weren't aware
that most of them (70–75%) fail to meet expectations,
and it's getting worse. You should be aware of this
destructive phenomenon, its wide-ranging adverse consequences, and the ways to avoid it, all outlined in detail
in this fully evidence-based book.

We open this book with a bird's-eye view of the M&A
scene – a discussion of three highly consequential
acquisitions: a smashing success ("the good"), a
resounding failure ("the bad"), and an embarrassing
fiasco ("the ugly"). We draw important preliminary
lessons from these three acquisitions in this chapter.

M&As today are nothing like those of yore, and
understanding the historical trends of M&A is crucial
for improving acquisition decisions. This chapter focuses
on changes in merger characteristics, like the large
increase in the almost extinct conglomerate (business-
unrelated) acquisitions and their hazards, and the steep
rise in acquisition prices (premia).

This chapter continues the historical analysis of the preceding one, focusing on the growth of M&As in recent decades (numbers and volume), the increasing impact of technology acquisitions, and the perplexing deterioration in the profitability of buyers, which doesn't bode well for the success of acquisitions.

Practically every business capability acquired by mergers, such as research and development (R&D) capacity, patents, trademarks, brands, new customers, etc., can be developed internally by companies. There are, of course, different costs, uncertainties, and time to market involved in the choice between acquisitions and internal development, which we discuss. We document that the benefits of internal development far exceed those of acquisitions, and therefore, here is our advice: don't rush to acquire businesses before you fully consider the alternatives.

Conglomerates – entities composed of business-unrelated units – fell from grace in the 1980s to the early 2000s because they are devoid of business logic, but came back in the past 10–15 years, particularly among tech buyers. Is this a new trend or a resumption of an old folly?

The M&A literature is replete with claims that there are opportune times to acquire businesses: buy when capital markets are hot, or when your industry peers are buying. Buy during recessions when target prices are low. We analyze empirically, using our sample of 40,000 acquisitions, the consequences of acquiring businesses during those "opportune times," and find most of them to lead to failed acquisitions. In M&As, avoid the "wisdom of the crowds."

We continue our examination of the alleged "good times to buy," focusing on internal opportunities, like a new chief executive officer (CEO) taking the helm, or a business reorganization. We document once more that these buying "opportunities" are illusory, and establish empirically the *really* good acquisitions opportunities.

Integrating the target with the buyer comes at the conclusion of the acquisition process, when the major players – CEO and chief financial officer (CFO) – return to their regular work. The hard and crucial integration is often left to staff and consultants. Consequently, target integration is where most acquisitions fail. To assure successful integration we provide you in this chapter with an evidence-based list of "integration risk factors," like the target is a foreign entity, to enable you to plan and assign the needed personnel for a successful integration and acquisition.

Corporate quarterly and annual financial reports – income statements, balance sheets, and cash flow statements – are jolted by acquisitions. The consolidation of the buyer with the target's accounts changes almost everything. Items with strange names, like *goodwill* and *in-process R&D* appear on the buyer's balance sheet, and comparability with the past (like sales growth) is distorted. We explain all this in this chapter, and draw your attention to important information you can obtain from the post-acquisition financial reports.

"Prepare the gallows." Well, maybe it's not that dramatic. A killer acquisition means that the buyer acquires, and then terminates the target to avoid competition with its own products or services. Such acquisitions aren't numerous, but they exist, and they seriously inhibit competition and innovation. We offer a better way to avoid the kill.

We provide evidence that buyers (like many securities investors) hold on to lost-case targets for too long. Unfortunately, there are strong incentives for managers to do this, but the consequences are grievous: a waste of managerial time and a diminution of the target's salvage value. We propose ways to avoid this managerial distraction and corporate loss.

It seems simple: if the buyer has enough cash on hand, it should use it to pay for the target; if not, pay with stocks. Not so fast. Turns out that the means of acquisition payment provides investors and the target's employees with a strong message about the success likelihood of the acquisition. The choice of acquisition means of payment should therefore be considered carefully by the buyer, using our guidelines.

In this and the following chapter we turn the light on the human element of acquisitions. Here we deal with proven cases where executives cater to their own needs, or follow misguided (irrational) policies, thereby harming shareholders. We focus on realigning the managerial incentives that will avoid such adverse behavior.

Surprisingly, acquisitions, even failed ones, extend significantly CEO tenure and pay. However, the penalty for unsuccessful acquisitions is generally light. Here you have a major reason for the unusually high rate of acquisition failure. As for employees, successful acquisitions increase significantly the buyers' headcount, but the widely touted synergies (employee efficiency gains) fail to show up in the data.

This is one of the most important chapters of the book. It appears at the end because it builds on many of the concepts and conclusions we presented earlier. In this chapter we provide a first-of-its-kind 10-factor score-card aimed at *predicting* the success likelihood of a given acquisition. This is a vital tool for executives and directors considering a merger candidate, and for investors asked to vote on merger proposals.

We conclude the book by pulling together the main findings and conclusions drawn from our empirical analysis regarding the major drivers of acquisition success. Here we outline what to do and not do in acquiring business.

As advertised, our book is totally evidence-based; it includes facts, rather than conjectures, opinions, or views. This evidence, permeating the book, is based on three pillars: a large (40,000) acquisitions sample, a comprehensive measure (indicator) of acquisition success, and a multivariate (43 factors) statistical estimation model aimed at identifying the major acquisition success drivers. Details of all this are provided in the appendix.

Preface

Corporate mergers and acquisitions, often the largest investment a company makes, fail to fulfill their expectations at an alarming rate of 70–75%. You wouldn't know this grim and highly damaging fact if you just followed the uniformly upbeat and enthusiastic merger announcements made by the acquiring and acquired executives, replete with highly optimistic promises of substantial synergies (cost savings), development of revolutionary products and services, or new markets to be penetrated by the proposed merger partners. Alas, most of those statements are sheer wishful thinking and sometimes hype, designed to garner investors' support for the merger. The fact, backed by our rigorous evidence, is that most mergers and acquisitions (M&As) fail, causing massive losses to shareholders of the acquiring companies, and serious dislocations to employees, customers, and suppliers. The acquisitions' high failure rate is a widespread, and still growing, debacle.

In this fully evidence-based book, we first empirically substantiate our contention that M&As are largely a "failure trap" and then unveil the reasons for the persistence and even increase in the disappointment from corporate acquisitions. Most of these failure drivers will surprise you. We then use a very large sample of 40,000 acquisitions, coupled with advanced statistical techniques to identify the major attributes of successful acquisitions, aimed at springing the M&A failure trap. Finally, we develop a first-of-its-kind and easy-to-use 10-factor scorecard designed to predict the success likelihood of a proposed acquisition, to be used by executives and directors currently considering a proposed acquisition, or by shareholders asked to vote on a merger proposal. Importantly, no technical or statistical knowledge is required to benefit from this book.

This book will be of considerable interest to corporate executives and directors, who will likely be involved in M&As during their careers; to investors asked to vote on merger proposals or who are considering investment in the acquiring companies; and to business professionals in general, economists, and university instructors interested in one of the most important and consequential economic events – business acquisitions.

We are grateful to Ms. Nancy Kleinrock for the outstanding and very helpful editing of this book, to Wiley's editors for guiding us through the book's publication process, and to Eli Amir, Rachel and Tom Corn, Elizabeth Demers, and Michael Mauboussin for helpful comments on parts of this book.

We sincerely hope that this unique and timely book will reverse the destructive path of corporate acquisitions.

Preamble: Why Should You Read This Book?

You probably believe that mergers and acquisitions (M&As) – often the largest investments companies make: think Exxon, paying $60B for Pioneer Natural Resources in October 2023, for example – are a boon for investors and employees, leading to new revenue and profit growth for the buying enterprise. How wrong. In fact, research shows that an astounding 70–75% of all acquisitions fail to live up to expectations, at shareholders' expense, of course. Sprint, the third largest U.S. wireless carrier, acquired Nextel, the fifth largest carrier, for $35B in February 2005. Executives of both companies waxed lyrical about the merger. Timothy Donahue, Nextel's chief executive officer (CEO), declared, "The new powerhouse company has the spectrum, infrastructure, distribution, superb and differentiated product portfolio that will drive our continued success." Cost savings of $12B were predicted from the merger. Alas, a mere three years later, Sprint wrote off – declared a loss of – $30B (86% of Nextel's acquisition price). This wasn't an aberration. It was more of the norm.

P.1 THE M&A FAILURE TRAP

A few are aware of this carnage. Warren Buffett, who knows a thing or two about corporate acquisitions, having done them all his professional life, declared metaphorically:

> Many managers apparently were overexposed in impressionable childhood years to the story in which the imprisoned handsome prince is released from a toad's body by a kiss from a beautiful princess. Consequently they are certain their managerial kiss will do wonders for the profitability of the company's [acquisition target]. . . . We have observed many kisses but very few miracles.

Nevertheless, many managerial princesses remain serenely confident about the future potency of their kisses – even after their corporate backyards are knee-deep in unresponsive toads.[1]

The valuation guru Aswath Damodaran (New York University) concurs: "If you look at the collective evidence across acquisitions, this is the most value-destructive action a company can take."[2] Harvard's late Clayton Christensen, of the "disruptive innovation" fame, reported that studies have documented an unbelievable M&A failure rate of 70–80%, while KPMG, a leading accounting firm, estimated more precisely the M&A failure rate at 83%.[3]

That "not acquiring" is often better than "acquiring" companies was demonstrated empirically by a clever academic study of contested (multibidder) acquisitions, where the successful corporate buyers were compared with the other, nonsuccessful bidders for the same targets. The researchers reported that the presumed "losers" – bidders that failed to buy the target – *outperformed* the "winners" by a substantial 25–30% risk-adjusted stock returns, over a three-year post-acquisition period. The researchers aptly titled their paper "Winning by Losing."[4]

The dismal performance of M&As, both in the United States and abroad, whether measured by buyers' post-acquisition sales and earnings growth or by their stock performance, did not go unnoticed by investors. In fact, in recent decades, a company's public announcement of a planned acquisition generally triggers a significant stock price *drop*, reflecting investors' dour expectations from the proposed acquisition. Thus, for example, on May 23, 2022, Broadcom announced its intention to acquire VMware for $60B and saw its stock price fall by 3% on the announcement day. Similarly, the stock price of Tapestry, which owns Coach, Kate Spade, and Stuart Weitzman brands, dropped by 15% on August 10, 2023, when it announced the acquisition of Capri Holdings, owner of Michael Kors, Versace, and Jimmy Choo, thereby reflecting deep investor concerns about the prudence of the acquisition and its terms.

---

[1] Buffett, W., 1981, Berkshire Hathaway, Annual Report. (Quoted by Malmendier and Tate, "Who Makes Acquisitions? CEO Overconfidence and the Market's Reaction," *Journal of Financial Economics* 89 no. 1 (2008): 20–43).
[2] Quoted from McCaffrey, P., 2019, "Aswath Damodaran on Acquisitions: Just Say No," CFA Institute, February, 28.
[3] Christensen, C., R. Alton, C. Rising, and A. Waldeck, "The Big Idea: The New M&A Playbook," *Harvard Business Review*, March (2011): 1–21.
[4] U. Malmendier, U., E., Moretti, and F. Peters, "Winning by Losing: Evidence on the Long-Term Effects of Mergers," *Review of Financial Studies* 31 (2018): 3212–3264.

Despite all that negativity, the pace of M&As does not abate; in fact, as we show in Chapter 3, it grows. And the architects of the mergers – CEOs of the buyers and targets – are as enthusiastic as ever about the mergers' prospects, uniformly predicting enticing synergies (cost savings) and fabulous revenue and earnings growth resulting from the mergers. How can this be? What's the basis for managers' continued trust in M&As, despite their dismal, proven record? Optimism in the face of destruction? That's one of the major questions we ask and answer in this book, which is fully evidence-based, using a sample of more than 40,000 actual acquisitions, analyzed by advanced statistical techniques. The answers will highly surprise you.

But we do much more in this book. We identify the *major reasons* for the success or failure of corporate acquisitions, many of which have not been highlighted or discussed in the vast extant literature and advice available on M&As. To top it all off, we develop in Chapter 15 of this book a unique, numerical *M&A scorecard*, aimed at assessing (predicting) the potential success of a specific acquisition, for the use of executives considering a merger proposal, corporate directors overseeing managers' decisions, and investors, who are sometimes asked to vote on a proposed merger or who want to make investment decisions regarding the merger partners.

Addressing these three major issues – explaining the persistence of the M&A phenomenon in spite of its harsh failure rate, identifying the major factors determining an acquisition's success, and developing a predictive numerical scorecard assessing merger consequences – should be of major interest to every businessperson, corporate manager, director, investor, economist, and business student, given the centrality of M&As in the economy and corporate success. Intriguingly, the urgency to address the merger growth conundrum is even greater, given our following finding that acquisition consequences deteriorate over time – a matter that is reported here for the first time.

P.2   M&A DECISIONS ARE GETTING WORSE

Do executives learn at least from their failures? The *Wall Street Journal* thinks so, quoting merger advisers: "Companies can get better at doing successful mergers and acquisitions."[5] Perhaps they *can*, but they do not. M&As defy the universal *learning curve rule*: rather than benefiting from experience and improving their M&A decisions and consequences, executives' acquisition decisions are in fact *getting worse* over time. They are "unlearning," rather than learning. Using likely the largest sample assembled for

---

[5] Dummet, B., 2023, "It's far from a sure thing," *Wall Street Journal*, September 17.

M&A research – more than 40,000 deals conducted over 40 years[6]—along with a comprehensive *merger success measure* that we developed, reflecting both the financial (sales and gross margin growth) and market (stock returns) dimensions of acquisition success, we found that the M&A success rate over the past 40 years was roughly one out of three, falling recently to one out of four, largely in line with previous research.[7]

What we find startling, however, is the "reverse learning" (forgetting?) phenomenon exhibited in Figure 1,[8] which portrays the average annual failure rate of M&As. The figure shows clearly that the merger failure rate is *trending upward*. From typical 50–60% acquisitions failure rates in the 1980s and 1990s, the failure rate (buyers' post-acquisition financial and stock market performance lagging pre-acquisition performance) rose to 60–75% in the 2000s (for the sake of conservatism we eliminated from the figure the financial crisis years, 2006 and 2007, due to unusually high acquisition failure rate of 85–90% in those years). The regression trend line in the figure, reflecting the overall failure pattern, is significantly upward-sloping, indicating the *decreasing quality* of corporate M&A decisions over time. A slight improvement occurred in the post financial crisis years.

And yet, one hears from time to time, particularly from investment bankers and M&A consultants, that corporate acquisition decisions have been improved over the past decade or two.[9] So here is out of the mouths of (not babes, but) corporate managers their view of the quality of the M&A decisions they have made in the past 20 years. Figure 2 presents both the number and total volume of annual "goodwill write-off" (impairments) declared during 2003–2022. A goodwill write-off (fully explained

---

[6] There were, of course, many more M&A deals over the past 40 years than 40,000. As we explain later, for purposes of our research we required for many of our tests the acquiring firms to be *publicly traded* so that we could observe their stock prices (investor sentiment). This eliminates from our sample acquisitions by private companies. The target companies in our sample aren't restricted to public firms. Our sample, though, while restricted, contains most of the large and economically consequential deals performed during the past 40 years.

[7] We explain the details of our measure of firms' M&A success rate in the appendix of this book. Briefly, we define successful M&As as those meeting three requirements: the acquirer's three-year postacquisition, industry-adjusted sales growth is positive and/or gross margin growth is positive, the stock price of the acquiring firm does not decrease postacquisition, and the buyer experiences no goodwill write-off in the postacquisition period.

[8] Figure 1 ends in 2018 because our "acquisition success" measure (see the appendix) includes the acquirer's sales and cost of sales growth, as well as stock returns for the postacquisition three to four years, which extends to 2022 for the year 2018.

[9] For example, see the *Wall Street Journal*, September 17, 2023, ibid.

Average M&A failure rate increases

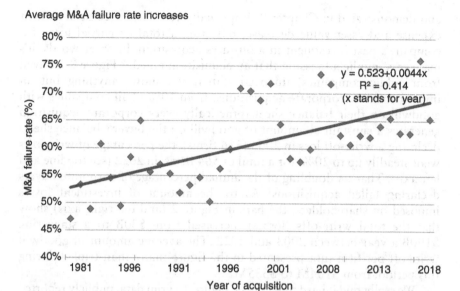

FIGURE 1   The Increasing M&A Failure Rate Over Time (The dots reflect average annual M&A failure rate for the period 1980–2018, excluding 2006–2007, plus a regression trend line.)

Percentage of firms writing off goodwill (left axis) and amount of goodwill write-off ($ billion, right axis): 2003–2022 (ex. 2008–2009 & 2020–2021)

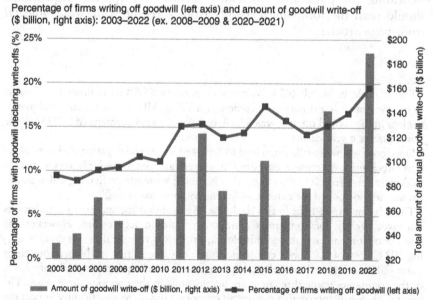

FIGURE 2   The Percentage of Firms with Goodwill from Acquisitions Writing Off Goodwill, and the Amount of Goodwill Write-Offs ($ Billion)

and demonstrated in Chapter 9) is a usually very large income statement expense and asset value decrease, reflecting a total or partial loss of a company's past investment in a business acquisition. In other words, it's managers' public admission that an acquisition failed.[10] Figure 2, derived from public companies' financial statements, shows anything but an improvement of corporate acquisitions: from 10% of all companies with goodwill on their balance sheet (practically every corporate acquisition generates a substantial amount of goodwill on the buyer's balance sheet) declaring a write-off loss in 2003 (316 firms), the percentage of write-offs went steadily up to 20%, for a total of 564 firms, in 2022 (see top line and left axis). That's a doubling of the annual percentage of corporate buyers declaring failed acquisitions! As to the amount of investment losses imposed on shareholders, the bars in Figure 2 (and the right axis) show that the total write-offs (losses) increased from $30B to a staggering $190B a year between 2003 and 2022. The average amount of goodwill write-off per firm (not presented in the figure) more than tripled during this period, from $104M to $335M.[11]

We really find it hard to reconcile Figure 2's grim data, publicly reported by the acquiring companies, with a view that the quality of corporate acquisitions improved over the past two decades.[12]

Finally, readers who may not be impressed by our statistical evidence indicating the poor and worsening record of corporate acquisitions should read the following excerpts from a recent *Wall Street Journal* front-page article:

---

[10] For example, in March 2024, Walgreens reported a $5.8B write-down in the value of its investment in primary-care clinic chain VillageMD. Consequently, Walgreens' net loss in the second quarter was $5.9B, compared to net earnings of $703M in the same quarter a year earlier.

[11] Since goodwill write-offs often lead to reported losses and negative investors' reaction (stock price decreases), corporate managers are understandably very reluctant to declare this event. It is thus likely that goodwill write-offs, reflecting failed acquisitions, are postponed for considerable time by some managers.

[12] There is one ray of light in this darkness. We find that the success of acquisitions improves slightly for companies conducting multiple acquisitions. However, the number of companies making multiple acquisitions is very small. For example, during 2022, 12% of the public companies made one acquisition in the previous three years (2019–2021), 4.5% of the companies made two acquisitions, and only 2.6% of the companies made three or more acquisitions in the previous three years. The latter is obviously too small a number of corporate buyers to significantly impact the overall quality of corporate acquisitions.

Big Media Deals Aren't Living Up to the Hype. Warner's CEO Wants to Do Another One

Streaming is losing money. Box-office receipts are underwhelming. Cable networks are dying. The entertainment industry is badly in need of a plot twist – and Warner Bros. Discovery boss David Zaslav is ready to supply one in the form of yet another blockbuster media merger. Zaslav met this week with Paramount Global CEO Bob Bakish and discussed the possibility of a deal between the media giants. . . . The logic of a Warner-Paramount pairing: overlapping cable networks and studio operations would translate into billions in savings. And Warner's Max streaming service would be supercharged with content. . . . If this story line sounds familiar, it's because it's a rerun played many times over the past decade. Giant mergers have been the response to virtually every big problem confronting the entertainment industry's titans. But so far, the results from these big deals aren't impressive. "These things just extend the runway, but they don't change the destiny of where they are going," said Andre James [Bain & Co.]. . . . Many media observers and analysts are skeptical about the merits of a Warner-Paramount deal. If the goal is a partnership in streaming, there are other models to explore – a bundled offering of services at a discounted price, or a joint venture – before jumping into an all-out merger.[13,14]

Thus, one bad giant deal is chasing another in a never-ending drama–farce, at shareholders' expense, reminding one of the tourist who saw years ago in New York harbor the magnificent yachts of J.P. Morgan, John D.

---

[13] Flint, J., Toonkel, J., and A. Sharma, 2023, "Big media deals aren't living up to the hype. Warner's CEO wants to do another one." *Wall Street Journal*, December 21.

[14] Reflecting on the poor records of past M&As by big media firms and the lack of merits in a Warner Bros. Discovery–Paramount merger, investors of *both companies* reacted *negatively* to the news of the merger talk, sending the share price of *both companies* down by nearly 30% over the subsequent three months. Among other issues, investors were concerned that Warner Bros. will have to raise billions of dollars of debt to acquire Paramount, which will further increase its already high debt level ("Why buying Paramount Global will not be easy," *Wall Street Journal*, February 1, 2024). Amid these heightened investor concerns and management realization of the lack of a clear pathway of integrating their businesses, Warner Bros. Discovery and Paramount discontinued their merger conversations in late February 2024, merely three months after the initial talk (Sherman, A., "Warner Bros. Discovery halts merger talks with Paramount Global, sources say," *CNBC*, February 27, 2024).

Rockefeller, and other finance and industry titans, and asked innocently: "Where are the customers' [investors'] yachts?"

This surprising finding of bad and worse acquisitions indicates one of two things: either corporate executives and directors, with their highly paid advisers, are getting worse over time at acquiring companies, or the personal acquisition motives of executives (higher compensation, empire building, and personal risk diversification; see Chapter 13) are getting stronger, overriding shareholders' interests. We will further explore this intriguing issue in a later chapter, but as for now the data speak loud and clear: as acquisition numbers and value increase, merger consequences are getting worse. No wonder investors are so antsy when learning about an impending acquisition and often dump the buyers' shares. Figures 1 and 2 obviously strengthen the need to fully understand the merger phenomenon and learn how to improve its consequences, which we do in this book by focusing on the following central issues.

P.3   THE CENTRAL ISSUES EXPLORED IN THIS BOOK

(A) *What explains the very high and increasing acquisition failure rate?*

Like post-mortems informing doctors how to improve health treatments, understanding the reasons for past acquisition failures is crucial to enhance the merger success rate. The failure of a complex and time-consuming process like a corporate merger cannot, of course, be explained by one overall reason. Life is complicated. Therefore, armed with a comprehensive measure of acquisition success (see the appendix), we analyzed more than 40,000 acquisitions worldwide to identify the major reasons for mergers' success and failure. Obviously, given the very high acquisition failure rate, we first focused on the reasons for merger failure. The following, in brief, are the major causes we identified for the persistent acquisition failure. In the book, we elaborate, with real-life examples, on these major causes for failure.

Insufficient attention to the acquisition alternative – internal development. Faced with lagging sales and earnings, chronically missing analysts' consensus earnings estimates, expiring patents, or a competitor's entry, and goaded by commission-hungry investment bankers, executives often panic and feel *they have to act* promptly and boldly, by "doing a big acquisition" (see the cases of Teva Pharmaceutical and Hewlett Packard in the next chapter). Sometimes an immediate corrective action has to be taken, but oftentimes, with some planning ahead, the *internal development* of new products and services and the restructuring of business processes are the better solution. New products can be developed internally rather than bought, production facilities can be built in-house, and new markets can be penetrated by expanding and improving the existing salesforce. As you will see in Chapter 4, our calculations show that the growth benefits of internal development are *substantially higher* than those of acquisitions. Surprising but true. Yet, internal development is rarely seriously considered as an alternative to acquisition. A panicked acquisition decision usually ends up with overpayment for the target and getting a business that is a strategic misfit. This overpayment and lack of strategic fit are among the major reasons for the observed high acquisition failure rate.

"Now is the time to buy." A second cause for acquisition failure is the widespread belief by CEOs that they can *time acquisitions* (akin to how investors try, and mostly fail, to time the market). This is often a chimera. For example, some say that when capital markets are up, better yet sizzling, you should buy a business because your shares (the acquisition currency) are high and perhaps even overvalued. Others prefer down markets, because target shares are depressed and you can acquire "bargains." Advisors will tell you that when your competitors are buying, you do not want to be the last standing with an empty bag. Thus, there is no scarcity of presumed "good times for acquisition." However, our comprehensive analysis, presented in Chapter 6, shows that most acquisitions that were made allegedly in "good times" actually failed. There are few good acquisition times, and we point them out, but, generally, rather than looking for good times, you should look for good targets; we also point those out.

The dire consequences of overconfident CEOs. Jeff Immelt, at General Electric, reportedly made 380 acquisitions while at the helm of the company.[15] Many of those acquisitions were not a good use of shareholders' money. You will read in Chapter 13 how *overconfident CEOs*, those overstating (in their own mind, or publicly) the expected benefits of their decisions, can be identified and that these executives – about 30% of all CEOs – are typically serial acquirers. Tracking the consequences of their acquisitions, we found that they are far from impressive. Being a gung-ho CEO is not a match for a

---

[15] Gara, A., 2017. "For GE's Jeff Immelt, hundreds of deals and $575B did not yield a higher stock return," *Forbes*, June 15.

thoughtful and careful corporate leader. So, here you have another, quite widespread reason for the growing acquisition failure rate – the overconfident CEO.

Conglomerate (unrelated) acquisitions. Amazon buying Whole Foods, Google acquiring Motorola Mobility, or Intel purchasing Mobileye are examples of conglomerate (core-unrelated) acquisitions. They were popular in the 1960s and 1970s and then fell from grace due to massive failures. Surprisingly, 10–15 years ago, conglomerates rose from the ashes, particularly among tech companies. As you'll see in Chapter 5, most of these conglomerate acquisitions are doomed to fail, in our opinion, because they lack business logic – shareholders buying the shares of the two merger partners achieve the same risk diversification as the acquiring company – and managing an enterprise outside a company's core competency is particularly difficult. The considerable number of conglomerate acquisitions made during the past decade or two have contributed significantly to the growing merger failure rate that we documented in the previous section.

Holding on to losers. An astute investor once said, "I made most of my money not from purchasing securities, but from selling them on time." The selling of an investment, particularly when it's not doing well ("out of the money"), is a wrenching decision for managers. It is hard to admit failure to yourself, and even harder to admit it to investors when the loss from the sale of a losing investment has to be reported in the income statement. Buyers' CEOs always hope that yet another reorganization, a change of target management, or the hiring of new consultants can prevent the target's failure, avoiding the investment write-off and the negative shareholder reaction. But this rarely happens. Rather, holding too long to failing targets drains executives' time and reduces the market value of what remains of the target. Big losses are often the result of retaining a failing target for too long.

Increasingly weak buyers. You read this here for the first time. Our sample analysis has revealed that the pre-acquisition performance of the sample buyers – as measured by their pre-acquisition three-year average return on assets (ROAs) – has been deteriorating over time. Stated differently, buyers are getting financially weaker, and that's likely a major reason for the acquisitions' failure to revive their performance and growth. Financially weak buyers cannot afford to acquire quality targets, they have to borrow heavily to finance the acquisition, and they aren't attractive to the target's top talent to keep working for them. These are all reasons for the acquisition's failure.

Summing up, there are, of course, additional reasons for acquisition failures that we investigate in the book: integration difficulties, cultural clashes, pre-acquisition target fraud, and misrepresentation (as in HP buying Autonomy, discussed in the following chapter) – but the six failure causes listed above account for the lion's share of the massive M&A failure trap. Later in the book we elaborate on each failure cause with real-life examples and provide suggestions for how to avoid them. With this, we accomplish the first major objective of our book: answering the perplexing question of why so many M&As fail and exposing the reasons that the failure rate keeps rising. But this is not just a book about post-mortems. It's mainly about how to *improve* the acquisition decision. So, let us move to the second major book objective.

(B) *How to enhance the likelihood of an acquisition success?*

There is no scarcity of M&A advice in the business literature and social media: you can find books by CEOs titled "What I learned from doing acquisitions"; numerous M&A advisors and consultants publish lists of "5 (or 10 or 15 or . . .) things to do to assure merger success"; economists report research results on issues like the hazard of CEO over-optimism, and the disregard of cultural differences between buyer and target employees; and board members inform on "how to prevent CEOs from committing acquisition failure." The usefulness of such advice is limited. All those M&A architects and experts recounting their experiences have, in fact, very limited M&A exposure (being typically involved in less than a handful of acquisitions), done under very special circumstances, like abnormally low interest rates, or in the wake of a financial crisis. There is not much one can generalize and learn from these public sources. As for investment bankers, their advice is often far from objective, given the fat fees they expect from an acquisition.

We use in this book an entirely different approach to improve acquisitions, whose main elements are as follows:

Comprehensive evidence: We assembled for this book a very large sample of more than 40,000 merger cases involving publicly traded buyers (the reason: some of our measures require share prices) from both the United States and abroad. Our targets are firms of all sorts, both public and private. Our sample covers the past 40 years. That's our database from which we draw inferences about the major determinants of M&As' success and failure. Our approach is thus *fully evidence-based*; it contains facts rather than conjectures, anecdotes, or some limited experiences.

A multidimensional success measure: A search for M&A success deter-minants requires a well-defined *success measure*, indicating what constitutes a winning acquisition. The M&A literature offers a bewildering array of success indicators: rising buyers' stock prices when the merger is announced, sales or earnings growth over three-to-five years post-merger, or new products or services emerging from the merger. Each of those measures captures an aspect of acquisition success yet misses other success dimensions. We, in con-trast, include three critical success dimensions in our measure. Specifically, we count an acquisition a success if it fulfills *all* of the following requirements:

(a) a positive buyer's sales growth and/or gross margin increase, over a three-year period after the acquisition, relative to its industry average growth (a financial performance dimension)

(b) the buyer's share price did not decrease over the three post-merger years (capital market performance)

(c) there was no accounting write-off of goodwill or of the merger investment (loss declaration) during the three post-acquisition years (an accounting perspective)[16]

Our acquisition success measure thus captures simultaneously the financial, capital market, and accounting aspects of the acquisi-tion. We aren't aware of any other M&A study that uses such a comprehensive success indicator. As for our sample, 36% of all acquisitions were successful by our measure over the 40 sample years. During the past couple of decades, though, the success rate declined to 30%. Thus, only three out of ten acquisitions currently fulfill their expectations. We also use state-of-the-art statistical analysis as follows:

An advanced statistical methodology: Most acquisition studies done by consultants, advisers, or financial institutions use simple correla-tion analysis, like the one we recently saw claiming that the larger the number of acquisitions a company makes, the higher its acquisi-tion success. This conclusion was derived from a correlation between the buyer's number of previous acquisitions and its post-acquisition share price changes. Simple correlation analyses,

---

[16] For the full details of our measure of acquisition success, see the appendix at the end of this book.

however, suffer from several serious statistical shortcomings, such as the "missing correlated variables" problem. Specifically, in the study mentioned earlier, the missing correlated variable may be the company's periodic cash flows. Firms flush with high and increasing cash flows tend to acquire more quality businesses *and* their share price rises quickly. So the real relationship may not be between the number of previous acquisitions and share price growth, as the consultants claimed, rather between operational success (high cash flows) and *both* increasing share prices and the number of acquisitions made. Accordingly, high cash flows may be the real driver of acquisition success, not the number of previous acquisitions. Statistics is an art as much as science.

In this book we use a multivariate regression analysis, which is the gold standard of economic and finance research (see the appendix for details). In fact, we *simultaneously* estimate the effect of more than 40 possible acquisition success determinants on the actual merger success. Those determinants include, among many others, the following:

- Target is a foreign entity.
- Acquisition payment is in the form of stocks.
- Buyer and target are business-wise unrelated (a conglomerate merger).
- Target is small relative to buyer.
- Target is a technology company.
- Target is a losing enterprise.
- Acquisition was made during rising capital markets.
- Acquisition premium is high.
- Merger is horizontal (the partners are business related).
- Buyer has considerable acquisition experience.

Our 43 variables model makes it unlikely that "missing variables" affect our inferences and recommendations and enhance the generality and usefulness of our findings. Thus, our substantially larger sample, more comprehensive acquisition success measure, and improved statistical methodology places this book on a substantially higher level than the available M&A literature. But we provide still more in this book:

(C) *A predictive merger scorecard*

The third theme of this book (after explaining the reasons for the very high and increasing acquisition failure rate and identifying the drivers of acquisition success) is the development of a predictive merger scorecard. We use our 43-variable acquisition success model to build a unique "merger scorecard," done here for the first time, to assign points to each acquisition success determinant (e.g., target is a profitable entity) and generate a summary score for a specific acquisition. This predictive merger score can be used by executives and board members, in comparison with the average scores of past acquisitions, to determine the likelihood of success of a proposed acquisition, and by investors asked to vote on an acquisition. In other words, our detailed acquisition scorecard provides decision-makers with a numerical forecast for an acquisition's success. We cannot overstate the importance of this new tool for people dealing with M&As. We deferred the development and exposition of the scorecard to Chapter 15, because its full understanding requires many of the concepts, findings, and recommendations we develop in the preceding chapters.

(D) *A spotlight on the human element: CEOs and employees involved in M&As*

We conclude the book with a thorough examination focused on the main acquisition players – the buyers' CEOs, and employees. This human resource aspect of M&As is rarely discussed in the acquisition literature. We empirically address questions like, are CEOs compensated for acquiring businesses, irrespective of their success or failure? Does acquisition failure hurt the CEOs' career and tenure? What happens to the buyer's and target's employees after the merger? In short, we examine here the human element involved in M&As.

P.4 FINALLY, WHO SHOULD READ THIS BOOK?

Everybody, of course. Seriously, if you are a corporate executive or a director considering a business acquisition, you will learn from this book how to avoid the major pitfalls dooming an acquisition, such as a conglomerate merger. You will also find out the major changes you should make in the acquisition terms, like substitute cash for stock payments, to improve the acquisition's success prospects and its reception by investors. Importantly, we also provide readers with a unique, predictive acquisition scorecard that will enable them to compare the prospects of the acquisition considered with those made by your peers. This information will enable decision makers to avoid the devastating "M&A failure trap."

If you are an investor asked to vote on an acquisition proposal, or consider whether to buy or sell the shares of the proposed merger parties, our book highlights for you the major acquisition and target attributes – like a target that is a foreign entity, a large debt raised to finance the acquisition, or the target sustaining a series of pre-acquisition losses – that will likely cause an acquisition failure. Our acquisition-specific scorecard will summarize for you the likelihood of an acquisition's success.

If you are a business professional, an economist, or just someone who is generally interested in economic issues and is perplexed by the frequent news about large merger failures or massive goodwill write-offs, our book will clarify for you the reasons for those, often colossal, managerial acquisition mistakes and how they could have been avoided.

Lastly, if you are a business school or economics university instructor, some of your courses likely deal with various M&A issues, such as the M&A role in business strategy, the financing of corporate acquisitions, or the accounting for mergers. Our book will be an easily accessible and readable reference for your students.

So, whoever you are, please join our following M&A journey to success.

CHAPTER 1

Appetizer

The Good, the Bad, and the Ugly

This "appetizer" chapter provides you with a panorama of intriguing and highly consequential acquisition cases concluding with important inferences about acquisition successes and blunders. It provides a triple-case, bird's-eye view of the mergers and acquisitions (M&A) scene, from one of the best acquisitions ever made to one of the worst, through the ugly and embarrassing.[1] We will draw from these cases certain preliminary – yet very interesting – conclusions regarding the factors affecting the consequences of corporate acquisitions. We will also indicate the limits of such individual case analyses, so popular in the media and business school classes. These limitations create the need for a rigorous, large-sample research into the factors contributing to the success and failure of corporate acquisitions to be reported throughout this book. Bon appétit.

1.1 THE GOOD: GOOGLE SNAPS YouTube AND ENTERS THE VIDEO-SHARING SPACE

It's October 2006. The world is stunned by North Korea's first nuclear test, while the tech community is startled by a different "bomb": Google announces the acquisition of the video-sharing startup company YouTube for a then eye-popping price of $1.65B – its largest purchase yet.[2] Back then

---

[1] The *Good, the Bad, and the Ugly* is the title of a 1966 hit movie directed by Sergio Leone and starring Clint Eastwood (Wikipedia).
[2] Allison, K. and A. van Duyn, 2006, "Google to buy YouTube for $1.65bn," *Financial Times*, October 9.

(2006), multibillion-dollar tech acquisitions, particularly of a one-year-old enterprise, were unheard of. Pundits were quick to proclaim that Google vastly overpaid for YouTube; Mark Cuban reportedly called the acquisition, burdened by various legal liabilities for content used, "crazy."[3] The overpayment claims were corroborated a while later by Google's own chief executive officer (CEO), who admitted that YouTube was acquired with a hefty premium.[4] As you'll see later in the book, contested (multibidder) acquisitions, like YouTube, often end up with the winner overpaying for the target – sometimes leading to a disastrous "winner's curse."[5] And YouTube's acquisition was indeed hotly contested – no less than Microsoft, Viacom, Yahoo!, and the News Corporation vied for YouTube's favors. Google's edge over other suitors was, in part, its commitment to retain the target's separate identity and managerial independence after acquisition.

Undeterred by criticism, executives of both Google and YouTube praised the deal effusively: Eric Schmidt, Google's CEO, proclaimed, "The YouTube team has built an exciting and powerful media platform that complements Google's mission to organize the world's information and make it universally accessible and useful." Google's cofounder, Sergey Brin, added, "We think one of the keys to comprehensive search experience will be video. On the whole, it is hard for me to imagine a better fit with another company." Speaking for the acquisition target, YouTube's cofounder Chad Harley claimed, "By joining forces with Google, we can benefit from its global reach and technology leadership."

This is typical of M&A announcements: irrespective of facts and circumstances, executives of both the buyer (acquirer) and the target (acquired) companies invariably wax lyrical about the acquisition, repeating ad nauseum the mantras of extraordinary *strategic fit*, large expected *synergies*, and hefty *value creation* for investors. After all, in some cases executives need shareholders' approval for the merger, and a bump in the buyer's stock price upon announcement will look good too. Yet, given the evidence that

---

[3] Luckerson, V., 2016, "A decade ago, Google bought YouTube – and it was the best tech deal ever," *The Ringer*, October 10.
[4] Sandoval, G., 2009, "Schmidt: We paid $1 billion premium for YouTube," CNET, October 6.
[5] The "winner's curse" is a phenomenon common in auctions where the ultimate winner in a contest is the one offering the highest price, often an overpayment, relative to intrinsic value, thereby acquiring a "cursed asset." (See R. Roll, "The Hubris Hypothesis of Corporate Takeovers," *Journal of Business*, 59 (1986): 197–216, for application of the winner's curse concept to M&As.)

most mergers disappoint, such uniform executives' praises are often sheer hype, laced with heavy wishful thinking, and aimed at affecting investors' acquisition perceptions, for which executives rarely pay a price when the acquisitions disappoint.[6] In general, executives' proclamations around merger announcements should be heavily discounted by investors.

In retrospect, YouTube's acquisition was a resounding success; some even call it the best tech acquisition ever (Luckerson, 2016). It is, however, difficult to accurately assess the degree of success, since Google—now Alphabet—while maintaining YouTube as a separate entity, had steadfastly refused to disclose key valuation metrics, like YouTube's contribution to Google's revenues and earnings. In 2020, however, under heavy pressure from analysts, Alphabet's CEO, Sundar Pichai, revealed for the first time that YouTube's 2019 revenues were $15.2B – still a partial figure (missing, for example, are subscription revenues from YouTube's TV). Applying a market multiple of six to seven times to YouTube's revenues – typical of successful social media companies, like Twitter of past – yields a YouTube's conservative, stand-alone value estimate of about $100B – an astounding return on a $1.65B investment. Also impressive is YouTube's enormous and continuously increasing footprint: over 2B registered users – a quarter of the world's population – growing from 50M at time of acquisition (Sorkin and Peters, 2006).[7] YouTube is second only to Facebook (and perhaps TikTok) in the number of users, with a constantly growing library of billions of videos, making it a leading player in the social network arena.

The dire concerns at acquisition of massive litigation against YouTube by original video and content owners also didn't materialize, as YouTube's executives smartly managed to avoid the most disruptive litigations and frictions with content owners.[8] And YouTube keeps evolving. It recently added, for example, YouTube Red, an ad-free paid streaming subscription service, pitting it against the likes of Netflix and Hulu. All these YouTube

---

[6] The number of class-action shareholder lawsuits alleging false acquisition promises and unmet synergies and value enhancement are very small, however, bolstering executives' acquisition hype.

[7] Sorkin, A. and J. Peters, 2006, "Google to acquire YouTube for $1.65 billion," *New York Times*, October 9.

[8] YouTube's executives developed good relationships with major content providers – signing deals with CBS Programing, Universal Music Group, and Sony BMG Music, among others, enabling it to use their videos.

achievements were made along with various contributions to Google by YouTube. So, this acquisition was definitely a "good" one, to put it mildly.[9]

But wait, is YouTube really a merger (like in merging, combining)? It was definitely an acquisition by Google, but did the operations of the two entities consolidate for *mutual benefit*? Were there substantial synergies involved? This is an interesting question, since corporate acquisitions are generally aimed at one of two objectives: to enhance the buyer's short-to-medium-term operating performance (like Hormel Foods' acquisition of Planters in 2021) or to transform its business model for the long-term (e.g., Olivetti – a business and office products maker – acquiring in 2003 Telecom Italia). YouTube's acquisition didn't fulfill either target. It obviously improved Google's consolidated financial results, but it didn't materially change Google's core business (information search).[10] YouTube's acquisition seems more like the investments made by Warren Buffett for Berkshire Hathaway over the years or by private equity firms rather than regular mergers. This distinction between mergers and investment in unrelated businesses operating independently after acquisition is important because such "independent" acquisitions don't raise the thorny issues of integration and "killer acquisitions," to be analyzed later in the book. Nevertheless, YouTube was definitely a smashingly "good" acquisition. It's time to consider a "bad" one.

1.2   THE BAD: TEVA BUYS ACTAVIS AND LOSES ITS FOOTING

"Generic-Drug Makers Are Too Frail to Cure," warned the *Wall Street Journal* on June 2, 2019, explaining "The calamity engulfing generic-drug stocks has many causes, but they are all made worse by one simple malady: *too much debt*. . . . Years of weak performance for these companies has lately broken into share-price crisis. . . . All of this would be far less scary to investors if generic-drug makers had managed their balance sheets more carefully in recent years. Instead, they *borrowed money for splashy acquisitions at high prices*. For instance, Teva bought Allergan's generic business for about $40 billion in cash and stock in 2016."[11] (Emphasis ours)

---

[9] Interestingly, investors didn't have a clue at the time of the acquisition announcement about the subsequent success of YouTube's acquisition. Google's stock price following the acquisition announcement (October 9, 2006) *decreased* by 0.5%.

[10] In fact, attempts by Google to use YouTube's subscribers' data raised serious concerns among users and were therefore stunted.

[11] Grant, C., 2019, "These drug companies are too frail to cure," *Wall Street Journal*, June 2.

Sadly it's true. In July 2016, Israel-based Teva Pharmaceutical Industries Ltd, the world's largest generic drug manufacturer at the time, acquired Allergan's generic business named Actavis Generics for $40.5B, paying for it mostly with borrowed money. The acquisition, not surprisingly, was praised by Teva's CEO as "Creating a transformative generic and specialty company well positioned to win in global healthcare." Left unexplained was how would adding one generic drug producer (Teva) to another (Actavis) be "transformative." Businesses transform by changing radically their business model, not by piling on the same businesses and, in this case, a lagging one. Interestingly, investors at the time of the acquisition announcement didn't question the "transformative" and other hyped claims, as Teva's stock price rose sharply upon the acquisition announcement (July 27, 2015). As P. T. Barnum said, "There's a sucker born every minute." Subsequent events, unfortunately, made the fiction of this "transformation" clear to all.

In fact, Actavis' acquisition seemed more like a desperate move than a planned transformation. Prior to the acquisition, Teva faced headwinds from two directions. First, competition among generic-drug manufacturers intensified by many new entrants and by the Federal Drug Administration (FDA) speeding up generic approvals, leading to substantial sectorial product price declines. Second, the imminent patent expiration of Teva's major proprietary (nongeneric) drug Copaxone (multiple sclerosis), hauling in $4B annual sales, which was sure to create a deep hole in Teva's revenues and earnings. Like many directors facing similar predicaments, Teva's board members believed that "a big acquisition" would be the only solution to the problem. Erez Vigodman was specifically hired as CEO to do just that: a major acquisition.

This, of course, is a familiar scenario that you'll see playing out again and again in this book, and much more frequently in the business world: when a company's sales and earnings stall, and leading financial analysts and active investors clamor for a growth restart, managers, egged on by commission-hungry investment bankers, opt for the seemingly quick solution: a big acquisition. The alternative: a serious strategic restructuring, including a business model change – like IBM's 1990s highly successful transformation from hardware to software – seems too slow and timid and is rarely seriously considered. A "bold acquisition" has the added advantage of shifting investors' attention from the company's deteriorating performance to the acquisition and gives a temporary boost to the company's top line (revenues) from aggregating the sales of the merger partners.

Regrettably, the main consequences of such hasty acquisitions are often a significant overpayment for the target and a serious strategic misfit. In Teva's case, the misstep was adding more generic capacity just when the sector was suffering from both falling demand and prices. Since when are two losers better than one? That was made even worse by the addition of a huge debt to finance the acquisition. All of these problems afflicted Teva's acquisition of Actavis.

In Teva's haste for a big deal, Actavis was, in fact, a second-best. Teva's first choice was Mylan Pharmaceuticals, a large generic and specialty drug company. But Mylan defended itself vigorously and evaded the clutches of Teva.[12] Like a scorned lover, Teva looked feverishly for an alternative and settled for Actavis, paying 83% of the acquisition price ($40.5B) in cash it had to borrow. This raised Teva's debt to $35B – an unsustainable burden for a company with only $1.6B earnings in 2015.

Irrespective of the adverse circumstances, the glowing merger forecasts made regularly by buyer's executives were also prominent in Teva's acquisition announcement: cost synergies and tax savings from Actavis' acquisition were estimated by Teva's management at $1.4B annually, and the following year (2017) revenues and earnings before interest, taxes, depreciation, and amortization (EBITDA) were predicted to be $26B and $9.5B, respectively. Gullible investors fell for the enticing acquisition prospects, as Teva's share price rose 16% upon the acquisition announcement, on July 27, 2015! This is yet another example of investors being generally clueless about a merger's prospects and largely believing managers' hype.

Reality, however, was far different: actual 2017 revenues were only $22.4B, and EBITDA was only $6.7B. The departure of Teva's CEO, the architect of the acquisition, in 2017 was unavoidable. Worse yet, Teva's operations didn't improve in the following years. In fact, in 2018, revenues fell sharply to $18.9B, and earnings turned to a *loss* of $2.47B. Not unexpectedly, Teva's share price fell from $51.63 in July 2016 to $9.56 on January 2, 2020, in the pre-COVID market (an 81% decrease).

To be fair, the acquisition of Actavis wasn't the sole trigger of the carnage at Teva. The continuous softening of generic prices and the loss of exclusivity of its proprietary best-selling drug Copaxone took their toll, as did various legal issues concerning Teva's opioid selling in the United States

---

[12] In the fierce public exchange between Teva's and Mylan's executives, the latter's CEO wrote, "Bringing Teva's dysfunctional culture to the region could disrupt the core of our business, result in the flight of key talent. . ... This challenged culture at Teva is, we believe, a direct result of a board of directors that refuses to change, lacks adequate global pharmaceutical experience, and consistently meddles in company operations. This is the same board that was described like a nuthouse. . ..." (Hagai Amit, "Teva Cuts 14,000 Jobs," *Haaretz,* December 17, 2017). Surely this was a gross exaggeration by Mylan, even defamatory.

and alleged price fixing, but Actavis' failed acquisition and the burden of the huge debt owed were undoubtedly the major factors in Teva's downfall, from which it didn't fully recover until this writing.

Later, there was some mildly good news too: two new Teva's drugs were approved by the FDA in 2017 and 2018 (Austedo and Ajory), and in 2023 Teva partnered with Sanofi to develop an immunology drug (a skeptical market, however, reacted negatively with Teva's price dropping 4.3% at the news). But as the *Wall Street Journal* article quoted earlier noted, "All of this would be far less scary to investors if generic-drug makers had managed their balance sheets more carefully in recent years. Instead, they borrowed money for splashy acquisitions at high prices." The large Actavis acquisition rendered Teva particularly frail. As recently as July 2023, Teva's total debt was still $21B with razor-thin cash flows from operations of $1.6B in 2022. We emphasize the large debt issue because, as you'll see later, a heavy debt is a common drag on the performance of acquisitions.

Summarizing, Teva's 2016 decision to double-down on generic-drug operations by purchasing Actavis was evidently the wrong thing to do, particularly in the face of relentless downward pressure on generic drug prices. In retrospect, Actavis was far from transformative and did not contribute materially to Teva's operations. It would have been far better for Teva to avoid the "big acquisition" in 2016 and spend at least part of Actavis' price tag ($40B) on developing proprietary drugs to replace the patent-expiring Capaxone, or on an acquisition of a specialty (proprietary) drug or a biotech company to bolster Teva's product development. That's where the big money is rather than in generics. But the pressure in 2016 to quickly do "a big strategic move" was apparently irresistible. In our "good, bad, and ugly" classification, Teva's acquisition of Actavis was undoubtedly "the bad."[13] But there is worse.

1.3   THE UGLY: Hewlett-Packard PICKS UP AUTONOMY AND ALMOST LOSES ITS OWN

Here is a familiar scenario: a storied company hits the breaks – sales slow down, the pipeline of new products/services dries up, and earnings disappoint. Investors and analysts get antsy. To make things worse for managers,

---

[13] In a sad postscript, in February 2022, Warren Buffett finally dumped all of his Teva's stock at a loss. Apparently, even famously patient investors like Buffett have a limit.

activist investors are circling the wounded company, calling for strategic and even managerial changes. Hewlett-Packard (HP) faced all this in the early 2000s. The company was founded in 1939 by the legendary William Hewlett and David Packard, Stanford-educated electrical engineers, who literally started operations in a Palo Alto single-car garage, thereby initiating the legend of garage or basement startups. HP subsequently emerged from the garage to grow into a worldwide, dominating technology enterprise with $126B annual revenues and 324,000 employees in 2010. The company was a major player in the personal computers, printers, copiers, scanners, and sophisticated tech equipment fields, with a reputation for innovation and high product quality. (One of us was an early and proud owner of an advanced HP, pre-computer, pocket calculator – the top of the market at the time.)

Alas, in the 1990s, most of HP's products were low-margin hardware boxes (printers, copiers) with little if any growth. Obviously, it was time for a change. Carly Fiorina was hired in 1999 to regenerate growth by innovation, but after trying mightily to innovate, she ended up buying another large, low-margin, hardware company, the personal computer manufacturer Compaq, against the advice of influential directors and investors. When this acquisition didn't do the growth regeneration trick – how could it? – the idea to shift from hardware to software was raised by HP's directors and investors. Didn't such a shift resurrect IBM in the 1990s? And who was better suited to navigate the shift than a CEO of a large software company? All eyes were therefore turned to Leo Apotheker, a German executive who was briefly the co-CEO of the software giant SAP; he was promptly hired by HP as CEO in 2010.

But how to quickly turn a behemoth like HP from a traditional hardware manufacturer to an agile software producer? You guessed it: by a bold, large acquisition. A quick (later discovered to be disastrously superficial) search and due diligence identified the "ideal" target: Autonomy Corp., a British software company founded in 1996, which specialized, it claimed, in big data analytics and information management and protection. By the time of acquisition, Autonomy was a U.K. tech star, reputed to be the largest British software company in 2010, and its founder and CEO, Michael Lynch, was widely celebrated and even referred to by the *Sunday Times* as "Britain's Bill Gates." So, Autonomy seemed to come with a pedigree, particularly if you relied on rumors and newspapers.

CEO Leo Apotheker strongly believed that Autonomy was an excellent fit for HP, ushering in the much needed strategic pivot to software and the cloud, and agreed to an exorbitant price: $11.1B for a company with $1B revenues in 2010 (later alleged by HP to be grossly inflated). The acquisition price, reflecting an astounding 80% premium over Autonomy's share price (typical acquisition premia are in the 35–45% range), was widely criticized by the media as "absurdly high," and the acquisition was referred to as a "botched strategy shift."[14] This time, the acquisition miscalculation was so obvious that even investors and the media got it right. Despite executives' hype around the acquisition, HP's stock price continued its downward spiral, but CEO Apotheker was unfazed, declaring in August 2011, "Together with Autonomy we plan to reinvent how both structured and unstructured data is processed, analyzed, optimized, automated, and protected." That was a mouthful indeed. He also promised, "Just to make sure everybody understands, Autonomy will be, on Day 1, accretive [presumably in EPS terms] to HP." What more do investors need?

Left unanswered was the strategic question, How could Autonomy with only $1B annual sales, later revealed to be grossly inflated, significantly change the course of a $127B revenue company (HP's sales in 2011)? It was a scooter's engine installed in a semi-trailer. So, despite the optimistic statements, the wide criticism of the deal and of Apotheker's leadership of HP didn't abate, and in September 2011 he was fired, after just 11 months at HP's helm – a record, even for HP. And this was *before* the acquisition of Autonomy closed.[15] Don't cry for Apotheker, though; he reportedly took home $25M in severance pay. Even failure in corporate America often gets rewarded. To mend things, HP hired Meg Whitman as CEO, an experienced technology executive and a former CEO of eBay.[16]

The more experienced Whitman perhaps had a golden opportunity to cancel or renegotiate the Autonomy deal, but Autonomy was acquired nevertheless in October 2011, and HP's press release on October 3, 2011, was ebullient: "The acquisition positions HP as a leader in the large and growing enterprise information management space. Autonomy's software offerings power more than 25,000 customer accounts worldwide." Not surprisingly, given the exorbitant acquisition price and premium paid, Autonomy's CEO, Michael Lynch (the "British Bill Gates") was ecstatic, stating, "This is a historic day for Autonomy, our employees and the customers we serve. . . .

---

[14] Wikipedia, HP Autonomy.
[15] HP's share price during the third quarter of 2011, when the acquisition was discussed, plunged by more than a third. One wonders how HP's directors could ignore such a uniformly negative shareholder view? As reported, they also ignored a letter sent to them by HP chief financial officer (CFO) Cathie Lesjak, expressing grave misgivings about the Autonomy deal.
[16] *CNN Money*, September 22, 2011.

We are at the dawn of a new era." HP's new chief executive, Meg Whitman, a former HP board member, publicly expressed in November 2011 her full support of Autonomy's acquisition by saying "I am really excited about this acquisition, which would be priority 1, 2, and 3 for 2012." Autonomy indeed became a priority for HP, but not as intended.

As became widely known soon thereafter, Autonomy's acquisition was an unmitigated disaster. Shortly after the acquisition, Autonomy's sales plummeted, and roughly a year after the acquisition, HP wrote off – declared a loss of – $8.8B of Autonomy's investment, a full 80% of the acquisition price, stating that it had uncovered serious accounting improprieties at Autonomy, including "outright misrepresentations" of sales and earnings that occurred before HP acquired the company. As expected, CEO Whitman blamed her predecessor Apotheker and HP's head of strategy Shane Robinson for the Autonomy fiasco. Whitman added that the company filed a fraud complaint against Autonomy and its executives with the U.S. Securities and Exchange Commission (SEC), as well as with British law enforcement, and that it intends to file civil charges against Autonomy's past executives to recoup shareholders' losses. However, not to raise investors' expectations for a quick resolution and compensation, she added that she expected the legal process to be a "multiyear journey." ("Nightmare" would have been more fitting.)[17] HP shares plunged a further 13% on the announcement. What else?

As expected, Lynch dismissed all fraud charges and blamed HP's leadership for botching the acquisition, threatening to countersue the acquirer. In May 2023, after a protracted legal battle, the United Kingdom extradited Lynch to the United States to face criminal fraud charges, from which he was exonerated, and in August 2024 he was killed in a freak boat accident. In 2020, a U.S. appeals court upheld Hussain Sushovan's fraud conviction and five-year prison sentence for his role, as the CFO of Autonomy, in the 2011 Autonomy acquisition and its various misrepresentations. It was a total mess. We believe most readers will agree with our designation of Autonomy's acquisition as "ugly" in our good/bad/ugly classification. Not only was it a financial disaster, but it was also an embarrassment to a storied company like HP as well as to HP's highly experienced executives and directors. That's how strong the appeal of the so-called transformative acquisition apparently is. A postscript: HP never fully recovered from the Autonomy

---

[17]David Goldman, "HP takes $8.8 billion writedown on Autonomy," *CNN Business*, November 20, 2012.

debacle. In 2015, it split under activists' pressure into two companies—Hewlett Packard Enterprises and HP Inc.—separating its personal computer and printer businesses from its technology services, but even this split didn't return HP to its glory days as a leading technology company.[18] Ugly and sad.

1.4 PRELIMINARY LESSONS

So there you have it: the good, the bad, and the ugly acquisitions. What can we learn from these cases? Quite a few things.

1.4.1 Acquisitions Under Duress Generally Fail

Many successful companies, like Teva Pharmaceutical and HP, sooner or later reach a maturity stage; the uniqueness of their leading products or services peters out, some of their patents expire (Teva's Capaxone), or they face a disruption when competitors improve their own products (Apple's iPhone terminating Nokia's leadership). Sales and share prices consequently stall, and management is under heavy pressure of investors, analysts, and activists to regenerate growth *quickly*. The common prescription is a "transformative acquisition."[19] This, however, is easier said than done. There are very few readily available acquisition candidates capable of such a transformation, and the managers/owners of those few are aware of the buyers' desperate situation and drive the target prices up to the stratosphere (Autonomy's $11.1B absurd price tag). Such hasty acquisitions, goaded by commission-hungry investment bankers, are not only expensive, but they also often end up as strategic misfits, as when Teva dug itself deeper into the deteriorating generic-drug sector with the acquisition of Actavis. Teva and HP made exceptional blunders, but in reality such hasty acquisition failures are more the norm, as our analysis will show.

The natural phase of business maturity and the consequent slowing-down of growth doesn't necessarily call for an implant (acquisition). Such business cycles aren't secret, or unexpected, so the ideal course is to identify the looming crisis *at an early stage*, well before patents expire or

---

[18] To add insult to injury, Warren Buffett's Berkshire Hathaway sold $158 million of its HP's shares in September 2023.
[19] Some managers of slowing-down companies can't resist the temptation to commit financial statement fraud to portray continued growth. See, for example, the case of Satyam (2009), India's biggest financial reporting fraud.

competitors' products become dominant, and to develop a cool-headed restructuring plan. An acquisition may be part of such a plan, but not necessarily so. In 2021, for example, several major oil companies, realizing the increasing public headwinds facing fossil fuels, reorganized to enhance renewable energy production, often without major acquisitions. Similarly, Intel, which experienced a serious loss of market share and sliding stock price in 2020, recruited a new CEO who announced (in March 2021) a bold reorganization plan that included increased outsourcing, a $20B commitment for new production facilities, and enhanced research and development (R&D). This wide-ranging reorganization plan gained shareholders' approval and drove Intel's share price up more than 5%, but it didn't include an acquisition. So, our first lesson is that in most cases there is no need for a hasty, large acquisition to save the day, which, in any case, is rarely saved by acquisitions anyway (recall the 70–75% acquisition failure rate).

1.4.2   Debt Matters, a Lot

What almost crushed Teva was mainly the large debt raised to acquire Actavis. Our multivariate model (see the appendix) confirms on a large sample that acquisitions that significantly raise the *financial leverage* (debt-to-equity ratio) of the buyer often fail, because the forecasted synergies and revenue increases expected from the merger are frequently grossly optimistic and fall short of the large debt servicing payments, let alone generate a profit. Furthermore, often ignored by buyers and their investors are the prospects of unexpected future shifts in customer demand, new technologies developed, or changes in economic conditions, which adversely impact the consequences of the acquisition. Buyers often fail to balance the unchanging requirement to service a large debt against the considerable uncertainty of the acquisition's benefits. So, a large acquisition financed mostly by debt will likely adversely affect the buyer's operations and solvency, sometimes even leading to its failure.

1.4.3   Know Thy Target

Autonomy, acquired by HP for $11.1B, was apparently an empty shell, since HP in short order wrote off – recognized as a loss – 80% of Autonomy's balance sheet value. How could this happen to a large and experienced technology company like HP? Where were the experts expected to pour over Autonomy's books and the due diligence of Autonomy's business? Where were the advising investment bankers, which profited handsomely from the acquisition? And where were HP's board members? Sound asleep apparently, or falling for the U.K. hype surrounding Autonomy and its founder

Lynch? And why didn't anybody pay attention to the red alerts of falling HP share prices throughout the acquisition process and the highly critical financial experts who warned against the deal?[20]

And most important, how could two HP CEOs, Apotheker and Whitman, both with considerable technology expertise, enthusiastically endorse and push for Autonomy's acquisition? The fact that, in most cases, executives and board members involved in failing acquisitions don't pay a price for the debacle they caused certainly contributes to such careless target examination. "Other people's money" matters less.

Part of the problem, confirmed by our multivariate model, is that acquisitions' examination and due diligence are more problematic when the target is a foreign entity (cross-border acquisitions), like Autonomy. Distance matters to information acquisition, and the integrity (truthfulness) of financial reports is compromised in many countries around the world (although not in the United Kingdom). That's one of the reasons that our model indicates (see the appendix) that foreign targets often detract from the acquisition's success. Furthermore, cross-border acquisitions are much more difficult to integrate (merge) than domestic ones, due to different cultures, norms, and laws. A case in point is GE and the protracted problems and difficulties it encountered when acquiring and integrating the power division of the French company Alstom.

Accordingly, the botched acquisition and integration of Autonomy highlights the importance of the target's due diligence and thorough examination, along with holding financially responsible the acquisition's architects.

1.4.4 Investors Are Mostly Clueless

At the time of the merger announcement, investors cheered up the subsequently failed acquisition of Teva (a 16% share price rise) yet viewed warily the highly successful YouTube's purchase (Google's 0.5% share price drop).

---

[20] The signs of Autonomy's misrepresentations could have been detected before acquisition. Jack Ciesielski, a veteran analyst and forensic accountant, wrote a few years later that in each of the 10 quarters preceding Autonomy's acquisition it had reported revenues that were within 4% of analysts' expectations – a suspicious consistency. Ciesielski notes that Autonomy inflated revenues by coaxing its resellers toward each quarter-end to "buy" the software for deals close to be completed (but not yet recognized as revenues). This trick enabled Autonomy to inflate its quarterly revenues by about 15%. Of course, once this so-called channel stuffing had ceased, upon Autonomy's acquisition, its revenues plummeted. See, Jack Ciesielski, "How Autonomy Fooled Hewlett-Packard," *Fortune*, December 15, 2016.

However, investors correctly predicted the Autonomy debacle. Overall, and this is confirmed by research, at the time of acquisitions, investors are generally concerned with their consequences, as evidenced by the frequent negative share price reaction to managerial acquisition announcements, yet investors are rarely able to distinguish ahead of time between successful and unsuccessful acquisitions. This is, however, understandable, given the uniform and often irresponsible hype of acquisitions by the buyer's executives[21] and the paucity of substantive, objective information about the forthcoming merger and the associated risks. This lack of information is a serious concern, particularly for policymakers (SEC), because investors are sometime asked to vote on significant mergers, but there isn't much beyond managers' hype to base such a vote on. So, what's the use of requiring investors' M&A approval? Our multivariate model (see the appendix) and the "acquisition scorecard" we propose (Chapter 15) will assist investors in voting on mergers and in the related investment decisions they may choose to make.

1.4.5 Any Positive Lessons?

So far we have pointed out several negative inferences from HP and Teva's acquisitions. Can we find anything to be positively learned from the successful YouTube purchase? Two things stand out comparing the highly successful YouTube acquisition by Google with the failures of HP and Teva. First, in contrast with the underperforming buyers, HP and Teva, *at the time of acquisition*, Google was a very successful, up-and-coming tech company, leading its field at the time of YouTube's acquisition. Second and even more important, the target (YouTube) was unusually successful pre-acquisition: it was a fast-growing company in a new, highly promising sector (video-sharing), where Google had no operations. So, acquisitions by successful companies of up-and-coming targets are often highly likely to succeed. Furthermore, the target's pre-acquisition financial health and growth trajectory are crucial for the acquisition's success.

Interestingly, a few years after the YouTube acquisition, the same highly successful Google attempted another "transformative" merger. In August 2011, it acquired for $12.5B (a hefty 63% premium) Motorola Mobility Holding, the cell phone arm that split earlier from Motorola. The transformation expectations were made clear by Larry Page, Google's cofounder,

---

[21]Managers' uniform hype at acquisition announcements is a combination of natural excessive optimism and often insufficient knowledge about the target's expected benefits (recall Autonomy) and the integration challenges. Indeed, managers' overconfidence and excessive optimism are well documented; see Chapter 13.

who praised the acquisition thusly: "Motorola is a great American tech company that has driven the mobile revolution . . . including the creation of the first cell phone. . .. And as a company who made a big, early bet on Android, Motorola has become an incredibly valuable partner of Google. . .. [I]t's a great time to be in the mobile business, and that's why I am confident Dennis [Motorola's chief] and the team at Motorola will be creating the next generation of mobile devices that will improve lives for years to come."

So, Google clearly planned a business model change by entering the cell phone market with Motorola's "next-generation mobile devices." This entry attempt, however, failed miserably. Slightly over two years after acquisition (January 2014), Google sold Motorola Mobility to Lenovo for a mere $2.9B and Motorola's cable set-top box business to a private equity firm for $2.3B. Google, however, kept Motorola's large patent portfolio, likely to protect its own Android patents against infringement claims. Why the different acquisition consequences, YouTube vs. Motorola? It's obvious: YouTube was a young, upcoming, and highly sought after company, while Motorola Mobility was a has-been in the wireless industry. Indeed, our model shows that the *premerger performance of the target company* has a significant positive effect on the merger success. There are very few successful turnarounds of lagging targets (toads kissed by princesses in Buffett's metaphor).

1.5 FINALLY, A WORD OF CAUTION

We were able to draw various interesting inferences and lessons from the "good, bad, and ugly" acquisition cases presented in this chapter, but these inferences are based on just three *individual and highly prominent* mergers. Can these lessons be generalized? Could you say definitively, for example, that acquisitions financed by a high level of debt should be avoided or that an underperforming target should be shunned? Definitely not, based on a sample of three and without considering the special circumstances surrounding the acquisitions. It may be, for example, that an underperforming target acquired by a successful company with special expertise in its business (e.g., if Samsung were to acquire Motorola Mobility) could have been turned into a success story. That's why we developed for this book a multivariate statistical model estimated on a large sample (40,000 acquisitions) to overcome the limitations of a few individual cases, like the good, the bad, and the ugly presented in this chapter.

So, we have served an appetizer. The main course is yet to come.

CHAPTER 2

The Ever-Changing Nature of M&As (1)

Deal Characteristics

The merger and acquisition (M&A) scene is changing quickly, rendering past writings and personal experiences largely dated. To gain recency, this chapter and the next one provide a 40-year perspective of the changes in 10 key attributes of the "market for corporate control" – namely, mergers and acquisitions. Some of the changed attributes, like the growing number and size of acquisitions, or the high correlation between mergers and capital markets activity, were noted earlier, while others, like the return of the conglomerate mergers, are new and highly surprising. All in all, M&As today are very different from those of yore, and understanding these trends will improve M&A decisions. This chapter will focus on changes in deal (acquisition) characteristics, while the next chapter highlights trends in deal size and capital markets.

"History is more or less bunk."

—Henry Ford

In 1985, the consumer products company R.J. Reynolds acquired Nabisco, an established food producer, for $4.9B. This was a straightforward horizontal (same industry) merger. Nabisco was obviously within the "knowledge domain" of Reynolds, easy to value and integrate. Fast-forward to 2017, Intel, a leading semiconductor designer and manufacturer, acquired the young Israeli company Mobileye for $15B (an eye-popping 50% premium over market price). Mobileye is a designer and distributor of autonomous driving technology – not even close to Intel's core business. This demonstrates significant M&A shifts: the return of the conglomerates, which we will discuss briefly here and more fully in Chapter 5; and the strikingly large acquisitions prices and premia typical of recent acquisitions.

2.1 CONGLOMERATES RISE FROM THE ASHES

This finding surprised us most: Figure 2.1 portrays the share of conglomerate acquisitions – buyer and target operate in different industries – of all acquisitions. The conglomerates share was roughly 40% in the early 1990s, decreased to 35% in 2008–2010, and then rose sharply to almost 50% – a historic high – as of late. And we thought that conglomerates were a dying breed. Dinosaurs.

Some may recall that conglomerates were in vogue until the 1980s – Ling-Temco-Vought (LTV) and ITT Corp. were just a few of the famous, large conglomerates of the 1960s and 1970s – arguably enjoying the economic benefits of scale, internal capital and labor markets, and overall risk diversification due to operating in unrelated industries. Conglomeration

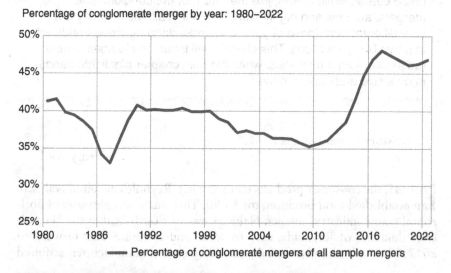

Percentage of conglomerate merger by year: 1980–2022

FIGURE 2.1 The Resurgence of Conglomerate Acquisitions

seemed then to be the winning business model. Some pundits even predicted that a few conglomerates will ultimately control the entire U.S. economy.[1]

As we will argue in Chapter 5, conglomerates never made economic sense. If investors want to diversify and invest in, say, airlines, banks, and biotech, they can just buy shares in companies operating in these industries. Investors don't need companies to do the involved and costly merger-based risk diversification for them. Furthermore, conglomerates are very difficult to manage. Most chief executive officers (CEOs) barely cope well with one industry. How are they expected to succeed in a multisector, multiple-technology environment? And the alleged synergies of conglomerates are hard to come by because the merger partners operate in different industries. So, it wasn't surprising that over time most conglomerates petered out. In recent years, the last of the seemingly invincible big conglomerates – General Electric – also met the inevitable fate of all its peers and is now a shadow of its former self. Other operating conglomerates, like United Technologies, Honeywell, ThyssenKrupp, and Siemens, are breaking up and spinning off unrelated operations. So, we strongly believed that the conglomerate phenomenon was all but extinct. How wrong we were.

As Figure 2.1 makes clear, conglomerates were recently resurging. The dinosaurs are back. In the past 10–15 years, conglomerate acquisitions rose sharply, now reaching more than 45% of all acquisitions. But here is the difference: the buyers are now mostly large tech and Internet companies, like Google acquiring YouTube (Chapter 1), Amazon buying Whole Foods and Twitch, AT&T merging with Time Warner (recently separated amicably), and Comcast purchasing Sky (a European broadcaster). Time will tell whether this new breed of conglomerates will be more successful and enduring than its predecessors (more on this in Chapter 5). We are very skeptical. The absence of economic justification of the conglomerate business model will be hard to overcome. What doesn't make economic sense (like Amazon owning Whole Foods and Twitch) falls sooner or later by the wayside (AT&T and Time Warner, for example). As usual, investors will pay the price of such managers' follies.

---

[1]This seemingly absurd prediction appears now to come true. The "magnificent seven" (Apple, Microsoft, Alphabet, Amazon, Nvidia, Tesla, and Meta Platforms) are practically all conglomerates, and they largely control the U.S. stock market, at least in performance and size (for the dominance of the "magnificent seven" in the U.S. stock market in recent years, see, for example, the *Wall Street Journal*, "It's the magnificent seven's market. The other stocks are just living it," December 17, 2023).

2.2   BUYERS ARE BECOMING DESPERATE

Buyers' performance and business fundamentals leading up to the acquisition are crucial for understanding the motivation and outcome of the mergers. Recall (Chapter 1) the acquisition of YouTube by the up-and-coming, highly successful Google, which greatly supported the continued development of YouTube and, in contrast, Teva Pharmaceutical's weak performance pre-acquisition and its precarious financial situation (very high leverage), which helped doom the acquisition of Actavis. Figure 2.2 portrays our sample buyers' median return on assets (ROA), a widely-used indicator of profitability and performance, measured in the year before acquisition and adjusted for the industry average ROA (the industry average ROA of the same year was subtracted from the buyer's ROA). It is clear from Figure 2.2 that buyers' ROA prior to acquisition has been fast deteriorating over time. Specifically, buyers' industry-adjusted profitability fell from above industry average (1.1%) in 1980 to deeply below industry average (−1.5%) in 2022. From winners to laggards.

Buyers' deteriorating pre-acquisition performance in recent decades has led to managers becoming increasingly desperate to acquire businesses as a quick fix for their fundamental performance problems. Hard-pressed CEOs of underperforming firms who are in a hurry to reverse declining profitability, however, tend to overpay for targets and often choose the wrong ones, from a strategic point of view (recall HP, Chapter 1). Overpaying for acquisitions

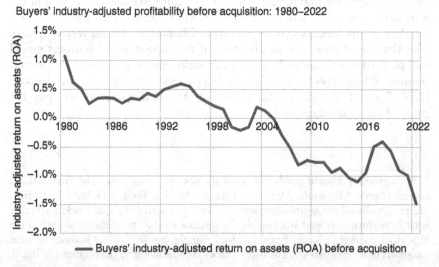

Buyers' industry-adjusted profitability before acquisition: 1980–2022

—— Buyers' industry-adjusted return on assets (ROA) before acquisition

FIGURE 2.2   Buyers' Decreasing Profitability Prior to Acquisition

is a highly problematic practice as it deprives buyers of resources that could have been deployed in other important uses, such as post-acquisition integration (e.g., offering attractive compensation packages to retain the key personnel of the acquired business).

Desperate CEOs also tend to overlook the poor fit of strategically unsound and hastily chosen acquisition targets. Acquiring a poorly fit target significantly dims the prospect of value-enhancing acquisitions, as there is likely little synergy to be extracted from such mergers. It also increases the difficulty and cost of post-acquisition integration. Thus, the potential pitfalls of acquisitions by underperforming bidders are indeed numerous and serious. This little-known fact – that buyers are increasingly poor performers – likely contributed substantially to the overall deterioration of acquisition success discussed in the preamble (portrayed in Figure 1).

2.3 INTERNAL DEVELOPMENT BECOMES A LESS ATTRACTIVE SUBSTITUTE FOR ACQUISITIONS

Patents can be bought or developed internally (with research and development, or R&D), customers can be acquired (buying a cellular phone operator, for example) or accumulated in-house by advertising and promotions, and gas reserves can be purchased or explored. This internal development option to acquisition is a fundamental consideration often overlooked by executives eager to make a "big, transformative acquisition." The substitution between acquisitions and internal development of capabilities is made clear by Figure 2.3, which shows for every five years the mean internal investment in the development of business capabilities (R&D, brand enhancement, customer acquisition, etc.), relative to total assets, made by companies that make acquisitions (left bar in each pair) compared with those that don't acquire (right bar). It is clear from the figure that in every five years, corporate buyers (left bar) are making lower investments in internal development (height of bar) than nonbuyers (right bar), indicating the substitution between acquisitions and internal development. It is surprising, however, that the difference in internal investment intensity between buyers and nonbuyers (the two bars) has grown dramatically over time.

Whereas in the early years, 1980–1999, the internal investment of corporate buyers was 75–80% of the internal investment of nonbuyers, in recent years buyers' internal investment *is less than half* of the internal investment of nonbuyers. As Figure 2.3 shows, this increasing difference is the result of both the increasing internal investment in development of nonbuyers (rising right bars), and the decreasing internal investment of companies engaged

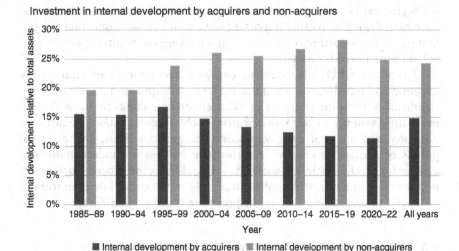

Investment in internal development by acquirers and non-acquirers

FIGURE 2.3 The Increasing Preference for External Acquisitions Over Internal Development

in M&As (decreasing left bars). It thus appears that in the past couple of decades, many corporate buyers have relied more and more on acquisitions and less on internal development as a substitute to acquisitions. In contrast, nonbuyers have substantially increased their investment in internal development. The trade-off between the two types of investment declined, and more companies became serial acquirers, as a matter of strategy.

This suggests that the decision whether to acquire a business or *alternatively* develop internally the needed capabilities is rarely considered nowadays. Most companies are either corporate buyers or internal developers as a matter of strategy, like Jeff Immelt at GE, who made 380 acquisitions during his tenure as CEO. We will dig deeper into this interesting development, discussed here for the first time, in Chapter 4, but at this stage it appears to us as an adverse development. Internal investments or acquisitions shouldn't be long-term strategies. Rather, they should be considered as alternatives in every specific case of a need for reorganization and business change.

2.4 THE ACQUISITION PREMIUM – UP, UP, AND AWAY

The acquisition premium is often measured by the excess of the price paid for the target over its market value prior to the first acquisition announcement. This premium may reflect various things: the synergies and other benefits expected from the acquisition, investors' undervaluation of the target's growth potential at time of acquisition, and/or buyers' *overpayment* for the target. It's difficult, of course, to pinpoint the exact reason for a specific acquisition premium before the acquisition's consequences become clear, but the trend and general impact of acquisition premia can be determined. To do that, we used our large sample.

Since our expanded sample includes nonpublic targets, having no share prices (private entities, subsidiaries of other companies), we measure the acquisition premium by the ratio of the price paid for the target to its recent annual sales. This mean ratio is portrayed in Figure 2.4. It is evident that the acquisition premium was relatively stable, though with significant gyrations, until roughly 2009–2010 (the aftermath of the financial crisis) but has been rising sharply since then. Apparently, the increasing demand for acquisition targets caused acquisition prices and premia to rise. That is basic economics. The premia for "large acquisitions," those with deal value exceeding 10% of the buyer's market value, has been noticeably higher than for all acquisitions, as was the premium rise after 2010 (top curve, Figure 2.4). This trend likely reflects the increasing importance of large acquisitions, perceived by buyers capable of quickly reviving lagging operations. So, not only are acquisitions on the rise, the prices paid for them are also increasing, with obvious negative consequences for the success of mergers.

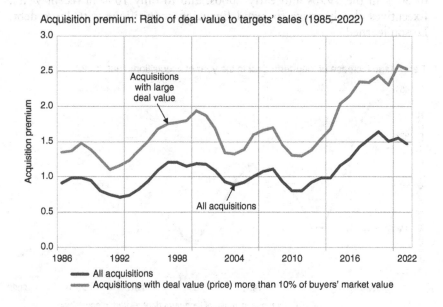

Acquisition premium: Ratio of deal value to targets' sales (1985–2022)

FIGURE 2.4   The Rising Acquisition Premium

Large acquisition premia, as in the case of HP's purchase of Autonomy (Chapter 1), likely include a *hefty overpayment* for the target that becomes a serious drag on the merger's success. Indeed, our multivariate model indicates a negative correlation between acquisition premia and merger success. The sharply rising premium for all acquisitions (bottom curve, Figure 2.4), and particularly for large ones (upper curve), is undoubtedly a major contributor to the increasing acquisition failure rate highlighted in our opening chapter (the "reverse learning effect," Figure 1).

2.5   THE USE OF DEBT IN ACQUISITIONS DECREASES

While the overall quality of M&A decisions by executives has been falling, one factor negatively impacting the success of acquisitions – debt financing (recall Teva Pharmaceutical in Chapter 1) – has been improving. It seems that executives internalized the fact that large debt is a drag on the acquisition's success. Figure 2.5 shows buyers' median annual percentage increase in long-term debt in the year of acquisition, adjusted for the industry-average median change. The curve has been decreasing sharply over time: the increase in long-term debt in the year of acquisition – mainly reflecting the debt raised to finance the acquisition – fell from over 40% in the 1980s to 30% in the 1990s and early 2000s, and to only 10% in recent years. Executives clearly strive to avoid financing acquisitions with large debt. Lesson learned.

Percentage increase of long-term debt in the year of acquisition: 1985–2022

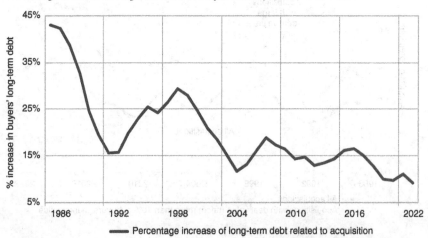

FIGURE 2.5   The Decreasing Use of Debt Financing in Acquisitions

TAKEAWAYS

The long-term trends in deal characteristics of M&As identified in this chapter – resurgence of conglomerate acquisitions, buyers' deteriorating performance pre-acquisition, increasing use of acquisitions as a substitute for internal development, and the rising acquisition premium – all point to key factors likely responsible for the persistently high and increasing M&A failure rate highlighted in the preamble to this book. The only "redeeming factor" – the sharp decline in acquisition's debt financing – has exerted a positive impact on the acquisition's success. The fact that four business factors are trending in a deleterious direction while only one is trending favorably provides a partial explanation to the sorry state of acquisition success these days. In the next chapter, we will explore the market conditions (stock market trends and geographic and industry settings where many acquisitions cluster) and trends in the size of M&A deals (changes in buyer and target sizes and growth in deal value over time), as these both hold further clues for why managers fail to improve merger decisions.

CHAPTER 3

The Ever-Changing Nature of M&As (2)

Markets and Merger Sizes

Mergers and acquisitions (M&As) are an integral part of the activities of companies and capital markets, so the key trends of M&As are expected to mirror those of the stock market and global economy. This chapter explores how M&As have changed relative to the markets over time, focusing on the industry concentration and geographic flows of impactful acquisitions, as well as the overall volume and value of M&As. We identify the rise of technology and globalization as potent drivers for the M&A markets in recent decades. We also highlight the relation between the volume and value of M&As and stock market boom-and-bust cycles. These attributes, together with those identified in the preceding chapter, provide a comprehensive view of the evolution of M&As over time. A thorough understanding of this evolution is a prerequisite for improving M&A decisions.

History tells us that M&A volume follows the stock market. Gains in stock prices tend to lift investors' and managers' optimism and inspire deal-seeking activities, so it is no coincidence that waves of large M&A deals usually occur with rising stock prices. The mega-deals of each decade often coincide with the peaks of the stock market. The largest acquisitions of the Roaring 20s, such as the acquisition of the Brooklyn Edison Company by Consolidated Gas Company of New York for $1B, occurred in 1928, shortly before the end of the decade's bull market of the 1920s. Other large M&A deals, such as Citicorp's purchase of Travelers Group for $70B in

1998 – a boom market year, Pfizer's acquisition of Warner-Lambert for $90B in 1999, and, of course, AOL's acquisition of Time Warner for $182B in the early 2000s, all occurred at the peak of the exceptionally strong stock market of the late 1990s.

Recently, more technology deals involving tech buyers and targets have joined the waves of large M&As (Microsoft's acquisition of Activision Blizzard for $68.7B and Broadcom's acquisition of VMware for $69B in 2022 are such examples). The pursuit of knowledge and innovation is clearly the catalyst of these technology deals. A case in point is Pfizer's early-2023 acquisition of Seagen, a biopharma company with no profit for more than 20 years, for $43B (with a 33% premium), a deal aimed at giving Pfizer access to Seagen's promising pipeline of cancer drugs. Although less prevalent than domestic acquisitions, large cross-border deals have also become more common with rising globalization (e.g., AB InBev of Belgium acquired UK's SABMiller for $107B in 2016 to build the first truly global beer company). But beyond the anecdotes, what were the main underlying developments?

3.1   THE GROWING VOLUME OF M&A DEALS

As economies develop and new business sectors emerge and grow (biotechnology, Internet services, financial technologies, and artificial intelligence [AI]), one would expect the volume of M&As to rise. This is indeed corroborated by Figure 3.1, which portrays the total *number* of M&A deals (continuous line), as well as the total annual *value* of acquisitions (bars), over the past 43 years.[1] It is clear from the deal value data (height of bars) that the M&A phenomenon is fast *increasing over time*.[2] This is particularly evident if you ignore the three tall bars of the late tech bubble period, 1998–2000, which was an abnormal time in terms of new company (mostly bubbles) formation and capital market frenzy, as well as the large number and value of acquisitions in those years. This aberration quickly vanished, and M&A activity returned to normal after 2000, as the tech bubble burst. So, ignoring the 1998–2000 bars in Figure 3.1, the remaining bars, reflecting the total annual M&A deal value, were fast increasing over time. Deal value is clearly on the rise.

---

[1]To provide an improved impression of the historical development, the annual amounts presented in several figures in this chapter represent three-year moving averages, made in order to smooth somewhat the choppy nature of annual data.
[2]To ensure its comparability over time, we adjusted the annual value of acquisitions for inflation measured by annual consumer price index (CPI) using the 2022 dollar value (i.e., the value of acquisitions in all years is based on the dollar value of 2022).

Total deal value (adjusted for CPI and based on 2022 dollar value), number of deals, and S&P 500 index:1980–2022

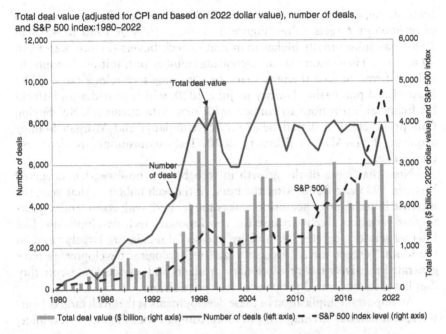

FIGURE 3.1 The Growth of M&A Deals and Stock Market Trends, 1980–2022

The number of acquisitions (solid line) also rose quickly from 1980 to roughly 2007–2008 (the financial crisis) but decreased slightly thereafter, indicating that in the past decade and a half value-per-deal increased substantially, on average. For example, some of the largest acquisitions ever occurred in recent years, such as Exxon Mobil announcing in October 2023 the acquisition of Pioneer Natural Resources for $59.5B and Microsoft acquiring Activision in the same month for $68.7B. So overall, the M&A phenomenon is central to developed economies, and it's also steadily growing along with the world's developed countries, clearly deserving the attention it gets in this book. A business phenomenon valued at over $3T a year globally definitely warrants careful analysis and thorough understanding.

3.2 TECHNOLOGY IS FLOURISHING IN ACQUISITIONS, TOO

The ascent of tech isn't limited to daily life (smartphones, online shopping, information searches, AI, etc.); it also is clearly manifested in the M&A statistics. Figures 3.2 (buyers) and 3.3 (targets) show the continuous rise in the share of both technology buyers and technology targets relative to all acquisitions, with a moderation in the 2000s. Note that the rate of growth of *technology targets* value (Figure 3.3), from 10% in 1980 to 45% in 2020, was substantially higher than that of tech buyers (Figure 3.2), from 20 to 40%. The reason was an increasing number of traditional (nontechnology) firms entered the tech space by acquiring technology targets, like MasterCard purchasing Finicity in June 2020, which provides a platform for financial institutions to connect with new data streams; CNN buying Canopy in 2020, a digital news service company; and Morgan Stanley acquiring E*TRADE in February 2020. Tech acquisitions are definitely on the rise.

Note that most of the growth in tech buyers, however, has occurred between 1985 and 2000. After the burst of the tech bubble in that year, the increase in technology acquisitions was moderated, with considerable year-to-year variation, likely because the revolutionary tech developments, like Internet services, wireless technology, and social media, are largely "long in the tooth," except for AI. Recent years' technological developments have generated relatively few revolutionary products and services, an eventuality that has also moderated the pace of tech acquisitions.

An important implication of these developments is that tech targets (software, autonomous driving, AI) are more complex and difficult to evaluate,

Percentage and relative value of deals by technology buyers: 1980–2022

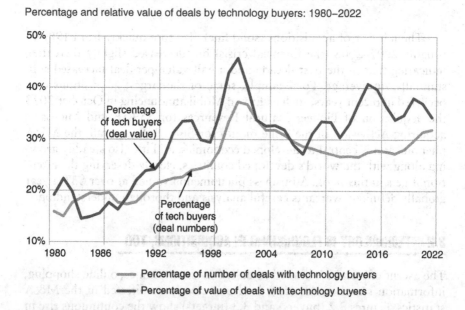

FIGURE 3.2 The Rising Share of Technology Buyers

Percentage and relative value of deals with technology targets: 1980–2022

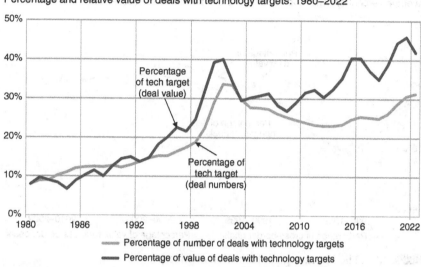

FIGURE 3.3   The Rising Share of Technology Targets

price, and integrate than other targets (retail, transportation). This likely contributed to the rise over time in acquisition failure, noted in the Preamble.

3.3   M&A GOES GLOBAL

Figure 3.4 shows the value and number of *cross-border deals* (buyer or target is a non-U.S. company), relative to all deals. The share of such deals is clearly growing, indicating an increasing globalization of M&As, reaching currently 25–30% of all deals. Like in the technology mergers of the previous section, the main rise occurred until roughly 2010, with slower growth thereafter. As we will discuss in Chapter 8, due to integration difficulties, acquiring a foreign entity detracts, on average, from the merger's success and the buyer's value, which has been likely a contributing factor to the decline in overall *acquisition success* discussed in the Preamble. Merging operations in different countries involves the complex tasks of combining diverse cultures, laws, and institutions, as well as rising difficulties in performing target due diligence in countries with different accounting systems and lax enforcement of securities laws. These factors contributed to the relative lack of success of many cross-border acquisitions, although it's important to note that not all cross-border deals are failures, as demonstrated by the successful Sanofi (France)–Genzyme (U.S.) merger, among others.

Average percentage and relative value of cross-border deals: 1980–2022

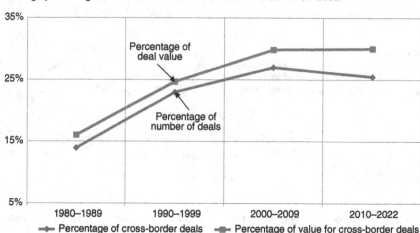

FIGURE 3.4   The Increasing Globalization of M&A Deals

3.4 THE CLOSE RELATION BETWEEN M&A AND INVESTORS' SENTIMENT

Look back please at Figure 3.1. The broken line represents the S&P 500 index, reflecting the aggregate stock price movement of large U.S. companies and the changes in investors' sentiments. Note the high correlation between M&A activity, particularly in terms of annual deal value (bars) and the stock market level. The measured correlation between the annual changes in investors' sentiments (S&P 500 index) and the annual number of deals is 83%![3]

The main reasons for such high correlation are as follows. First, high stock prices provide buyers with more potent currency (their stocks) to finance deals, although the prices of targets also increase with the level of capital markets. Second, improved investors' sentiments (higher share prices) signal better economic activity in the future, leading executives to prepare for expansion and future growth by acquisitions, among other means. Third, some executives may even believe that as share prices rise, their shares become *overvalued* (priced above fundamentals), which offers them an opportunity to buy businesses with "cheap currency." This, however, is a

---

[3]The year 2023 (not included in Figure 3.1), though, was a striking exception: while global M&A value fell 20%, the S&P 500 index rose 24.2%.

grave mistake, as we show in Chapter 6.[4] Fourth, certain executives even acquire businesses during prospering capital markets as a defensive mechanism, following this dictum: if you don't acquire in good times, you'll be acquired by others. Whatever the reason, the evidence is clear: M&A intensity closely follows capital markets activity.

That M&A activity is positively correlated with capital markets is quite known. However, an important issue, rarely raised, is whether good capital markets are conducive to *successful deals*. Does a market-buying frenzy lead to acquisitions that create value, and vice versa for M&As in lean markets? In short, should you follow the crowd in buying businesses when markets are hot? We deal with this important question fully in Chapter 6, but here is the essence of our findings, and it is surprising: our statistical model includes a variable for "market conditions," reflecting the 12-month change in the S&P 500 index *prior to* acquisition. This variable in our model is found to be *negative* and is highly statistically significant, strongly indicating that acquisitions frenzy during periods of booming stock prices yields largely unsuccessful deals and *shareholder value destruction*. This is an important lesson for corporate executives. Equally surprising is the finding that deals made following poor capital markets or crisis periods (e.g., the 2007–2008 financial crisis) are generally well chosen and executed. It is counterintuitive but true. Apparently good economic times and high stock prices make acquirers lax, rushing into half-baked deals and often overpaying for the targets whose prices are also high in hot markets. The lesson you'll see us draw again and again in this book is that following the crowd is rarely a recipe for success in business, and definitely not in M&As.[5]

3.5 BUYERS AND TARGETS GET MODERATELY LARGER

Figure 3.5 portrays the growth in median total assets of corporate buyers and targets over time: from 1989–2005 to 2006–2022. The median buyer grew from $3B of total assets in 1989–2005 to $3.4B in 2006–2022 (left

---

[4] Some academics (e.g., A. Shleifer and R. Vishny, "Stock Market Driven Acquisitions," *Journal of Financial Economics* 70, no. 3 (2003): 295–311) seem to suggest that buyers use inflated shares for acquisitions.

[5] A case in point: research has shown that buying highly ranked mutual funds or exchange-traded funds (ETFs) and selling low-ranked funds – "following the crowd" – is a losing proposition (see, for example, Voorhees, A., 2021, "Why chasing winners rarely works," *Financial Field Notes*, September 27).

axis of Figure 3.5), and the median target grew from $333M in 1989–2005 to $442M in 2006–2022 (right axis). These growth rates seem rather moderate, and they are, because we adjusted buyers' and targets' total assets by the CPI (Consumer Price Index) deflator to 2022 dollars. It doesn't make economic sense, indeed it's misleading, to compare dollar changes over 34 years without adjusting them for inflation (price changes), hence our CPI adjustment in Figure 3.5.[6] As Figure 3.5 shows, targets (top line) grew somewhat faster than buyers. The buyer-to-target average size multiple has shrunk from about 10 times in 2008–2012 to six to seven times in 2018–2022, reflecting buyers' increasing appetite in recent years to acquire *larger* targets. Parenthetically, our statistical model (see the Appendix) shows that large targets are more difficult to integrate with the buyers, and hence detract, on average, from the acquisition's success.

Importantly, the size growth portrayed in Figure 3.5 isn't accompanied by an increase in the *quality of acquisitions*, as Figure 1 in the preamble clearly shows. Distressingly, the rate of shareholder value destroying acquisitions keeps rising over time. This reminds us of a clever comment made by one of our instructors: "Quality times quantity is a constant."

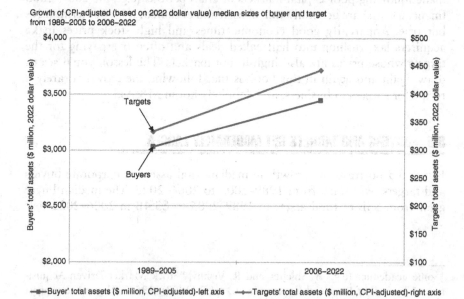

Growth of CPI-adjusted (based on 2022 dollar value) median sizes of buyer and target from 1989–2005 to 2006–2022

FIGURE 3.5   CPI-Adjusted Median Change of Buyers' and Targets' Size from 1989–2005 to 2006–2022

---

[6]The unadjusted data show that the median buyer grew over the period by 150%.

3.6   RESOLVING THE M&A FAILURE CONUNDRUM: WHY THE HIGH AND INCREASING FAILURE RATE?

This chapter explored five trends relating to the markets and sizes of M&As in recent decades. These trends, together with the five deal characteristics highlighted in the prior chapter, provide preliminary answers to the two fundamental questions raised in the preamble to our book: Why is the M&A failure rate so high (70–75%), and why isn't there an improvement (managerial learning) of the merger failure rate? Answers: When buyers' operating performance increasingly deteriorates pre-acquisition (trend #2, Chapter 2), leading to desperate acquisitions (overpayment, poor strategic fit and poor integrations); when the acquisition premium constantly rises (trend #4, Chapter 2); when conglomerate (unrelated) acquisitions, mostly doomed to fail, are on the rise (trend #1, Chapter 2); when the often better alternative to acquisition – internal development – is chosen in fewer and fewer cases (trend #3, Chapter 2); when more acquisitions involve technology targets that are hard to evaluate and difficult to integrate (trend #2, Chapter 3); when acquisitions of foreign targets having complex and difficult integration issues become more prevalent (trend # 3, Chapter 3); and when rising stock prices cause futile acquisition frenzies (trend #4, Chapter 3), a large and increasing number of failed acquisitions is inevitable. So, both trends in deal characteristics and capital markets conditions adversely affect merger success, shown in the grim overall outcomes of acquisitions.

In the following chapters, we will dig deeper into the main culprits of the merger failure trap and focus on the remedies that will enable executives to avoid them.

CHAPTER 4

Internal Development
The Alternative to Acquisitions

Recall Teva Pharmaceutical's (Chapter 1) rush to make a "big acquisition" to regenerate growth, even hiring a new chief executive officer
(CEO) for the task. But, before making the acquisition decision –
which flopped famously – did Teva's executives and directors seriously consider the alternative: *develop internally* an improved
capacity for generic manufacturing or enhance the development of
proprietary drugs to replace the expiring ones? No such consideration is in the public record, and none was apparently done. In fact,
most acquired business capabilities – research and development
(R&D) capacity, new customers, patents, brands, new markets, or
new products – can be developed internally. There are advantages
and disadvantages to acquisitions over internal development, but
acquisitions aren't always the winner. Shortly, you'll be highly surprised to see that the benefits of internal development in generating
growth and reducing risk are substantially higher than those of
acquisitions, on average. The main lesson, therefore, is to not rush to
acquire a business until you are convinced by solid analysis that
internal development is an inferior action to acquisition. Consider
carefully the alternatives.

4.1   REGENERATING GROWTH WITHOUT ACQUISITIONS

This section presents several notable examples of strategic decisions made to
regenerate growth and gain market share that relied primarily on internal
development without "big acquisitions."

4.1.1 Verizon Teaches AT&T a Lesson

As the wireless industry in the United States started to mature around 2010, the two leading players – Verizon and AT&T, which walked mostly in tandem until then – parted ways and chose contrasting strategies to deal with slowing sales and profits: acquisitions versus internal development. AT&T decided to expand bigtime into content creation (entertainment, advertising), intended to be streamed over its vast telecommunications network, by conducting massive, multibillion-dollar acquisitions. Starting in 2014, AT&T announced its intention to acquire DirecTV for $67B, thereby increasing substantially its market share in the pay-TV sector. This was only the opening shot of a buying spree. Some smaller acquisitions followed and then came the "big one": Time Warner (HBO, TNT, CNN), with all its extensive content, purchased for almost $110B. Given AT&T's size and market share, big acquisitions are legally complicated because of antitrust regulations. They cost a fortune in fighting regulatory challenges all over the world and shareholder objections, and, of course, they cause a total managerial distraction from the growing problems of the core telecom market. Furthermore, all those acquisitions by AT&T were financed primarily by debt, which has to be serviced irrespective of the acquisition success. Alas, all was for naught. In 2021 and 2022, AT&T publicly declared defeat and began unwinding its massive acquisitions of DirecTV and Time Warner, respectively. Very rarely is a significant strategic shift by a major corporation so strikingly and publicly repudiated as was AT&T's. The loss to shareholders from all those failed acquisitions ran into the tens of billions of dollars; see Figure 4.1.

Verizon, meanwhile, doubled down on its core wireless business.[1] There were no splashy acquisitions of content creators and media companies, just updating and enabling commercial (along with individual) use of 4G and, thereafter, 5G technology. There was a clear focus on internal development. Verizon did not give up completely on streaming content, of course, but it did it without major acquisitions by striking partnerships with key content creators, like Netflix and Disney. This did not call for raising large debt and paying heavy annual service charges. This is a tale of two same-sector companies pursuing different growth strategies. The fortunes of AT&T and Verizon have diverged substantially, reflecting the different consequences of the strategies, as shown in Figure 4.1. From 2010 to 2022, while Verizon almost tripled its market value, AT&T saw

---

[1] In 2013, Verizon announced its decision to acquire the remaining 45% stake that it did not already own in Verizon Wireless from its joint venture partner Vodafone Group Plc (Verizon Communications' 8–K report, September 2, 2013). This buyout, completed in 2014, gave Verizon the full ownership and control of its wireless business.

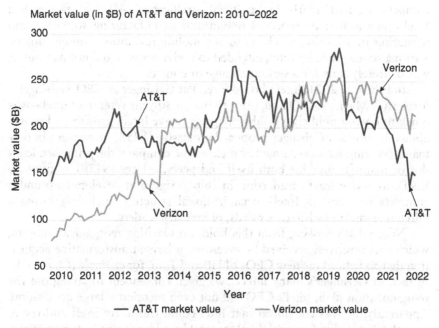

Market value (in $B) of AT&T and Verizon: 2010–2022

FIGURE 4.1 The Market Values of AT&T versus Verizon: 2010–2022

its market value virtually unchanged. It was a lost decade for AT&T's shareholders. Since 2014, when AT&T began its acquisition spree, it has lost nearly 20% of shareholder value. Verizon's market cap, in contrast, has gained more than 50%.

4.1.2 Intel Gets a Facelift (Reorganization)

The next example, Intel, is less decisive. It's still a work in progress but once more demonstrates planning for growth without big acquisitions. Intel is a storied enterprise. Founded in 1968 by tech legends Gordon Moore and Robert Noyce and led subsequently into sector leadership by Andrew Grove (*"Only the Paranoid Survive"*), it is among the world's largest semiconductor developers and marketers, and at $63B sales in 2022, Intel ranks 64 among the top U.S. companies by revenue. But even the mighty stumble. Intel's revenue fell 12.5% in the four-year period of 2019–2022, and its net earnings dropped by a whopping 62% during that time. Far from the stellar performance of yore. Intel's stock price, not surprisingly, followed suit and declined 39% during January 2019–October 2022. Reasons for this disappointing performance abound: the pace of new chip development by competitors, particularly for artificial intelligence (AI), was faster than Intel's, aggravated by repeated design and manufacturing stumbles, and hesitation in adjusting products to the mobile revolution, among others. Various acquisitions by Intel, intended to revive growth, did not pan out. It was definitely time for a serious change of course.

In February 2021, Intel's board hired Pat Gelsinger as CEO. Gelsinger – formerly VMware's CEO and, prior to that, a 30-year veteran of Intel – was quick to lay out publicly a bold strategy to revive Intel's growth and profitability. In essence, Gelsinger proposed a massive ($25B) investment in new manufacturing facilities, aimed at making the company the prime semiconductor manufacturer for both itself and peers; a large ($15B) addition to R&D, to revive Intel's leadership in chip design and development; and a complete overhaul of Intel's organizational structure, including hiring a "dream team," in Gelsinger's words, of industry leaders.

Note what's missing from this bold, far-reaching reorganization plan, which was positively received by investors: a large, transformative acquisition that so enticed the new CEOs of HP and Teva, for example (Chapter 1). In fact, in Gelsinger's many interviews given subsequent to laying out the reorganization plan, Intel's CEO did not even mention a large acquisition. Apparently, he was convinced that Intel could transform itself and revive growth from within (internal development) by adding manufacturing capacity, enhancing R&D, and substantially upgrading managerial capacity.

It wasn't all smooth sailing. Given the reorganization's recency to this book's writing and the general high-tech slump in 2022 and early 2023, the jury is still out on Intel's new reorganization success, although, after some initial setbacks, Intel's stock price rose nearly 90% in 2023 against a 25% rise of the S&P 500, but gave it up in July-August 2024. As we said: Intel is still a work-in-process.[2]

4.1.3 Merck Goes for Collaborations

While the acquisition spree of AI startups is currently heating up, Germany's Merck KGaA decided to part ways with the acquirers:

> Germany's Merck KGaA is betting on artificial-intelligence partnerships to develop new drugs, but refraining from bringing in external expertise through acquisitions, . . . Pharmaceutical companies are increasingly looking to AI tools for everything from designing new

---

[2] At its AI Everywhere event on December 14, 2023, Intel launched new chips for generative AI software to enable customers' AI solutions ("Intel accelerates AI everywhere with launch of powerful next-gen products," *CNBC*, December 14, 2023).

experimental drugs to predicting the response patients will have to treatments. Merck . . . sees greater value in teaming up with independent AI companies, rather than in an outright acquisition of a company that specializes in the technology.[3]

Merck prefers AI partnerships to acquisitions, it explained, because the AI field is moving and changing so fast and unexpectedly that acquisitions can lead the buyer down the wrong path. Partnerships, in contrast, are substantially less expensive than acquisitions and more flexible.

Merck recently entered into AI drug-development collaborations with American-Israeli biotech company Biolojic Design and with U.S. company Caris Life Sciences. Last September, the company forged alliances with U.K.–based AI specialists Benevolent-AI and Exscientia, aiming to significantly reduce drug discovery timelines.[4]

So, there you have it – various major companies using different approaches at developing key capabilities without acquisitions.

4.1.4   And That's Not All

Older and proven examples of successful internal reorganizations without "big acquisitions" abound. For example, Starbucks was forced in 2008 to close 600 losing outlets, after a profit drop of 28% from 2007, and closed another 300 stores in 2009. It also laid off 6,700 employees. All in all, it was a serious downturn and crisis for the erstwhile coffee star. Howard Schulz, Starbucks' former and highly successful CEO, on retirement, was called back in January 2008, and upon his return, he substantially overhauled the company' menus, particularly its breakfast offerings, introduced Starbucks' very successful app, and refreshed its management team. Consequently, the company emerged a winner from its doldrums, without major acquisitions. Yet another example is the Lego Group, which in 2004 saw its sales drop 40% in just two years and its debt soar to $1B. The major problem, which sounds like a joke, was that the sales price of many of the new Lego sets did not cover their cost of design and manufacturing. In addition, Lego suffered a complete breakdown of its management team and control systems. In 2005, a new management team was installed that sold various

---

[3] Amolak, H. and S. Haxel, 2024. "Germany's Merck bets on AI drug-design partnerships, rules out acquisitions – Interview," *Wall Street Journal*, June 7.
[4] *Wall Street Journal*, ibid.

unrelated units, while also bringing costs and prices under control. The company soon regained its leadership in the toy industry and returned to profitability, once more, without a major acquisition.

The preceding cases aren't promotion for internal development. They are just intended to show that it's possible to reverse slowdowns, and even performance declines, by clever reorganizations, based on internal development, without substantial acquisitions.

4.2 REFRESHING WEARY BUSINESS MODELS

The choice between internal development and acquisitions is not limited to companies that face the immediate challenges of reversing sales growth declines or a slowdown in earnings but also includes enterprises that consider how to breathe new life into age-old business models. The following are examples of two enterprises that chose differently between internal development and acquisitions.

4.2.1 Johnson & Johnson Ramps Up Drug Research

Johnson & Johnson (J&J), the large drug and medical instrument company, recently decided to ramp up its core business of developing new drugs and diagnostics by integrating it with data science, AI, and machine learning.[5] J&J has hired 6,000 data scientists since 2019 and opened in the San Francisco Bay Area an advanced data science research site in 2022. Capitalizing on its massive database of clinical-trial results and patient records, J&J integrated its data scientists with the company's strategic research decision-makers by having the data scientists work alongside its drug development scientists and health specialists and thereby guide the company's research efforts. Early results from J&J's new integrated approach are promising. For example, the Federal Drug Administration (FDA) has granted "breakthrough device" designation to an algorithm developed by J&J to expedite the diagnosis of pulmonary hypertension, a life-threatening disease whose early diagnosis is difficult but vital for long-term survival. The algorithm "learned" from more than eight million electrocardiogram readouts to shorten the detection time of pulmonary hypertension by 12–18 months, achieving a critical milestone for the FDA's approval.[6]

---

[5] "J&J hired thousands of data scientists. Will the strategy pay off?" *Wall Street Journal*, November 30, 2023.
[6] On May 24, 2022, the day of this news announcement, the stock price of Johnson & Johnson rose 2.1% relative to the market, and its market cap gained $5.1B.

4.2.2 Prudential Tries Acquisition but Fails

Prudential Financial, a large finance company, also sought to modernize its core business with data-driven technologies. Instead of investing in the development of such technologies, as J&J has done, in 2019 Prudential acquired Assurance IQ, a data science startup, for $2.35B, planning to leverage Assurance's algorithms and machine learning capabilities to develop new financial products and market them digitally and directly to consumers. Prudential, however, failed to get what it expected from this acquisition and was instead shocked by the revelation that Assurance's key technology was vastly hyped and its sales projections overly optimistic. "A really poor acquisition, a head scratcher, value destroying, and vastly overpaid" was the verdict of the acquisition by some analysts within a year of the deal. "We wish we would have paid less," the head of Prudential's U.S. businesses admitted.[7] Worse yet, Assurance's marketing tactics became the subject of regulatory scrutiny soon after the acquisition. Faced with this litany of disappointments in 2021 and 2022, Prudential wrote off $1.96B of goodwill from the Assurance acquisition, wiping out 83% of the $2.35B price tag of Assurance IQ and 92% of the goodwill value ($2.13B) from the acquisition. Prudential's hope to modernize its core business (financial services) was stunted by a "head scratcher" acquisition.

4.3 SO, WHAT DOES IT ALL MEAN?

The point we want to stress by the preceding cases is that in most occurrences of business slowdown or even retreat, when analysts, investment bankers, and influential investors are clamoring for a quick turnaround by a major acquisition, a thoughtful reorganization by the internal development of existing and new capabilities is a preferred alternative to acquisitions. The same holds for a company that wants to refresh and modernize its core business model. The choice between acquisitions and internal development, or a combination of both, should therefore be thoroughly considered and discussed with directors and consultants, particularly because, as you'll shortly see, in many cases, internal development is empirically superior and more profitable than business acquisitions.

Come to think of it, this is not really surprising. As we have seen, most acquisitions fail, and many such failures lead to total investment loss

---

[7] Scism, L., 2022, "How Prudential's big tech bet went sour," *Wall Street Journal*, April 29.

(HP–Autonomy, for example). In contrast, internal development can be terminated at any development stage (Phase I drug clinical tests, for example), as success indicators are missed and thereby the investment loss minimized. Change, of course, is also easier to usher in (integrate) with internal development than with an acquisition, given the lower integration costs of the former (no cultural or legal conflicts, for example). Acquisitions, of course, also have advantages, particularly in shorter time of implementation and lower product development uncertainty. So, our message is this: before you rush to acquire a business, reflect seriously on the alternative: internal reorganization and development.

4.4 THE TRADE-OFFS

The vast extant merger and acquisition (M&A) literature offers only a sporadic discussion of the trade-offs between internal development and acquisitions. In most cases, this discussion boils down to the *speed* of implementing the desired business change, like regenerating sales growth or enhancing product development. Proponents of acquisitions claim that internal development is too slow and uncertain to achieve these objectives in time. Recall the case of Teva Pharmaceutical (Chapter 1), whose sales slowed down due to increased generic competition and the near patent expiration of its main proprietary drug Copaxon. A quick change of Teva's course was deemed essential, and a substantial acquisition seemed the only solution. Developing alternative drugs for the patent-expiring Copaxon may have taken several years – far too long to wait – and development success wasn't guaranteed. Acquisition, therefore, appeared the only viable option for Teva.

Upon reflection, though, the urgency argument for acquisitions often indicates poor management. Any reasonably run drug company would have known years in advance that its leading drug will ultimately lose its patent protection and embark on developing alternative products well ahead of the patent termination day. So, internal development commenced years ahead of patent expiration is almost always an alternative to an acquisition. Of course, specific situations will vary with respect to the timing, cost, and uncertainty aspects involved in the choice between internal development and acquisitions, and no general rule applying to all circumstances can be formulated. What we can do here – and this will be very useful to managers and directors – is to analyze our sample regarding the actual use of acquisitions versus internal development and ascertain the benefits of each course of action. That's next.

4.5 INTERNAL DEVELOPMENT AND ACQUISITIONS ARE SUBSTITUTES

Figure 4.2 shows, for the period, 1985–2022, averaged over every five years, that internal development and acquisitions are indeed *substitutes*. We measure internal development as spending on R&D, capital expenditures, and "organizational capital" (such as AI).[8] In Figure 4.2, firms making acquisitions (buyers) are divided into two groups: those with "low internal development" (below industry median) and those with "high internal development" (above industry median), and the average value of acquisitions (divided by total assets) is recorded for each group. It is clear from the figure that in every 5-year period, companies that *invest less* on internal development (depicted by the left bar in each pair) spend *substantially more*

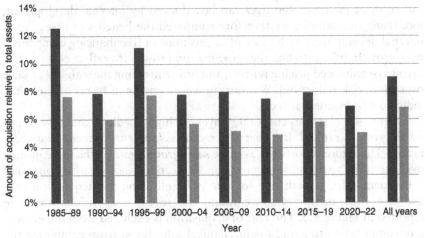

Value of acquisition by firms with low vs. high internal development: firms with low (high) internal development spend more (less) on acquisition

■ Amount of acquisition by firms with low internal development
▨ Amount of acquisition by firms with high internal development

FIGURE 4.2 The Substitution Between Internal Development and Acquisition, 1985–2022

---

[8] We measure organizational capital outlays as one-third of firms' total selling, general, and administrative (SG&A) expenses. Prior studies suggest that up to one-third of firms' SG&A expenses represent investment in various types of organizational capital, such as information technology and brand enhancement. See, for example, L. Enache and A. Srivastava, "Should Intangible Investments Be Reported Separately or Combined with Operating Expenses?" *Management Science* 64, no. 7 (2018): 3446–3468.

on corporate acquisitions than those that spend more on internal development (right bar). The left bars (acquisitions by low-internal-development
companies) dominate in every 5-year period the right bars. For all years
(far-right pair of bars), the difference in spending on acquisitions between
the low and high-internal-development companies is about 25%. So, internal
development and business acquisitions are in real life substitutes.[9] This substitution clearly supports our recommendation that, prior to embarking on
an acquisition, the alternative of internal development should be seriously
considered by executives and directors.

4.6   THE MEASURED BENEFITS OF INTERNAL DEVELOPMENT VS. ACQUISITIONS

Acquisitions are generally made to spur revenue growth, to decrease production costs, or to change the buyer's business model. As we have seen
earlier, most of these objectives can be achieved by internal development,
too. Using our sample, we therefore compared the benefits of investing in
internal development with those of acquisitions in (i) enhancing companies'
sales growth, (ii) increasing the gross margin growth (to reflect cost of sales
savings or enhanced pricing power), and (iii) reinforcing the stability of sales
over time (risk reduction). We thus measure benefits in terms of three key
indicators of business success.

Figure 4.3 classifies corporate buyers in high, medium, and low equal-
sized groups, ranked by their *internal-development-to-acquisition* cost
ratio.[10] The figure reports the average *sales growth rate* of the three groups
over the three years subsequent to the acquisition year. We also computed
subsequent sales growth rate for one year following the acquisition year
and five subsequent years; we found the results very similar to those
reported in Figure 4.3. The year of acquisition is excluded from the growth
rate computation to avoid the mechanical sales boost from combining the
sales of the buyer and target in the acquisition year. The figure shows (left
three bars) the clear sales growth advantage of firms focusing on investment in internal development. As the ratio of internal development to
acquisition increases (from left to right of the three left bars) so does the
growth of future sales.

---

[9] In Section 2.3 and Figure 2.3, we noted that this substitution has declined over the
past two decades, as more companies became serial acquirers as a matter of strategy.
[10] The internal development-to-acquisitions cost is measured as the ratio of internal
development annual cost, consisting of R&D, capital expenditure, and organizational capital, to the cost of acquisitions.

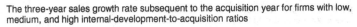

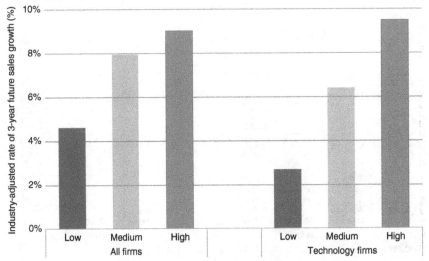

The three-year sales growth rate subsequent to the acquisition year for firms with low, medium, and high internal-development-to-acquisition ratios

Low, medium, and high internal-development-to-acquisition ratio

FIGURE 4.3   Internal Development Beats Acquisitions in Spurring Sales

The (industry-adjusted) sales growth of the "high" ratio – 9% – is twice as high as the growth of the "low" ratio companies. The sales growth advantage of internal development over acquisitions is even higher for *technology firms* (the three bars on the right side of Figure 4.3). The average future sales growth rate of technology buyers with high internal-development-to-acquisition ratio is close to 10% (right bar of Figure 4.3), which is more than three times the growth rate of technology firms with low internal-development-to-acquisition ratio (2.7%). Figure 4.3 thus shows that increasing internal development pays off handsomely in terms of spurring sales growth.

Figure 4.4 shows similar findings for the gross profit (sales minus cost of sales) growth rate, adding to our analysis the dimension of cost of production efficiencies. It is evident that the growth of gross profit after corporate acquisitions increases with the ratio of investment in internal development to acquisitions. The three bars (indicating growth rates) are increasing for both all firms (left) and technology firms (right), as one moves from left (low internal development) to right. Once more, the rate of gross profit growth is particularly pronounced for technology companies (the three bars on the right side of Figure 4.4).

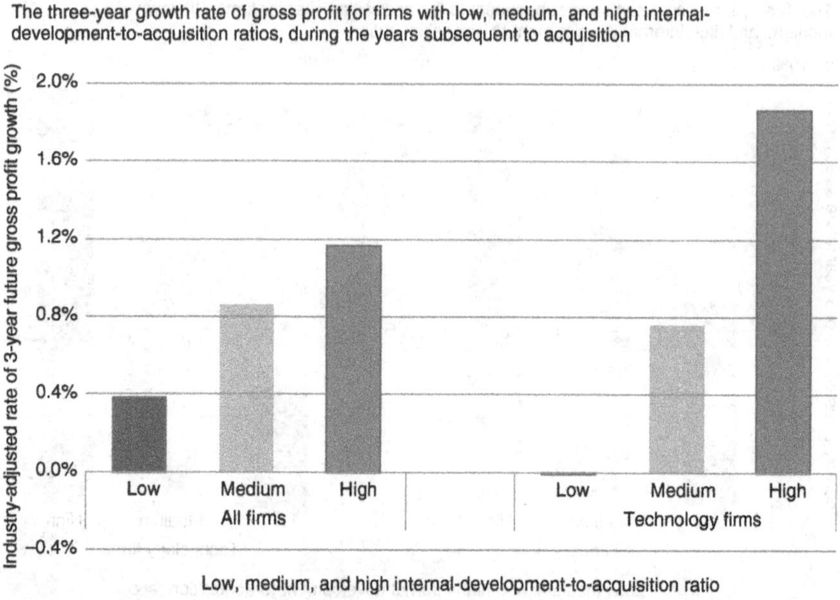

The three-year growth rate of gross profit for firms with low, medium, and high internal-development-to-acquisition ratios, during the years subsequent to acquisition

Low, medium, and high internal-development-to-acquisition ratio

FIGURE 4.4   Internal Development Generates Higher Gross Profit Growth Than Acquisition

Finally, high sales growth rates usually come with increased volatility or uncertainty (risk) of sales. It's therefore particularly important to examine the effects of internal development and acquisitions on the *volatility of sales*, as shown by Figure 4.5. Surprisingly, the figure indicates that as the ratio of investment in internal development to acquisitions increases (from left to right of the three bars), sales volatility, in fact, *decreases*, namely, sales become more stable with internal development.[11] We obtained very similar results for the volatility of future sales growth rates.

A different perspective is provided by Figure 4.6, which shows that investment in internal development (upper line) has a greater (more positive) effect on the post-merger three-year growth rate of industry-adjusted gross profit in every year (1985–2022) than investment in acquisitions (lower line), whose effects on gross profit growth are in fact negative in most years. These results are derived from regressing companies' post-merger growth rate of industry-adjusted gross profit on their investment in internal development and their spending on acquisitions (and a host of other

---

[11] Sales volatility was measured as the standard deviation of sales divided by total assets.

The volatility of future (subsequent to acquisition) sales for firms with low, medium, and high internal-development-to-acquisition ratios

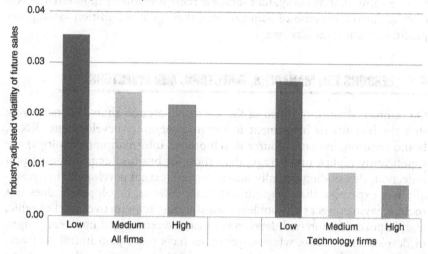

FIGURE 4.5 Internal Development Enhances Sales Stability

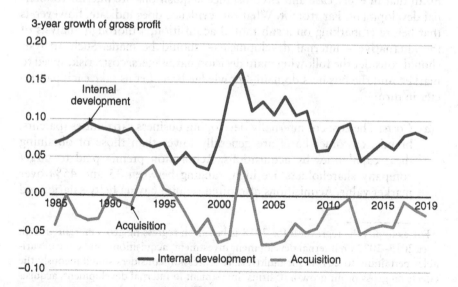

FIGURE 4.6 The Yearly Effect of Investment in Internal Development and Acquisitions on the Industry-Adjusted Three-Year Growth Rate of Gross Profit, 1985–2022

potential growth contributors, including company size).[12] Thus, our compu-
tations show that as companies increase their investment in internal development (at the expense of acquisitions), their post-acquisition sales, gross
profit, and sales stability rise.

4.7 LESSONS FOR MANAGERS, DIRECTORS, AND INVESTORS

Our empirical work outlined in the preceding section showed conclusively
that the benefits of investment in internal (organic) development (R&D,
brand creation, human resource development, information technology) are
significantly higher, on average, than those of business acquisitions. Upon
reflection, this finding actually makes sense. Internal development is generally less expensive than acquisitions, since internal development does not
require paying target shareholders a substantial premium over market value,
and, importantly, internal development can be terminated upon early signs
of development failure while acquisitions have to be paid in full up front.
Furthermore, the integration of internal development with other company
activities is often substantially easier and faster than that of acquisitions.

But recall that our empirical findings are "on average." They do not
mean that in every case and circumstance acquisitions are inferior to internal development. Far from it. What our evidence does indicate, however, is
that before embarking on a substantial acquisition, a thorough analysis of
the alternative – internal development – should be made. Such analysis
should consider the following main decision parameters: costs, risk, speed to
market, and the business domain–knowledge base. Let us take each param-
eter in turn:

(a) *Costs:* The costs of internally developing business capabilities (patents,
   brands, customer base) are generally lower than those of obtaining
   these capabilities by acquisitions. Acquisition premia paid to target
   company shareholders are high, ranging between 35 and 45% over
   market value. Acquisitions also often require paying hefty salaries and

---

[12] For example, the regression for 2018 is based on regressing gross margin growth
over 2019–2022 on internal development investment, acquisitions, and control variables pertaining to 2018. Our multivariate regression considers simultaneously the
effects on gross profit growth of firms' investment in internal development, acquisitions, and other potential growth contributors. This approach thus documents more
reliably the effect of investment in internal development versus acquisitions on the
post-merger growth of gross profit by ensuring that these effects are not due to the
contributions of other factors.

bonuses to retain target company management and talent, with less so for internal development. Integration costs are also substantially lower for internal development than for acquisitions. And most importantly, internal development can be terminated at any stage upon signs of development snags while acquisitions must be paid in full and up front. So, in terms of *costs*, internal development generally has a clear advantage over acquisitions.

(b) *Risk:* By risk we mean the likelihood that the projects or capabilities under development will fail to live up to their technological expectations, like a software product failing a beta test, or a drug under development crashing clinical trials. This risk is generally lower for acquisitions than for internal development. The latter often starts the project from scratch (like building a customer base), whereas acquired capabilities are generally at an advanced, or even completed stage (acquiring an enterprise with patents, or an insurance company with a stable customer base). Thus, the risk of technological developmental failure in acquisitions is substantially lower than that of internal development. So, for acquisitions, they cost more but bear a lower development risk.

(c) *Speed to market of products or services:* The advantage here seems clearly on the side of acquisitions. However, well-run organizations do not wait for their capability's demise, like Teva Pharmaceutical facing the patent expiration of its blockbuster drug Copaxon. Rather, they start the internal development of capabilities well ahead of a looming crisis. In those cases, acquisitions do not always have an advantage over internal development in terms of speed to market. But in cases of distress, such as the loss of a major customer, when something has to be quickly done to spur growth and keep the trust of investors, acquisitions, if successful (a big if), have a clear speed advantage over internal development. This seems to leave us in a quandary: the speed (sometimes) and risk factors favor acquisitions, whereas the cost factor is definitely on the side of internal development. We need a tiebreaker here. Fortunately, there is one that should often determine the decision to buy or internally develop:

(d) *Business domain or knowledge base:* As we have seen, Verizon, Starbucks, Lego, and Johnson & Johnson reorganized themselves and achieved considerable growth and value enhancement without acquisitions, while Google (YouTube) and CVS (Oak Street Health) resorted to relatively large acquisitions. Is there a business logic underlying these different strategies? Indeed, there is.

When businesses reorganize to regenerate growth or revive profitability and regain market share, the reorganization plan or new strategy might call for staying *within the core* – business domain (industry) and knowledge base of the company – and just do things better, more efficiently, or on a larger scale. Alternatively, the reorganization plan might call for a change of a maturing or a decaying business model or adding a new, emerging business model. These different strategies should be the main determinant of the choice between internal development and business acquisitions, subject to considerations of the previous parameters: costs, risk, and speed to market. Let us explain.

Internal development is preferred for reorganizations staying within the company's core, or business domain and knowledge base, such as in the opening Verizon case. Company executives are familiar with the technologies, personnel, and regulations required for internal development within the core. Cost, risk, and sometimes even speed to market favor in this case internal development. That's the reason Verizon, Starbucks, and Lego, which stayed within their core business domains, chose internal development over acquisitions and were ultimately successful.

In contrast, Google and CVS clearly looked for a change in or a substantial extension of their business model. Google wanted to extend operations to the video-sharing sector and CVS, a pharmacy, to primary care medical centers. Such changes of business models require a new knowledge base and are best achieved by successful acquisitions.

So, when considering a reorganization or a strategic shift for regenerating growth, start with this question: Do we want to change the core business model and knowledge domain of the company, or do we just want to improve the operation of the current model? This will indicate the preferability of business acquisitions (new knowledge domain) over internal development. Then the secondary issues of cost, risk, and speed to market will have to be considered to cement the final choice.

CHAPTER 5

The Folly of the Conglomerate Acquisitions

Conglomerate companies – business enterprises comprised of unrelated units – were the toast of the town in the 1960s and 1970s. Some even predicted that three or four conglomerates would ultimately dominate the U.S. economy. But reality was very different. Conglomerates never overcame the glaring absence of economic justification for their business structure and operating model. Indeed, the 1980s and 1990s saw the failure and disappearance of most conglomerates, leading in the past few years to the downfall of the largest of them all: General Electric. So, we thought that the conglomerates met the fate of the dinosaurs, but – surprise – in the past two decades, conglomerate acquisitions came roaring back. And yet, conglomerates still don't make economic sense, so why are they back, and how are they faring?

5.1 A CONGLOMERATE ACQUISITION: INTEL–MOBILEYE

Intel, the storied American tech company founded in 1968 by the legendary Gordon Moore and Robert Noyce, was for a long time the world's leading semiconductor designer and manufacturer. In 2020, Intel ranked 45th on the Fortune 500 list of the largest U.S. corporations by revenue. Intel supplies microprocessors for the leading computer systems manufacturers and also designs and manufactures motherboard chipsets, network interface controllers, and integrated circuits, along with other devices related to communications and computing. In short, Intel is a vital link in the ever-expanding communications and computing spectrum. As of late, however, Intel has faced growing competition in both the design and manufacturing of its major products, which has had serious adverse effects on its growth, profitability, and share prices.

Intel's revenues declined 12% from 2019 to 2022, and its net income fell a whopping 62%. Intel obviously struggles to keep its former leading position. This is, of course, a familiar scenario for many longtime leading companies hitting plateaus, reminding one of Xerox, IBM, and Cisco.

What did Intel do to regenerate its growth and regain its leading position? A big acquisition, of course. Indeed, in August 2017 Intel acquired the Israeli company Mobileye for an eye-popping price of $15.3B, amounting to a multiple of 43 times Mobileye's 2016 revenues ($358M) and a 141 earnings multiple ($108M).[1] Not surprisingly, most analysts reacted negatively to the acquisition, focusing on the exorbitant price apparently paid. The fact that earlier (2010) Intel bought the software security company McAfee for $8B and spun it off in 2016 for less than $5B didn't lend much credence to Intel's acquisition prowess. But there was something else disconcerting about Mobileye – it was a conglomerate acquisition.

Mobileye, at the time of its acquisition, was a leader in a new and fast-growing field – autonomous driving, developing self-driving technologies and driver assistance systems. It already had development agreements with several major car manufacturers, like BMW. The company, which was founded in 1999, was valued at $1.5B in 2013 and went public in 2014. But Mobileye's business was *inherently unrelated* to Intel's. How could its acquisition solve any of the competitive and design challenges of Intel? Where would the synergies come from? Apparently, from nowhere, like any typical conglomerate acquisition.

All this quickly became clear, and in December 2021 cash-strapped Intel started unloading Mobileye. It announced plans to take Mobileye public via initial public offering (IPO) and sold its shares to the public, while retaining control of Mobileye. For the IPO, Intel valued Mobileye at $16B–17B, very close to its acquisition price, while the S&P 500 advanced 93% over that period! Currently, Mobileye is no longer the only game in town. Many competitors are operating in its space, and it's still unclear what Intel's objectives were in acquiring Mobileye. Like with other conglomerate acquisitions, the objectives of Mobileye's purchase were dubious and the results disappointing.

5.2 THE ALLEGED BENEFITS OF CONGLOMERATES

Who still remembers the corporate names International Telephone & Telegraph (ITT), Litton Industries, Gulf and Western, Textron, or Ling, Temco, Vought (LTV)? We bet only a few, if any, and yet, throughout the 1960s and

---

[1] Reed, J. and M. Murgia, 2017. "Intel buys Mobileye in $15.3bn deal," *Financial Times*, March 13.

1970s, these companies were the darlings of shareholders, leading corporate America. They played a central role in the media and investment worlds, and their chief executives were adorning the covers of all the major business magazines. Those were the leading conglomerate companies, namely, business enterprises comprised of unrelated entities, like finance, manufacturing, and retail. LTV, for example, was involved in aerospace, airlines, electronics, steel manufacturing, sporting goods, meat packing, car rentals, and pharmaceuticals, among other businesses. Gulf and Western, once parodied as "Engulf+Devour," operated businesses in entertainment, financial services, and various unrelated consumer products. One wonders, managing all these unrelated businesses, how did their chief executive officers (CEOs) have the time to frequently appear on TV and pose for magazine covers?

For the individuals building the conglomerate behemoth, like James Ling, the founder of LTV, or Charles Bluhdorn of Gulf and Western, the motivation appears to be sheer greed and empire building. Running a conglomerate empire was highly remunerative, and its leaders were the toast of the town, occupying the boards of glittering charitable institutions. Jack Welch, the legendary CEO of the largest and longest surviving conglomerate – General Electric – was truly a celebrity. It was common to name Welch the CEO of the century, among other adorations. Business schools competed on inviting him to talk to their graduate students, magazines vied for his interviews, and books were written about his innovative management style and business methods. It's very difficult to reach this level of reverence and remuneration running a single-business company, even a very successful one.

So the personal motives of the conglomerate founders and CEOs are easily understandable. But why did fund managers and shareholders tolerate this activity, particularly when the operating performance of conglomerates was in most cases mediocre? It's simple – as with most fads, many investors were allured by the promise of the great future of the conglomerates, an expectation bolstered by academics and consultants who provided the economic "justification" for the conglomerate business structure. The conglomerates were rationalized – even hailed – as a winning business organization, generating financial and managerial efficiencies, as well as risk attenuation.

The alleged financial efficiencies of conglomerates generally went by the name of *internal capital markets.* Financing growth (research and development, capital expenditures) generally requires ample external funds (loans, bonds), which is quite expensive. But if one unit of a conglomerate can transfer its excess cash to another unit – internal fund transfers – the cost of funds may be substantially reduced. So the transfer of corporate funds among conglomerate units, according to need and opportunity, went the argument, created for the conglomerates considerable financial efficiencies, unavailable to single-business enterprises. So, for example, having a stable cash-producing insurance company in one's group will support several other cash-starved units, without resorting to external capital markets.

As for the managerial efficiencies, proponents of conglomerates claimed that by their sheer size and diversification of activities, conglomerates could draw top managerial talent who were less attracted to "boring" specialized firms. Conglomerates could also pay executives better, and the expectation of moving from one industry to another within the company would be a special attraction to venturesome, risk-taking employees. This superior managerial team would be deployed across the conglomerate units to maximize the use of employee and managerial skills. A special term was also coined for this advantage – *internal labor markets*. Large corporate centers of R&D and IT would be well funded by conglomerates and efficiently serve the disparate business units. So there you have it – a perfect economic justification of the conglomerate form of business organization.

Add to this the powerful argument of *enterprise risk reduction* through the diversification of unrelated business activities – same as the diversification of one's securities portfolio – and the argument for conglomerates' superiority seems compelling. Conglomerates were expected to "inherit the earth."

The CEO of the Century

There was never a better example of a company that appeared to be reaping all the conglomerate efficiencies than GE's 20 years (1981–2001) under Jack Welch. As for financial efficiencies – the famed internal capital market – GE went further than other conglomerates and actually owned one of America's largest financial institutions: GE Capital. In addition to traditional banking and investment banking activities, GE Capital financed, and even supported, various GE units in need of funds for working capital, R&D, loan repayments, and sometimes even covering losses.

Regarding managerial efficiencies, GE maintained advanced executive programs – "GE's business school" – and groomed managers by moving them across the conglomerate's units. Being a top GE executive under Jack Welch guaranteed one a CEO position in many major companies (Jim McNerney at Boeing and Bob Nardelli at Home Depot, for example).

Most importantly, Jack Welch delivered for the conglomerate shareholders. GE's revenues rose from $25B to $130B, and profits too kept pace under his leadership. Analysts' earnings consensus estimates were regularly beaten, sometimes with the help of selling assets and recording capital gains, and the stock price kept rising. Everyone – investors, directors, employees, customers, and suppliers – participated in the party.

But this beautiful facade apparently stood on shaky grounds and unraveled under Welch's successor, the unlucky Jeff Immelt. Despite 380 acquisitions and numerous strategic turnarounds – like GE's focus on renewables and, later, software (GE Digital) – GE's stock performance under Immelt was among the worst of any major U.S. company, leading ultimately to its current sorry state: the famed conglomerate split into three companies in 2021, none of them with stellar performance so far. The magic has finally gone from GE and for good reason – there was never a compelling business justification for the company, or for any other conglomerate.

5.3 AND THE FUNDAMENTAL SHORTCOMINGS OF THE CONGLOMERATES ARE. . .

There is a fundamental principle in business organization that many managers ignore (or aren't aware of) and investment bankers abhor: don't do things that your shareholders can do on their own. Applied to conglomerates, this principle implies that there is no justification for a company to operate, say, a bank, TV station, jet engines production, and appliance manufacturing, because investors who want to invest in these industries can easily buy shares in such stand-alone companies – and do it much cheaper than by corporate mergers. Moreover, each investor can allocate their funds according to individual preferences (say, 60% manufacturing and 40% insurance), whereas the conglomerate company forces a specific allocation on all its shareholders.[2] So why should investors own GE stocks when they can easily have a portfolio of its units – manufacturing, finance, and entertainment (GE owned for a while the television network NBC) stocks – and reap the expected benefits and risk diversification provided by such a portfolio?

Thus, when a specific business organization lacks an economic justification or rationale, it is not sustainable. And this, sooner or later, led to the demise of practically all the big conglomerates. Simply speaking, who needs conglomerates?

5.4 BUT WAIT: WHAT ABOUT THE CLAIMED EFFICIENCIES?

If you, an investor, own Nvidia and Prudential (an insurance company) stocks, you get a certain risk diversification, but you can't transfer

---

[2] The same fundamental principle underlies the seminal Modigliani and Miller (both Nobel laureates in economics) paper "The Cost of Capital, Corporation Finance, and the Theory of Investment" (*American Economic Review*, 48 (1958): 261–297), which argued that there is no reason that a specific capital structure (debt-to-equity ratio) maintained by a company will affect its value, since shareholders can achieve any capital structure they desire by holding different quantities of the firm's stocks and bonds (or debt).

Prudential's excess cash to Nvidia when the need arises, but if both companies were owned by a conglomerate, central management could initiate such a fund transfer and spare Nvidia raising expensive funds externally. So, there seems to be an important efficiency (internal capital markets) available to a conglomerate but not to its individual shareholders.

This argument for conglomerates is appealing in the abstract but has failed in reality because excess cash of certain conglomerate units was frequently used to prop up other *failing units* that were better sold off or terminated. Conglomerate executives, reluctant to admit that they botched certain acquisitions or mismanaged them, often supported these failing businesses with funds transfers from healthier units, thereby prolonging the losses and value destruction of the failing business and weakening the healthy ones. Thus, for example, GE acquired the French company Alstom's thermal, renewables, and grid businesses in November 2015 for $13.5B, integrating it with GE's power division. But the power market softened soon after the acquisition, and the French subsidiary was subject to severe regulatory and other restrictions (no employee layoffs) that seriously hampered GE's power division and the company as a whole. Nevertheless, GE continuously tried to reorganize Alstom and likely supported its waning cash flows with internal funds transfers. As of this writing, GE still tries to shrink its underperforming power division, and in late 2022, the company announced its intention to sell its nuclear steam turbine segment. Conglomerate executives were generally loath to terminate losing operations and committed to prop them up with internal fund transfers.[3] The alleged "internal labor markets" advantage of conglomerates – grooming and promoting managers by moving them across units – also rarely worked as advertised, because such transfers were frequently used to promote well-connected and influential executives rather than those with the greatest talent.

But the most destructive shortcoming of conglomerates is the absence of the "market discipline." The monitoring of public companies by investors and the consequent changes in stock prices are replaced in conglomerates by internal performance evaluation, which was often heavily influenced by corporate politics and power positions. Conglomerates avoid the harsh but rather quick and objective judgment of the market (investors) regarding the performance of their business units and are thus hothouses for inaptitude, nepotism, and influence peddling. This was clearly shown by several academic studies that established the existence of a "diversification discount" – a

---

[3] We explain later in this book why managers have strong incentives to hold on to losing investments, such as failed acquisitions, and continue supporting them for too long (Chapter 11).

measure of conglomerate inefficiencies. The researchers compared the market value of conglomerates with that of stand-alone companies that replicated the conglomerate's business units. Thus, for example, GE's value was compared with the sum of stand-alone finance, appliances, manufacturing, and TV networks. This research conclusively showed that the combined value of the stand-alone companies exceeded that of the conglomerates by 25–30%.[4] This came to be known as the *diversification discount*, clearly reflecting the inherent inefficiencies of conglomerates.

And those inefficiencies weren't late to show up. By the 1980s and 1990s, most conglomerates were gone, kaput: LTV, IT&T, Litton, Gulf and Western, and TRW are all now relics of the past. Even the longest standing of them all (140+ years) – GE – is now a shadow of its former self. There seems to be no escape from the cardinal rule: if it doesn't make economic sense, it's unsustainable.[5]

5.5   SO, HOW SURPRISED WE WERE . . .

Some readers may ask at this stage why we need to know all about conglomerates if they are extinct. Because – surprise, surprise – they are back in the form of a surge in conglomerate acquisitions. Just look at Figure 5.1, which portrays the percentage of conglomerate acquisitions (when the target's business is unrelated to the buyer's) out of all of our sample acquisitions. As expected, the percentage of conglomerate acquisitions declined in the 1980s and 1990s, as investors observed the implosion of one big conglomerate

---

[4] See, for example, D. Hoechle, M. Schmid, I. Walter, and D. Yermack, "How Much of the Diversification Discount Can Be Explained by Poor Corporate Governance?" *Journal of Financial Economics* 103 (2012): 41–60.

[5] GE, like many other conglomerates, cannot avoid the fate of subsequently breaking up its businesses in order to save itself. After resisting for years intense investor calls to break the company apart, in November 2018 GE's CEO Larry Culp finally announced the decision to split GE "into three public companies, drawing the curtain on an era of modern business – the dominance of industrial conglomerates" (Gryta, T., 2018, "The end of the GE we knew: Breakup turns a page in modern business history," *Wall Street Journal*, November 9). Three years later in November 2021, GE announced that it would split into three separate publicly traded companies – healthcare, aviation, and energy (Pound, J., 2021, "GE to break up into 3 companies focusing on aviation, health care, and energy," *CNBC*, November 9). In April 2024, GE completed the final step of its breakup ("GE's final split: A breakup 130 years in the making," *Wall Street Journal*, April 2, 2024).

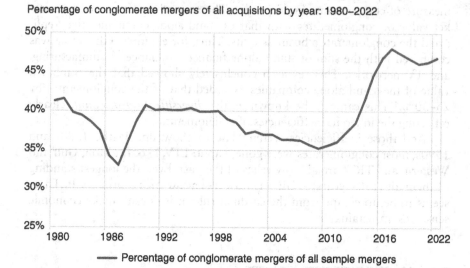

Percentage of conglomerate mergers of all acquisitions by year: 1980–2022

FIGURE 5.1   The Resurgence of Conglomerate Acquisitions

after another and realized that most conglomerates were doomed to fail. And yet – and this is the surprise – during the past decade or so, conglomerate acquisitions have been on the rise, bigtime. Currently, *almost half* of all acquisitions are conglomerates! The zombies rise from the dead? This astounding finding seemed to escape the media and commentators, since we haven't seen serious discussions of this recent economic development.

What's also surprising is that many of these conglomerate acquisitions, particularly the large ones, are made by big technology companies, such as the Intel–Mobileye merger mentioned earlier, along with Amazon–Whole Foods, Microsoft–Xbox, Google–various autonomous cars developers, Apple–SoundJam MP (iTunes), and the list goes on. What explains this acquisition shift? Perhaps these highly successful tech companies, which are flush with cash, are concerned that their core business is maturing and therefore are looking for growth opportunities elsewhere. These cash-rich companies are willing to spend considerable resources on the "next big thing" in an unrelated business. Due to the near-monopolistic position of some of these companies (Microsoft, Amazon), they are prevented by antitrust regulators from acquiring sizable companies in, or near, their core business. Conglomerate acquisitions are, in contrast, tolerated. Or perhaps it's the hubris of managers who were very successful in their initial endeavor (creating and managing Google, Amazon, and Apple), believing that they can repeat their erstwhile success in a new field. It remains to be seen whether these newcomers to conglomeration will fare better than the conglomerates of yore. We doubt it very much. The early lackluster experience of Intel–Mobileye or

Amazon–Whole Foods, as well as Amazon's ten-year travails to make Twitch (video broadcasts) profitable, seems to support our misgivings, though there were some great conglomerate success stories as well, like Google buying YouTube or Amazon developing AWS (cloud services). So, we'll postpone our final judgment of this recent rise in tech conglomerate acquisitions and say, "The jury is still out." And yet, we can't conclude this chapter without repeating the warning: be wary of conglomerate acquisitions.

Why are we so confident about the futility of conglomerate acquisitions? To bolster our conceptual arguments about the fundamental flaws of conglomerate mergers and their harm to shareholders, we demonstrate in Figure 5.2 the effects of conglomerate mergers versus horizontal (same-industry) mergers on the *acquisition success*. These effects are derived from the coefficients of our comprehensive statistical model (introduced in the appendix). The percentages (vertical axis) in Figure 5.2 reflect the effect on the average acquisition success rate of each type of merger: all buyers (left two bars), technology buyers (middle two bars), and financial services buyers (right two bars), while taking into account in our model the effects of other acquisition success determinants. Figure 5.2 clearly shows that for all types of buyers conglomerate mergers detract, on average, from acquisition success – the conglomerate acquisition bars in the figure are *all negative*,

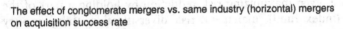

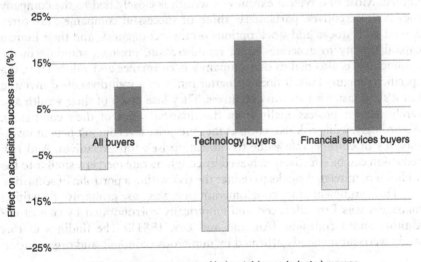

FIGURE 5.2 The Effect of Conglomerate Mergers vs. Same-Industry Mergers on the Acquisition Success Rate

indicating that conglomerate mergers *decrease* acquisition success rate. Same-industry mergers (the right bar in each pair), in contrast, significantly increase acquisition success rate (positive bars).

5.6   FINALLY, BEWARE THE SELFISH CEO

We dismissed the risk-reduction motive of conglomerate acquisitions – if unit A falls on hard times, a successful unit B will stabilize the company's operations – because individual shareholders can achieve such (or any other) risk reduction level by owning the shares of companies whose businesses parallel those of units A and B. But what if corporate managers have a different agenda than their shareholders? What if conglomerate risk reduction serves managers' own interests, irrespective of whether it benefits shareholders or not? Such divergence of preferences between managers (the agents) and their shareholders (the principals), and the consequent harm to shareholders, is known in economics as *agency costs*. In this case the agency costs are those of conducting unnecessary (from shareholders' perspective) conglomerate mergers.

The reason for suspecting such divergence of preferences is as follows: while investors can diversify and adjust the risk of their portfolios to the extent they want, even maximizing risk reduction by holding a part of the entire market (index fund), managers' risk diversification ability is very limited. Most of a typical executive's wealth is closely tied to the company they run. Executives, particularly those of successful companies, are often loaded with stocks and stock options on their companies, and their human capital (ability to generate future remuneration, prestige, standing in the community) is also tied to the company's performance and value. Thus, if a specific company fails, it doesn't matter much to a well-diversified investor, but it's a disaster for its top executives. They lose much of their wealth and rarely recover professionally from the financial ruins of their companies. Accordingly, while risk reduction at the enterprise level doesn't benefit investors, it's of considerable value to the enterprise's top executives. And risk reduction can be effectively achieved by conglomerate mergers, similar to the addition of unrelated stocks to reduce the risk within a portfolio of securities.

This argument for conglomerate mergers as primarily benefiting managers was first advanced and empirically corroborated by one of the authors and a colleague (Amihud and Lev, 1981).[6] The findings of this study were subsequently affirmed by numerous economic and organization

---

[6] Y. Amihud and B. Lev, "Risk Reduction as a Managerial Motive for Conglomerate Mergers," *Bell Journal of Economics* 12 (1981): 605–617.

researchers. Specifically, Amihud and Lev classified public companies into two groups: those controlled by a small, cohesive group of owners, like in Ford or Google, and those with widely dispersed ownership among many shareholders, thereby effectively controlled by their managers. If conglomerate acquisitions benefited mainly managers, then the latter group of companies, those controlled by managers, would conduct a significantly larger proportion of conglomerate acquisitions than the first (owner-controlled) group. And that's indeed what the researchers found, lending strong support to managers' (but not shareholders') preference for conglomerate acquisitions.

This conclusion has particular relevance to corporate directors who oversee managers. The justification for conglomerate acquisition proposals has to be carefully examined by directors and major shareholders and the expected benefits *to the company and its shareholders* substantiated rock solid. Otherwise, such acquisition proposals should be rejected. Remember, conglomerate acquisitions are bad for corporate health and shareholder wealth. They should be avoided in most cases. When executives insist on such acquisitions, they should present a credible case, with measurable targets, supporting their proposal.

CHAPTER 6

Are There "Best Times" to Acquire Businesses (1)?

External Opportunities

The literature on mergers and acquisitions (M&As), along with M&A advisers and investment bankers, often suggest that there are opportune times to buy companies and that managers should exploit these opportunities. Thus, for example, when capital markets are thriving, buyers' high share prices facilitate acquisitions; or, when your peers are all consolidating, don't remain on the sidelines. New chief executive officers (CEOs) are often advised to make their mark early on with a big, transformative acquisition. In this and the next chapters, we use our sample of 40,000 acquisitions to systematically examine the various claims for "best times to buy." This chapter focuses on *external opportunities*, such as booming stock markets or an industry acquisition frenzy, while the next one explores internal opportunities, such as a new CEO taking the helm or a reorganization and restructuring plan. For both types of opportunities, we have a big surprise for you: most of the presumably "best times to buy" are, in fact, the *worst times*. They are serious "M&A traps." Just avoid them. But, not to worry: we also offer several proven "best times to buy."

"It was the best of times, and it was the worst of times."

—Charles Dickens (*A Tale of Two Cities*)

6.1   STAY AWAY FROM HOT CAPITAL MARKETS

We have shown in Chapter 3 that there is a significant positive correlation between the state of capital markets (high or low stock prices) and merger activity. Thus, for example, in late 2022 and the first quarter of 2023, a period characterized by fear of recession, the S&P 500 declined to 4,109 on March 31, 2023, from 4,530 a year earlier – a 9.3% drop. The total M&A activity, in tandem, dropped during that period to $575.1B, an astounding 48% decrease, compared to the same period a year earlier. In Europe the fall was even sharper – 70%.[1] Obviously, it's easier to finance acquisition with stocks, fully or partially, during hot markets, when share prices are high and conditions for issuing new shares are favorable. In addition, rising stock markets signal investors' optimism about future economic conditions, incentivizing managers to expand capacity and innovation and seek new markets, often by acquisitions. The reverse holds true, too, as in the 2022/2023 example discussed earlier. So, it's not surprising that merger activity is positively correlated with capital market conditions.

But should managers rush and buy businesses when the market is hot, like so many are doing (hence the correlation)? The answer seems to be yes. Isn't the "wisdom of the crowds" generally right? Not in this case, though, as Figure 6.1 demonstrates. The figure is remarkable in its simplicity and emphatic in its message. We have at our disposal a very long period of acquisitions (1980–2022), allowing us to examine up and down capital markets. We then use our measure of merger success (reflecting the buyer's post-acquisition sales and gross margin growth, positive stock returns, and no goodwill write-offs) to evaluate the success of acquisitions made during the up and down market years. Simple, yet powerful.

Specifically, we ranked our sample acquisitions (40,000) by the S&P 500 change in the 24 months prior to the acquisition and classified the acquisitions to three groups: low, medium, and high market conditions (pre-acquisition). Figure 6.1 exhibits the three market situations: low, medium, and high markets (left bar in each pair). The bars to the right of each market situation depict the average success of the acquisitions made during these three periods. The message is loud and clear: as conditions of capital markets improve (from left to right of the figure), the success of

---

[1] ynet.com, Israel, March 31, 2023.

Average acquisition success rate in low, medium, and high capital markets, measured by the 24-month S&P 500 return (price change) prior to acquisition

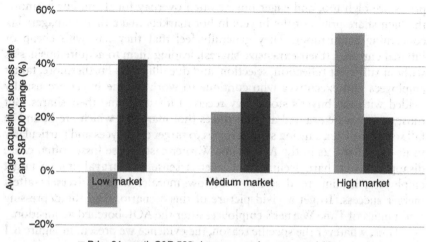

FIGURE 6.1　The Average Success Rate of Acquisitions During Periods of Low, Medium, and High Capital Markets, as Measured by the Pre-acquisition 24-Month Change in S&P 500

acquisitions *worsens*.[2] From a 41% acquisition success rate in poor capital markets (second from left bar) to 20% in booming markets (right bar), the *number* of acquisitions grows during good markets, but their success rate declines. This message is, to the best of our knowledge, new to the M&A literature: purchasing businesses in hot capital markets, as so many recommend – and as many managers do – is a bad idea. No wonder so many acquisitions fail (70–75%).

---

[2] Figure 6.1 was constructed by first measuring for all our sample acquisitions the 24 months' record of the S&P 500 index prior to the acquisition, indicating the pre-acquisition market conditions. Next, acquisitions under all market conditions (S&P 500 index change over the prior 24 months) were ranked and classified into three groups: acquisitions following poor markets (in fact, negative S&P 500 change) on the left of the figure, acquisitions following intermediate markets (middle pair of bars), and acquisitions following booming markets (right two bars). The average acquisition success of each of the three groups is indicated by the height of the right bar of each pair, which drops (from left to right), from a more than 40 to 20% acquisition success rate.

There are several reasons for the surprising failure of corporate acquisitions made in hot capital markets. First, in such markets, target company prices are high too, and eager buyers often overpay for them. Furthermore, the high share prices of the buyers in hot markets make their managers lax concerning acquisitions. They generally feel that they pay with cheap or inflated currency (their expensive shares), leading them to acquire businesses without sufficient reflection, selection, and due diligence. Furthermore, target employees and executives who continue to work for the buyer are usually loaded with the buyer's stock they received for tendering their shares. But those stocks were granted at peak prices (hot markets), which are bound to fall sooner or later, causing serious losses to target employees and particularly to its executives, as in the AOL–Time Warner case. These losses often cause disappointment, hard feelings, and even a sense of betrayal among target employees, leading to desertion and low morale, which adversely affect merger success. To get a vivid picture of this scenario, read the depressing testimonies of Time Warner's employees after the AOL botched acquisition.

Thus, whatever the specific reason, the evidence we present in Figure 6.1 is clear: buying businesses in hot capital markets is, on average, a losing proposition; in contrast, buying in low markets will allow you to carefully select good matches – potential winners – and avoid paying exorbitant acquisition prices. So, just reverse your advisors' suggestion (more on that later).

6.2   DON'T SUCCUMB TO PEER PRESSURE TO ACQUIRE

You sometimes hear from directors and investment bankers: "All our peers are currently acquiring businesses and getting ahead; what are we waiting for?" Indeed, it is a fact that acquisitions are to some extent contagious: when several industry peers start acquiring, others in the sector don't want to be left empty-handed without a good mate. A sectorial rush to buy is often irresistible.

Indeed, history provides numerous examples of industry-concentrated acquisition sprees, like the post-deregulation airline consolidations of the 1980s and 1990s, big pharma's rush to buy small biotech companies (which still goes on), financial services firms in the early 2000s acquiring fintech companies, or wireless operators' mergers subsequent to that industry's deregulation. *The Economist* (July 17, 2020) reported on such a rush to buy in Europe: the EU General Court approved the €10.2B merger between O2 (owned by Telefonica) and Three (owned by Hutchinson), both wireless companies. A bit earlier, in April 2020, the $26B merger between T-Mobile and Sprint was also approved. A deal between Telia and Telenor in Denmark in 2015 was announced but later abandoned due to regulators' objections. And in October 2022, the French telecom group Orange and the Spanish peer MasMovil picked up Romania's Digi company's assets the regulators previously required to divest for securing the approval for their merger deal of $19.7B in Spain.

Currently, the sectorial acquisition frenzy focuses on generative artificial intelligence (AI). Forbes notes:[3]

> Since the release of ChatGPT shook the entire world in November 2022, FOMO (Fear Of Missing Out) has gripped the corporate world. In Silicon Valley I hear discussions predicting that new companies driving search, database, enterprise resource planning, supply chain management, etc. will be cropping up – all based on AI as its foundational layer. Incumbents in these enterprise sectors are feeling the pinch and getting paranoid about their relevance in the new Generative AI-dominated era. Hence, the Generative AI gold rush is ushering in a wave of mergers and acquisitions. . .

Reasons for industry-wide merger frenzies abound. Deregulation, like in airlines in the late 1970s, often leads to multiple consolidations. Relaxation of antitrust rules, as during the Trump administration, naturally enhances industry merger waves. The emergence of a new technology, like wireless communications, or currently AI, often leads to merger waves, particularly due to the fear that the industry will transform to a "winner takes all" situation.[4] And let's not forget the fads, like the special-purpose acquisition companies (SPACs) of the 2020s, which generated lots of acquisitions while they lasted.[5] Naturally, when the rush to acquire is on, you feel you don't want to be the only one left out. Sounds compelling, but is it really a good idea to join an industry rush to acquire? The evidence, surprisingly, says no.

---

[3] Pang, S., 2023, "FOMO-driven generative AI acquisition spree has begun," *Forbes*, August 5.

[4] For example, amid the frenzied AI arms race, driven by leading tech firms' large increases in capital spending on AI infrastructure (e.g., graphics processing units [GPUs] and data centers), it is reported that "SK Telecom said it is seeking to merge its AI chip start-up Sapeon with South Korea–based chip designer Rebellions to create a 'homegrown company' to lead the global AI race. They aim to complete the merger by the third quarter [of 2024]." (Clark, A., 2024, "Nvidia gains. What Oracle's earnings mean for the AI chip leader," *Barron's*, June 12).

[5] A SPAC is a public company, usually inactive, that raises money for acquiring other operating companies. In 2020, 247 SPACs were created, and in 2021, 613 SPAC initial public offerings (IPOs) were recorded. This phenomenon quickly faded (see, Kiernan, P., 2024, "SPAC mania is dead. The SEC wants to keep it that way," *Wall Street Journal*, January 24).

Figure 6.2 is constructed as follows: we identify an industry rush and peer pressure to acquire businesses by three alternative measures, all provided basically the same negative finding: (i) the number of acquisitions made in the industry (three-digit Standard Industrial Classification [SIC] code) during the past 12 months; (ii) the sum of deal (acquisition) values across all deals in the industry in the past 12 months; and (iii) the largest deal in the industry in the past 12 months. We then rank and classify our sample of buyers into three groups by the industry pressure to acquire that buyers faced in their respective industries: buyers facing low, high, and very high industry pressure to buy. Finally, we measure the average *acquisition success rate* for all acquisitions made in the three pressure (intensity) groups.

As Figure 6.2 clearly shows, as the industry pressure to acquire intensifies (increasing left bars in each pair), the average acquisition success (right bars in each pair) plummets: from 40% acquisition success (second from left bar) in industries without the pressure to buy, the success rate drops to less than 20% for acquisitions (right bar) made under intense industry pressure to acquire. That is a 50% success drop. Thus, acquiring businesses during an industry spree, as so many do, is obviously a bad idea. How come? Can all those "experts" pushing managers to join the industry rush to buy be wrong?

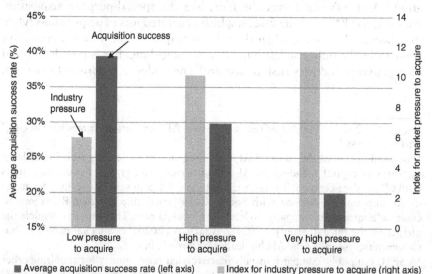

Average acquisition success rate for low, high, and very high *sectorial pressure* to acquire businesses

FIGURE 6.2 The Average Success Rate of Acquisitions Made During Low, High, and Very High Sectorial Acquisition Spree Periods (Measured by the Size of the Largest Acquisition in the Industry in the Past 12 Months)

Evidently, yes, mainly because the supply of targets that fit the buyer's strategy, and sold at a reasonable price, is at any point in time very limited, particularly when all your peers are looking for the same thing. There are very few low-hanging good acquisition candidates. Eligible targets, like small promising biotech companies or currently successful generative AI startups, have become quickly aware of their attractiveness to larger companies, often noticing multiple offers come their way. They accordingly bid up their prices substantially and quickly make themselves hard to get. They initially object to being acquired, put up outrageous demands (like staying independent after acquisition), and delay the acquisition process to garner more bids. All this significantly hurts the acquisition's ultimate success.

And then there is an even more damaging factor: if you just follow your peers' acquisitions, it means that a merger wasn't really in your strategic plan and probably not needed for your operations. Stated differently, acquiring just because others do doesn't make much economic sense and will therefore likely fail.

Whatever the reasons for failure, the facts remain (Figure 6.2): acquiring in a hot acquisition climate in your industry isn't a winning proposition, unless you are among the lucky few who were first to acquire and got a bargain. Avoiding the industry rush to buy reminds us of what one of us recently heard: "Better alone than in bad company," which was the welcome given to one of us by a restaurant owner who saw him enter the restaurant by himself.

6.3 DON'T BUY DURING ECONOMIC RECESSIONS

A *Harvard Business Review* article recently suggested three reasons that recessions are a good time to acquire businesses: "(i) [since] recessions are typically short-lived and followed by long period of growth and prosperity . . ., recessions present an opportunity [to buy] because they separate the wheat from the chaff, the winners from the losers; (ii) [recession] is also an opportune time to acquire companies and buy assets at fire-sale prices; [and] (iii) companies can now [in a recession] hire those engineers and information technology professionals who are being laid off during recessions."[6] This seems like sound advice: recessions provide an opportunity to pick up "Rembrandts in the attic" at fire-sale prices.

Sounds good, except that this recommendation flies in the face of our evidence. Figure 6.3, left side couple of bars, shows the average success rate

---

[6] Govindarajan, V. and A. Srivastava, 2022, "How companies should invest in a downturn," *Harvard Business Review*, June 17.

of acquisitions made during U.S. formal recessions (leftmost bar) and in regular years (bar to its immediate right).[7] The average success rate of recession acquisitions (left bar) falls short by 4–5% compared with acquisition made during nonrecession years. The difference in acquisition success between recession and nonrecession years is accordingly not negligible, and it definitely doesn't support the maxim: buy during recessions!

While the *Harvard Business Review* authors make reasonable arguments in favor of recession acquisitions, our hunch is that they don't work in reality because recessions in the United States are often short-lived (typically one to two years), thereby not allowing buyers sufficient time to carefully search and pick up winners (those that will survive the recession) from losers, nor for target prices to fall to fire-sale levels. Furthermore, given the relatively brief U.S. recessions, businesses are reluctant to lay off key talent, like R&D scientists, to be picked up by buyers.

Accordingly, we decided to give the process of separating successful from unsuccessful targets some more time and to examine the acquisitions made during the two years *following a recession*. This is the time when the

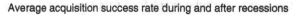

Average acquisition success rate during and after recessions

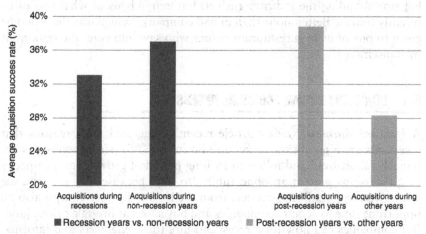

FIGURE 6.3 The Average Success Rate of Acquisitions Undertaken During and After Economic Recessions

---

[7]We followed the Bureau of Economic Research in defining recessions (two consecutive quarters of GDP decline). The modern recession years were 1980–1982, 1990–1991, 2001, and 2007–2009.

real recession winners separate themselves from the losers by quickly turning the corner in terms of sales and profits, retaining talent, and enjoying a slow but sure share price recovery. Our post-recession period is still close enough to the recession so that the low recession share prices didn't return all the way to their pre-recession levels and capital markets are far from hot. It is a narrow but interesting window of opportunity.

The two right-side bars of Figure 6.3 show the results of our post-recession acquisitions, compared with those in regular years. It is evident that the immediate post-recession period is the best time to acquire businesses. Post-recession acquisitions had an almost 40% success rate (second bar from right), compared with 28% average success rate for acquisitions made in other years (rightmost bar).

We accordingly found a relatively narrow window of opportunity – a couple of years immediately following a recession – which is ripe for acquiring companies that are showing early signs of turning the corner (e.g., experiencing a growth of sales and recovery of profits), didn't lay off major talent, and still have stock prices below previous peak. These are real bargains, as our evidence shows.

8.4 DON'T BUY WHEN YOUR STOCK IS OVERVALUED

"Using overvalued shares as a means of acquisition payment enhances the claim on capital of the bidding [acquiring] shareholders . . . using these [overpriced] shares to buy assets available for $p < s$ is better than not buying [these] assets. . . . The analysis also suggests some reason why making acquisitions with [overpriced] stocks might be better than issuing (new) stock and holding cash." That's the recommendation of two renowned economists (Shleifer and Vishny, 2003; 2001).[8] So, the economists' advice to managers of companies with overvalued (inflated) shares is to use these shares primarily to acquire other businesses. We will shortly examine the wisdom of this advice, but first, what exactly are overvalued (overpriced) shares? How do they come about, and who knows about them?

Recall the late 1990s. In retrospect it was a crazed period where hundreds and perhaps thousands of "nothing companies" – those without a

---

[8] A. Shleifer and R. Vishny, "Stock Market Driven Acquisitions," *Journal of Financial Economics* 70, no. 3 (2003): 295–311. Shleifer, A. and R. Vishny, 2001, "Stock market driven acquisitions," https://papers.ssrn.com/sol3/papers.cfm?abstract_id=278563.

valid business model and often having no real revenues, while incurring massive losses – were nevertheless snatched by investors and given high stock market valuations, because they were deemed to be new-era tech start-ups. Amazingly, even several traditional (retail, manufacturing) companies that just added the charmed "dot.com" to their names saw their share price magically rise. This high-tech craze lasted a few years but then came to the inevitable screeching halt in the early 2000s, followed by the collapse of high-tech stock prices, or the burst of the tech bubble. Their main exchange, Nasdaq, lost 60–70% of its value in a couple of years. Given this monumental share price collapse, it's safe to say in retrospect that high-tech shares were *substantially overvalued*, relative to their true, intrinsic value, during the late 1990s. Share misvaluation – overvaluation or undervaluation – occasionally happens to whole sectors, like high-tech as just described, and also to individual stocks.

Share overvaluation essentially means that the share price of a public company is traded consistently above its intrinsic, fundamental value, which reflects the present value of its future cash flows – namely, investors' perceptions of the company's future cash flows rise substantially above what the company will be able to deliver. How do shares become overvalued? Various reasons: investors become excessively optimistic about the prospects of a new, exciting technology, like generative AI, currently, or about charismatic, hype-spewing CEOs, like Sam Bankman-Fried (FTX Cryptocurrency Exchange) or Elizabeth Holmes (Theranos) – both now in the slammer – who, for a while, were able to convince investors of the fortunes to be made from buying into their schemes. But most often, share inflation occurs when adverse information about the company, like a failed drug clinical test or a negative competitive development, isn't yet known to investors.

But, as Michael Jensen put it, "By definition, overvalued shares will sooner or later collapse to their real, intrinsic value, because otherwise, they were not overvalued in the first place."[9] Generally this occurs when the inside information, unknown to investors, becomes public. But while the "overvaluation party" lasts, managers are often tempted to exploit their "inflated currency" to buy businesses. A successful acquisition, it is sometimes argued, may even eliminate the share overvaluation by generating new growth and avoid the share price collapse in the future.

So let's look at the facts. Figure 6.4 shows the average success rate of acquisitions by firms that were classified into seven groups in ascending

---

[9] M. Jensen, "Agency Costs of Overvalued Equity," *Financial Management* 34 (2006): 5–19.

order (from left to right) of share overvaluation.[10] The figure portrays an almost perfect *negative relation* between share overvaluation and acquisition success. Whereas the acquisitions made with fairly valued, or even low-valued shares had a success rate of 40–45%, on average (left bar of figure), acquisitions made with highly overvalued shares had a shareholder value-destroying success rate of 15–20% only (two right bars in Figure 6.4). Namely, only one in seven acquisitions paid for with overvalued shares fulfilled its expectations. What a waste of shareholders' money.

How can this be? The "logic" of using overvalued shares – "cheap currency" – for acquisitions seems so compelling. Well, actually not. First, share overvaluation is in most cases temporary, unless – and this is rare – it is hidden for an extended period by smart information manipulation by management. In general, sooner than later, news about the internal operating problems leading to the overvaluation (a sales slowdown, for example) leaks

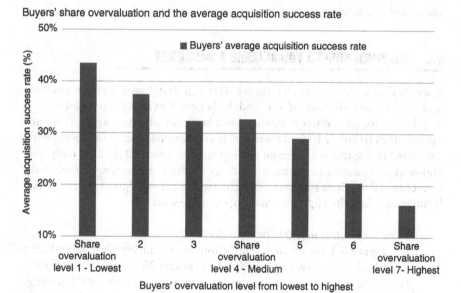

Buyers' share overvaluation and the average acquisition success rate

FIGURE 6.4 The Average Success of Acquisitions for Different Buyers' Share Overvaluation

---

[10]The exact measurement of share overvaluation is quite complex and will delay the flow of presentation here. For details, the reader is referred to F. Gu and B. Lev, "Overpriced Shares, Ill-Advised Acquisitions, and Goodwill Impairment," *The Accounting Review* 86, no. 6 (2011): 1995–2022.

out or is reported in a quarterly report. Knowing that, managers who want to exploit share overvaluation have to rush to buy businesses. They often overpay and acquire strategically misfit targets. Moreover, target executives and employees who continue to work for the buyers are loaded with the buyers' inflated shares they received in exchange for their own, and the prices of these shares will fall sharply when the overvaluation is revealed. Realizing that they were conned by exchanging their "good" shares for the overvalued ones, target employees and executives will leave the company or create an unhealthy business environment for their buyers (like Time Warner employees holding large quantities of the almost worthless AOL shares). All in all, acquiring businesses with overvalued shares is a recipe for failure, as Figure 6.4 clearly shows. Most important, a solid business enterprise cannot be built on trickery (paying for a target with temporarily inflated shares) and baseless promises about the buyers' illusory growth supporting the elevated share prices. A moral managerial behavior is the foundation of every successful business and acquisition.

6.5   SO, WHEN SHOULD YOU ACQUIRE A BUSINESS?

It seems that so far in this chapter we have rejected, based on solid evidence and arguments, all four of the widely believed external opportunities to acquire companies. What a downer for a book on M&As – aren't there any "good times to buy"? Indeed there are. If you watched our evidence closely – presented in Figures 6.1 through 6.4 – you have observed that the truly wise choice is to engage in acquisition activity in direct *opposition* to what the conventional wisdom suggests. So, here are the proven "good times" to buy businesses when the right external opportunities occur:

- *Wait for capital markets to slow down.*
  Figure 6.1 shows that acquisitions made during "hot capital markets" had a very low success rate, on average: 20% (right pair of bars). However, acquisitions made during *slow markets* had a 41% average success rate, well above our sample average (left two bars). Apparently, slow, or even losing, capital markets present buyers with especially attractive target opportunities. Competition in the "market for corporate control" (acquisitions) during slow capital markets is weak, and acquisition prices are low – an optimal time to pick up low-hanging fruit. If your stock prices are low too, pay for the acquisition with cash, or a combination of stock and cash. Most important, in slow capital markets you don't have to rush – take your time and acquire potential winners. Figure 6.1 (left two bars) shows that this is indeed successfully done in practice.

- *Let your competitors pay the high premia.*

Figure 6.2 shows that when your industry is in an acquisition frenzy, most buyers end up with "lemons," having an average acquisition success rate of only 20% (one in five), as indicated by the right two bars. No one should be surprised by this. Potential targets, like small promising biotech or generative AI startups, also notice the frenzy to buy and jack up their prices and other acquisition terms (like operating independently from the buyer). And in the rush to acquire you will likely miss the best targets. The evidence against buying in a frenzy (Figure 6.2) is quite compelling, but as the two bars on the left of Figure 6.2 show, buying, when only a few – or no – peers are acquiring, substantially improves the likelihood of your success. This is because of the same reasons as in the previous case: low target prices and ample time to search for suitable targets and conduct a thorough due diligence enhance acquisition success.

- *Buy post-recessions.*

Some believe that buying businesses during recessions is a good idea: business is slow, target prices are down, and boards of depressed targets are amenable to a deal. However, our evidence (Figure 6.3, left two bars) doesn't indicate a particularly high success rate for acquisitions made during recessions. Surprisingly, acquisitions made in the two *post-recession* years yield an above-average success rate. The reason is that recessions in the United States are relatively short – one to two years, leaving scant time to search thoroughly for good targets, bargain for a good price, conduct a thorough due diligence, and integrate the acquired assets. During the post-recession period, in contrast, target prices increase only gradually, and buyers are able to observe which targets show resilience and early signs of emerging successfully from the recession. These are the businesses worth buying.

TAKEAWAYS

The widely touted buying opportunities, such as hot capital markets or recession periods, don't actually turn out to be good times for acquiring companies. Buying during these times, in fact, sets buyers up for failed acquisitions. Our evidence shows that avoiding these frequently claimed buying opportunities can substantially improve the success rate of your acquisitions. The "wisdom of the crowds" and of many M&A advisors just doesn't work in the real world of acquisitions. In the next chapter, we will examine several firms' *internal conditions* that are also commonly believed to be "best times to buy."

CHAPTER 7

Are There "Best Times" to Acquire Businesses (2)?

Internal Opportunities

In the previous chapter we examined external (to the company) circumstances, like hot capital markets, which allegedly are good opportunities to acquire businesses. In this chapter, we focus on internal corporate events, like a change of chief executive officer (CEO), which are widely believed to offer "good times to acquire." We provide a thorough fact-based examination of whether these and other internal opportunities are indeed "best times to buy." As in the preceding chapter, we demonstrate that these presumably opportune times for acquisitions are in fact merger and acquisition (M&A) "traps" to be avoided. We offer other "best times," based on the buying firm's internal conditions.

7.1 AVOID HIGH ACQUISITION PREMIA

The 2006 acquisition of YouTube by Google (Chapter 1) required the payment of a hefty premium over market value, causing Mark Cuban to reportedly call it "crazy." And yet, YouTube turned out to be a fabulous acquisition. Perhaps acquisition targets are what economists call "Veblen goods," whose demand *increases* with their prices (like designer jewelry, luxury watches, yachts). A high acquisition premium (acquisition price substantially above the target's pre-announcement market value) may also signal a "diamond in the rough" – an unusual opportunity to turn around the target company or to use its hidden assets, like Sears Roebuck's real estate, when acquired by Edward Lampert in 2004. High acquisition premia can also be the result of multibuyer competition vying for an attractive target. In short, a high acquisition premium may signal a considerable untapped value. Should you go for it?

Upon reflection, though, a large acquisition premium may just reflect the buyer's delusion in assessing the value of the target, namely, exaggerating the expected value of cash flows to be created by the acquisition. A target's value assessment is often shrouded in uncertainty and is prone to be overstated by the optimistic, overconfident buyer's managers. Recall the highly exaggerated sales and profit forecasts made by the CEOs of Teva Pharmaceutical and HP prior to their disastrous acquisitions (Chapter 1). So, the wisdom of paying large acquisition premia is an open question, ripe to be answered by our sample of 40,000 acquisitions.

Figure 7.1 presents the relation between the acquisition premium paid (the upward-sloping line measured on the right axis) and the average acquisition success rates (the decreasing bars, from left to right). Specifically, we constructed Figure 7.1 by splitting our sample into three equal groups of low, medium, and high acquisition premia paid, and measured the average acquisition success rate in each group. The message of Figure 7.1 is clear: as the acquisition premium increases (the line rising from left to right), the acquisitions' success, on average, decreases (height of bars). A high premium is a recipe for an unsuccessful acquisition.[1]

The main reason for the sharply negative relation between acquisition premium paid and merger success is that large premia are often driven by buyers' *overvaluation* of the expected efficiencies and added value to be derived from the target. That is, buyers were excessively optimistic about the success of the merger. Indeed, studies have shown a positive relation between CEO optimism (or hubris) and the number of and prices paid for corporate acquisitions. Apparently, CEOs eager to acquire are caught by their own hype.

And then there is the unfortunate "winner's curse" syndrome associated with contested (multibuyer) acquisitions. Since the real value of a target to the buyer is never known for certain, it must be estimated (assessing expected future cash flows from the acquisition). In a contested acquisition, as in any bidding contest, where several buyers vie for a given target (like in the YouTube case), the various potential acquirers will bid for the target

---

[1] A quick note on our measurement: acquisition premium is usually measured as the price paid for the target over its capital market value before the acquisition announcement. Since in our test we include private targets and acquired subsidiaries of companies having no market value, we measure the acquisition premium as the acquisition price paid divided by the target's recent annual sales (e.g., an acquisition premium of 2.5 indicates that acquisition price paid is 2.5 times the target's recent annual sales). Since industries vary widely in their sales volumes, we adjust a specific company's acquisition premium by subtracting the average acquisition premium in its industry in the acquisition year from the company's acquisition premium. A positive premium means that the buyer paid for the target more than the industry average premium (market value over annual sales).

Average acquisition success rate for low, medium, and high acquisition premia groups

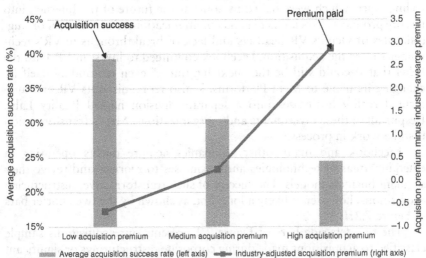

FIGURE 7.1 The Average Success Rate of Acquisitions in Relation to Premium Paid

according to their respective estimates of its value to them. The winner – the actual acquirer – will *by definition* be the one offering the highest price for the target, which will likely reflect the highest overvaluation among the various bidders. That's the "winner's curse" – the auction's winner is the one burdened with a highly overvalued and likely unsuccessful target.

Notwithstanding the specific reason for offering high acquisition premia, our evidence (Figure 7.1) is clear: when you have to pay a high (substantially above industry median) acquisition premium, stay away from the deal, or, at a minimum, go back to the drawing board and due diligence and carefully check the realism of your acquisition's value-added assumptions. Avoid the "winner's curse."[2]

7.2 SUCCESSFUL REORGANIZATIONS DON'T NECESSARILY CALL FOR ACQUISITIONS

Meta Platforms, Inc., formerly known as Facebook, is still struggling, at this writing, to gain successful footing in the new businesses developed from its acquisition of Oculus VR, a virtual reality (VR) gaming platform. Facebook

---

[2] On the "winner's curse," see, R. Roll, "The Hubris Hypothesis of Corporate Takeovers," *Journal of Business* 59 (1986): 197–216.

acquired Oculus for $2B in 2014, aiming to integrate its immersive VR technologies, which were hailed by some as the future of the Internet, into its core products in social media and communications. Despite years of sluggish sales of Oculus VR headsets and lack of breakthroughs in VR's technologies after the acquisition, Facebook continued to invest in VR with the belief that it could still be the "next big thing," even rebranding itself by changing its name to Meta Platforms. It also reorganized its VR and augmented reality businesses into a separate division named Reality Labs. Despite all of these investments and reorganizations, Meta's transformation is still a work in process.[3]

Facebook and many other companies acquire outfits operating in emerging areas of technologies and businesses to reorient and revive their stagnant business models. The success of such transformative, restructuring acquisitions, however, is likely a longshot, as shown by the two shorter bars of Figure 7.2.

The two left side bars of Figure 7.2 presents our acquisitions sample classified to acquisitions made during corporate restructurings or significant

Average acquisition success rate during restructuring vs. non-structuring periods

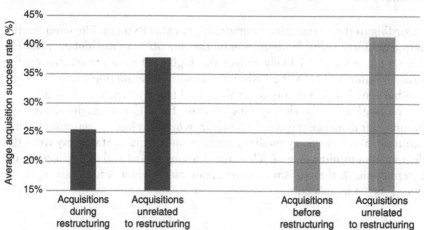

FIGURE 7.2   The Average Success Rate of Acquisitions Associated with Restructuring Initiatives

---

[3] According to Meta's 10-K filings, Reality Lab has raked in large annual losses: $13.7B in 2022 following $10B in 2021 and $6.6B in 2020. In its 2023 first-quarter earnings conference call, Meta disclosed that it expected Reality Labs to incur significantly greater losses in 2023. What a cheerful message.

strategic moves (like Facebook's) and those made in periods unrelated to restructurings or reorganizations. The bar height indicates the average success rate of the acquisitions made by the two groups. It is clear that acquisitions made during corporate restructurings had, on average, a very low success rate – about 25% – and substantially lower than acquisitions made in regular times: 38%.

Apparently, when a restructuring is centered around an acquisition, there is an eagerness to buy and a tendency to overpay for the target, which lessens its likelihood of success. In addition, there are very few targets capable of driving a successful restructuring in another company. Most do not. Motorola Mobility failed to do it for Google (Chapter 1); it was a similar case for Tumblr and Yahoo! (2013).[4]

Just to cover all bases, we have also examined the success of acquisitions that were made during the two years *prior* to reorganizations. The fate of these acquisitions is shown on the right side of Figure 7.2: outcomes were even worse than for acquisitions made during restructuring – a 23% average success rate for pre-reorganization acquisitions. So, no matter how you look at it, corporate acquisitions made in the context of a restructuring or a corporate strategic shift are, by and large, failures, unless a strategically fit target can be found for the right price – apparently a tall order. Corporate restructurings appear to be more successful when they are based on internal development efforts (see Chapter 4) than on pricey, ill-fitting acquisitions.

7.3 ACQUISITIONS WORK BEST FOR SUCCESSFUL BUYERS

Bayer, the inventor of Aspirin, among other products, saw its annual revenues grow moderately during 2009–2014, from $43.5B to $56.1B, and then hit a snag, dropping to $51.8B in 2016, and then plummeting to $39.6B and $46.8B in 2017 and 2018, respectively. Obviously, something had to be done to resurrect and stabilize Bayer's growth. The 2018, $63B acquisition of Monsanto seemed to be the needed tourniquet to stop the bleeding. It turned Bayer into the world's largest crop-science business, thereby reviving its sales and growth. Alas, the Monsanto acquisition quickly turned into a

---

[4] In 2013 Yahoo! acquired Tumblr, a social blogging platform, for $1.1B, hoping to inject a "cool factor" into its stalling Internet business to compete with the dominant social media players, like Facebook, Twitter, and Snapchat. The verdict for this acquisition came relatively swiftly – in 2015, merely two years after the acquisition, Yahoo! announced an impairment charge (loss) of $712M, as it wrote off 65% of the acquisition value of Tumblr. The announcement was later followed by the departure of Yahoo!'s CEO and main architect of the acquisition.

nightmare, as Bayer was besieged by a huge number of multibillion-dollar damage claims around the world over Monsanto's allegedly cancer-causing product Roundup.

Obviously, Monsanto wasn't the answer to Bayer's travails, but similar acquisition failures are typical of buyers in dire straits, rushing to find a savior. The standard suggestion of fund managers and investment bankers to companies that experience a slowdown, or even a reversal of sales or earnings growth, is to make a "big acquisition," but that, in fact, is often a bad idea, as demonstrated by Figure 7.3.

This figure was constructed as follows: we computed the sales growth rate for all the buyers in our sample during the three years prior to the acquisition year (that is, the sales growth rate from the third year before acquisition to the year before acquisition). We then ranked all the buyers by their sales growth rate, from lowest to highest, and sorted them into four equal groups: the 25% of companies with the lowest (negative) pre-acquisition sales growth rate (that is, companies facing serious operational challenges), the next 25% of companies with "low–medium growth," the 25% of companies with "medium–high growth," and finally, the highly successful 25% of the companies with the highest pre-acquisition sales growth rate. Since sales vary widely by industry, we adjusted each buyer's sales growth by subtracting from it the industry median sales growth to focus on its unique growth rate. Finally, for each of the four groups of buyers, we computed the average success rate of the acquisitions they made. These acquisition success rates are presented by the bars in Figure 7.3, while the average pre-acquisition buyers' sales growth rate is presented by the upward-slopping line (and the right axis).

It is clear from the left bar of the figure that the buyers with the lowest pre-acquisition sales growth – namely, those that desperately needed to regenerate stalling sales – made the worst acquisitions (32% success rate). Buyers with higher (positive) growth rate of sales – the middle two bars – had considerably better success in acquiring companies (37% and 41% success rates, respectively). Interestingly, buyers with the highest pre-acquisition sales growth rate (right bar of Figure 7.3) – the best pre-acquisition performers – had a somewhat lower acquisition success rate (35%). The reason for this outlier result (right bar) eludes us. But the three bars to the left of Figure 7.3 (75% of our sample) convey a consistent and important message:

Acquisitions aren't a magic solution for companies, including many mature ones, suffering from lagging sales and earnings. These challenged companies generally have meager funds and low share prices, making it difficult to find the right corrective target – one that is large enough to substantially reverse the fortunes of the acquiring company

Average acquisition success rate for buyers with low, low-medium, medium-high, and high industry-adjusted sales growth before acquisition

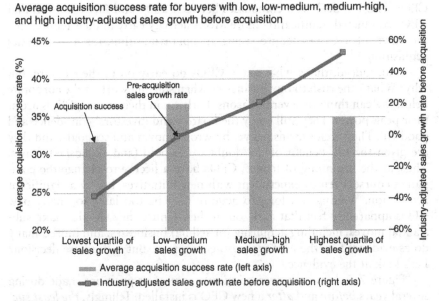

FIGURE 7.3   The Average Success Rate of Acquisitions by Companies, Classified by Pre-acquisition, Industry-Adjusted Sales Growth Rate

and is available to be acquired for the right price and the means available to the acquiring company. Just snatching a target that happens to be available in the market ends up worsening the buyer's situation, as Figure 7.3 confirms. The best acquisitions are conducted by financially fit buyers, like Google when buying YouTube (Chapter 1).[5]

7.4   CEOs SHOULDN'T INITIATE THEIR TENURE BY BUYING COMPANIES

Recall Meg Whitman (Chapter 1), who began her CEO tenure at HP in 2011 by completing the disastrous purchase of Autonomy, started by her predecessor. Apparently this wasn't an aberration. *McKinsey Insights* (April 13, 2017) in an article titled "A deal-making strategy for new CEOs," wrote: "More than half of new CEOs of S&P 500 companies launch some form of [acquisition/divestiture] transaction during their first two years in office.... A review of all mergers, acquisitions, and divestitures by the nearly 600

---

[5]This ironically reminds us of the quip that the only borrowers qualifying for a bank loan are those who don't need it. Not the needed consolation for struggling buyers.

CEOs who left S&P 500 companies between 2004 and 2014 showed that CEOs conducted significantly more M&A activity early in their tenure." So, the dawn of a CEO's tenure seems an opportune time for a substantial acquisition.

And, indeed, that's what many CEOs do early on in their tenure, but why? What's the rush to buy businesses when starting work at the corporate helm? We can think of several reasons. Early on in their tenure, CEOs are at their peak power. They still enjoy the board's and investors' confidence and goodwill. They aren't tarnished yet by wrong moves and scandals, and they are given the full benefit of the doubt to do bold (and expensive) things. Thus, at the beginning of tenure, CEOs have a license to change the company's course, even to experiment with new initiatives, led by a significant acquisition. Waiting too long to acquire may be too late. So, many new CEOs apparently feel that early on in their tenure they should make substantial moves, including acquiring (or selling) businesses, and indeed many do as evidenced by the *McKinsey Insights* report. But is it a wise decision? Let's look at the evidence.

Figure 7.4 shows the average success rate of acquisitions made during several years *before* and *after* a new CEO is installed. Tellingly, *the least successful acquisitions* are those made during the first two years of a new CEO (fourth and fifth bars from left) – achieving only a disappointing 18% and 22%, respectively successful acquisitions rate, well below our sample's

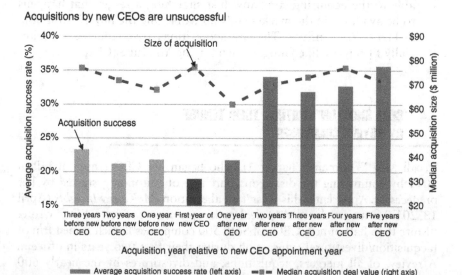

FIGURE 7.4   The Average Success Rate of Acquisitions Made Around the First Year of a CEO's Tenure

average success rate (35%). Note that these are the two years noted by
McKinsey Insights as most popular for acquisitions by new CEOs. These are
also below the success rate of the acquisitions made by their predecessors
during their last three years as CEOs (the three bars to the left of Figure 7.4)
and markedly worse than the acquisitions made by CEOs two to five years
into their tenure (the four bars to the right of Figure 7.4). Thus, the best
acquisitions, according to our evidence, were made during the two-to-five-year
period after starting the CEO tenure. The average success rate of the acquisitions made during those years – 33–35% – is, as expected, similar to the
average success rate of all acquisitions in our sample. But the acquisitions
made during the first two years of a CEO's tenure are often disastrous.
Whitman at HP was in "good company." Apparently, the halo of a new
CEO, the free reign given by the board, and the "honeymoon effect" are all
bad for acquisitions driven by the rush to complete a deal in the first year of
tenure. Taking time to familiarize yourself with the company's situation and
needs and carefully forging a new strategy are essential for successful acquisitions. This can rarely be done in a few months.

Finally, note the line on top of the bars in Figure 7.4. It denotes the
median _size of the acquisitions_ made around the installment of a new CEO.
It indicates that while acquisitions that were made in the first year of CEO
tenure were the _worst_, compared with previous and subsequent mergers,
they were among the largest acquisitions made (though the variation in
median size is not large): big and bad, what a poisonous combination to
start a CEO tenure with.

7.5   A BRIEF STATISTICAL NOTE (DON'T SKIP)

We have considered in this and the previous chapter eight circumstances
that are widely believed to be opportune times for corporate acquisitions. In
each case, we compared the rate of acquisitions success during the alleged
opportunity window (like, hot capital markets or during restructurings)
with the success of acquisitions made outside these opportunity periods,
drawing operational inferences from these comparisons. However, these
eight opportunity periods may not be _independent_, or distinct – they might
overlap. For example, there could be cases where the acquisitions made
during _restructurings_ were also those made by a new CEO, as some new
CEOs start their tenure with a corporate restructuring. For example,
Yahoo!'s acquisition of Tumblr in 2013 was made during the first tenure
year of its new CEO, Marissa Mayer, who envisioned the Tumblr acquisition
as a "game changer" for Yahoo!'s long-awaited turnaround. In such cases,
we are not presenting you with two distinct findings but with essentially one

acquisition opportunity: a restructuring made by a new CEO. This is a statistical yet important concern for the alert reader.

We want to assure readers that this potential confounding of opportunities was not the case with our eight inferences or recommendations presented in this and the preceding chapters. In our full multivariate model (see the appendix), all eight buying opportunities presented in this and the previous chapter were considered as *separate independent variables* (along with many other factors), some with interactions, enabling us to examine their *distinct effects* on the acquisition success. They were all found to be negatively related to acquisition success and statistically significant. Stated differently, the eight presumed acquisition opportunities presented here survived rigorous statistical, multivariate tests, each demonstrating a distinct negative effect on the ultimate objective: acquisition's success.[6]

7.6 FINALLY, WHEN SHOULD YOU ACQUIRE A BUSINESS?

As in the preceding chapter, we have, once again, using our large sample as a guide, ruled out several widely believed opportunities to acquire businesses. Specifically, we have shown that acquisitions should be avoided when firms face certain internal conditions, such as reorganization or restructuring, a sales slowdown, a new CEO taking the helm, and when the strong urge to buy will cost the buyer a hefty acquisition premium. In fact, these are some of the *worst times and circumstances* to acquire businesses. No wonder that with such "expert" advice, 70–75% of acquisitions fail. But what are the "good times to buy"?

- *Buy from strength.*

    Acquisitions are generally recommended to revive lagging, or even declining, sales and earnings. The problem is that businesses in these

---

[6] The distinct effects of the eight acquisition opportunities presented in this and the preceding chapter can also be demonstrated by comparing the success rate of acquisitions associated with *multiple buying opportunities* and conditions. For example, we find (but don't present here) that the success rate of acquisitions made during restructurings and by new CEOs is only 11%, which is substantially lower than the success rate of acquisitions with only one of the two factors – 24% success rate for acquisitions made during restructurings (Figure 7.2), and 18% for acquisitions made by a new CEO (Figure 7.4). Thus, restructuring and new CEO tenure each exerts its own negative effect on acquisitions' success. Similarly, the success rate of acquisitions made during a recession, along with a restructuring, declining company sales, and paid for with a high acquisition premium is only 7% (1 success for every 14 acquisitions).

situations, like Teva Pharmaceutical (Chapter 1), are in a weak position to conduct major and successful acquisitions; since such firms don't have the necessary funds for major transformative acquisitions and their share prices are too low to be used for acquisitions, they have to raise significant debt to acquire. Often the top talent of the targets deserts buyers with lagging operations, which adds to the difficulties of integrating the targets. That's the main reason for our finding (Figure 7.3, left bar) that companies with declining pre-acquisition sales made rather unsuccessful acquisitions. In contrast, acquisitions made by companies with positive sales growth (second and third bars from left in Figure 7.3) yield the highest success rates (35–42%). Accordingly, a good time to buy is when your earnings and stock prices are high and target executives are eager to come work for you. And what about the companies in distress? Forget about acquisitions. A thoughtful restructuring, a change of management, a joint venture, or, in extreme case, selling the business, are all preferred to a "big acquisition."

■ *Buy when needed.*

We have seen in this and the preceding chapter that there are several opportune times to acquire businesses: slowing capital markets, post-recession periods, robust pre-acquisition sales growth, etc. But, by and large, an acquisition should be made not during external "opportune times" but rather when it's absolutely necessary and called for by changing business circumstances, such as in one of the following times:

(i) You *foresee* a slowdown in operations, due to soon-to-expire patents, the end of major contracts, or changes in customers' tastes (toward electrical vehicles, for example). Such cases, planned ahead of a crisis, may call for an acquisition to spur operations, made with sufficient lead time to carefully look for a promising target.

(ii) You reach business maturity or face a significant change in competition. These circumstances generally call for a substantial change in your business model, like a switch from traditional (agent-based insurance) to online insurance. Under certain circumstances (see Chapter 4) an acquisition aimed at changing a business model will be preferred over alternative actions. Once more, don't acquire in a rush.

So, the most effective and opportune time to acquire a business is caused less by external circumstances (a recession, an industry acquisition frenzy, etc.) and more by an internal need for growth revival or business model change.

CHAPTER 8

Integration – The Achilles' Heel of M&A

The integration of the target's business into the buyer's is often downplayed by executives, yet integration is a highly important factor often determining the success of the acquisition. To prepare managers for a successful integration we provide in this chapter a *risk profile of integration challenges.* Awareness of the challenges that will likely be faced during the integration phase will enable managers to determine what resources, human and financial, will be needed for a successful integration. We identify eight major integration risk factors based on our sample evidence, such as acquisitions involving a foreign target (cross-border acquisitions) or acquisitions of a target whose founders continue to manage it after purchase. Our integration challenges risk profile is a new tool aimed at facilitating one of the most difficult stages of a corporate acquisition – its integration with the buyer.

> *"Wholeness is not achieved by cutting off a portion of one's being, but by integration of the contraries."*
>
> —Carl Jung

8.1 WHEN THE GOING GETS TOUGH, EVERYONE LEAVES

Most of the excitement, drama, and executive involvement in mergers and acquisitions (M&As) occur at the front end of the transaction: making the decision to acquire a business, conducting the search for an appropriate target, overseeing the due diligence, negotiating the target's price, and making public statements about the acquisition and running investors' and analysts' meetings. Once all this brouhaha is completed, however, the real hard work begins – integrating the target into the buyer's business structure. At that late stage, however, most participants in the merger vanish, and interest in the acquisition within the organization fades. Few top executives are interested in or have the time for the inglorious drudgery of merger integration. In particular, it gets harder and harder to draw the attention of top management needed for the crucial decisions required during the integration process, leading to inevitable delays and setbacks. Integration is therefore the stage where many acquisitions fail. The specialists, such as information technology (IT), finance, human resources, and marketing personnel, assigned to the integration are often overwhelmed by the task and left alone to cope with the very difficult issues and obstacles encountered during the merging of the buyer's and target's operations.

There is, however, little one can say about these challenges beyond the obvious, that integration is a vital stage of the acquisition process and shouldn't be left solely to specialists without "adult supervision." C-level involvement in the acquisition should stop at the *end of integration*, rather than at its beginning. But most people know that already. The problem is implementing this maxim.

What we can bring to the integration table is the very important, evidence-based risk profile of potential integration challenges: a list of factors adversely affecting the success of the acquisition and its integration in particular. The purpose of exposing these factors is to inform management how difficult the integration process will likely be and to delineate the specific areas that special attention and resources should be given to. This risk profile will allow top management to allocate sufficient time and resources to target integration and thereby assure the acquisition's success.

We aren't the first to talk about merger integration. In fact, a quick Google search of M&A integration difficulties revealed hundreds of items, most of them, though, of little use, in our opinion – admonitions like "pay attention to cultural issues," "engage customers," or "reduce employee anxiety." We haven't seen in this literature a comprehensive, evidence-based risk profile, like the one we provide in this chapter, that alerts management in advance to major integration challenges. But first, to focus the reader's attention, let's briefly consider the case of a seriously botched integration and draw from it some useful inferences.

8.2   SPRINT–NEXTEL: A BUNGLED INTEGRATION

"This new powerhouse company [Sprint+Nextel] has the spectrum, infrastructure, distribution, and superb and differentiated product portfolio that will drive our continued success. We are looking forward to competing with the Verizons and Cingulars [AT&T] of this world for the preeminent role in wireless and telecommunications." Thus spoke Timothy Donahue, chief executive officer (CEO) of Nextel, in February 2005, of the $35B acquisition of Nextel (the fifth biggest U.S. wireless carrier) by Sprint (the third largest). Alas, less than three years later (January 2008), Sprint wrote off (declared a loss of) a whopping $30.7B of the $35B acquisition price of Nextel (88%), which was supposed to play with Sprint "the preeminent role in wireless and telecommunications." What went so wrong? Almost everything, but particularly the integration of the two companies.

First, and weirdest, the management of the merged company decided to keep separate the two incompatible wireless systems of the buyer and target (iDen and CDMA), which caused total confusion among customers, particularly new ones who had to choose whether to join Sprint or Nextel's system, despite their celebrated merger. Second, customer relations, the key to subscribers' retention during integration, was a major victim of Sprint's CEO promise to investors to cut costs by $14B after acquisition. Customer service centers were among the first to experience the cost-cutting drive (service centers were closed, personnel laid off), just as subscribers needed support the most. This caused considerable resentment among subscribers, who left both Sprint and Nextel in droves. Only in January 2006 – a year after merger – were the two billing systems combined, yet unsuccessfully at first, with lots of billing mistakes, which added fodder to customer resentment. Not surprisingly, Sprint's churn (the percentage of customers leaving in a month) rose in 2006 to 2.4% – the highest rate in the industry. True to the nature of this failed integration, the merged company even kept the two, pre-merger headquarters separate. In short, there was never a productive integration between Sprint and Nextel. Instead of being focused from day one on retaining and adding customers and unifying the separate operating systems – what else is there to manage in a telecom company? – the integrators caused constant confusion among employees and massive customer defection.

But that wasn't all. Also driven away during integration were key employees of Nextel who saw the vision of a large, competitive company vanish before their eyes. Rather than merging the two headquarters and keeping the top talent, while letting others go, management of the combined company embarked on a bizarre policy of putting all positions at the merged entity up for competition among employees (which must have been a brilliant consultant's idea). Some employees even competed for their own jobs. This decision too caused confusion, discord, and resentment among employees and drove out many of them, particularly top executives at Nextel. As usual in these situations, "adverse selection" kicks in: those with good employment alternatives whom you want to keep leave, while others stay, with the expected degradation of the quality of the workforce.

All of this self-inflicted harm was in full view of investors, leading, by September 2006 – a mere half a year after the merger – to a 36% drop in Sprint–Nextel's stock price. By the second quarter of 2008, the merged company's stock price dropped by an astounding 93% to $1.91, from which recovery is highly improbable. The inevitable, almost total acquisition loss declaration – an 88% write-off – naturally followed.

Finally, in July 2013, Softbank purchased 72% of Sprint–Nextel, putting an end to this sorry merger saga. It was practically an act of mercy. There are few as poorly executed integrations as that of Sprint–Nextel, but there are many that are close, making this chapter's subject – acquisition integration – so critical.[1,2]

8.3   AN INTEGRATION RISK PROFILE

Given the importance of the integration phase of an acquisition, and the natural urge of top management to distance itself from the acquisition after its completion and return to their "day job," it's important to provide management with an *integration risk profile* to indicate the acquisitions for which integration will likely be smooth, and can be largely left to subordinates and specialists, and those that will probably encounter serious challenges and will require continued involvement of top management and perhaps outside advisors. In what follows, we develop an integration risk profile, starting with the acquisition of a *foreign target*, one of the major causes of integration failures.

8.3.1   The Challenges of Integrating a Foreign Target

Integrating foreign targets is often very demanding. Consider, as an example, the 2015 acquisition by GE of the French company Alstom's power division, for $13.5B. GE's announcement (November 2, 2015) was, as usual, cheerful and hopeful: "GE announced today that it has completed the acquisition of Alstom's power and grid businesses. The completion of the transaction follows the regulatory approval of the deal in over 20 countries and

---

[1]Some of the information in this section was drawn from "Analysis of a failed merger: Sprint–Nextel case," by Celiktas, M., 2016, Naval Postgraduate School, working paper.
[2]Time is a great healer. In 2020, T-Mobile acquired Sprint and merged it into its own operations (this time, successfully). The merged entity is a considerable success. T-Mobile's stock performance since the Sprint acquisition on April 1, 2020, until the end of 2023 was 92%, compared with the S&P 500 increase of 85%.

regions, including the European Union, United States, China, India, Japan, and Brazil [a full-employment act for lawyers and accountants]. . . . The completion of the Alstom power and grid acquisition is another significant step in GE's transformation [from what to what?]. . . . The complementary technology, global capability, installed base and talent of Alstom will further our core industrial growth. We are open for business and ready to deliver one of the most comprehensive technology offerings in the energy sector to our customers." What could be better for GE's customers and shareholders? But lurking behind this euphoria was a host of problems, including severe restrictions placed by and commitments made to the French government by GE to enable Alstom's acquisition, which greatly hindered the integration process.

What followed was a sad spectacle. In its zeal to acquire Alstom, GE failed to appreciate the worldwide shift of focus to renewable energy, while GE's power division, including Alstom, was mainly in the business of fossil fuels, and particularly natural gas. The inevitable drop in demand hit GE and Alstom hard. Added to the integration challenges was the fact that Alstom was a French company, leading to harsh conditions set by the French government to allow the acquisition. In particular, not only was GE prohibited from firing any of Alstom's employees – a key merger-efficiency move in the face of dropping demand – it instead committed to create 1,000 new jobs. So, as the market for its products softened and GE power laid off thousands of employees all over the world, it had to ramp up Alstom's production in France, increase excess inventories, and *add* employees (it managed to add only about 350 employees of the 1,000 promised and paid a multimillion-dollar fine for failing to reach the target). GE thus maintained an island of tranquility (Alstom) amid an industry turmoil – not the best way to integrate an acquisition. In the final analysis, Alstom's integration largely failed, and the rosy promises were unfulfilled.

Foreign acquisitions, while mostly not as painfully inhibited as Alstom's, usually come with heavy baggage. The different cultures of the merger partners often burden the integration of employees and customers, and different laws and regulations in the target's country of origin substantially increase the cost of integration. The closing of foreign facilities and headquarters and the relocation of employees to the buyer's home country often create hostile public opinion and negative media in the foreign country because of the loss of national pride and domestic employment. Legal and accounting costs generally mount in these cases.

Foreign targets are also subject to different accounting rules, and frequently to a lower level of *enforcement* of these rules (financial disclosure, insider trading) than in the United States, creating painful surprises during the integration stage, such as finding out that the target's revenues were seriously inflated or that various obligations were missing from the target's balance sheet, such as in the Autonomy's (UK) acquisition by HP (Chapter 1).

All in all, when acquiring a large foreign target, be prepared for a challenging and costly integration and the need for continued involvement of top management and legal staff during integration. Our overall statistical model (see the appendix for details) indeed shows that foreign acquisitions, on average, *detract* from the acquisition's success. Exceptions to this "on average" negative finding obviously exist (e.g., Sky Plc's acquisition by Comcast), but they are scarce.

8.3.2 The Problematic Integration of "Potentially Related" Targets

The integration of horizontal (same industry) or vertical (an entity and its supplier) acquisitions is relatively straightforward since both merger partners generally share the same technologies and knowledge base. The "integration" of conglomerates – unrelated entities – is also straightforward in most cases (like Google and YouTube, or Amazon and Whole Foods) since the target is often left to operate largely independently – so, in fact, there is no real integration in these cases (think Berkshire Hathaway's multiple acquisitions).

It is the cases where the targets' products or services are unrelated to the buyers' but the acquisition is aimed at integrating them to provide a more comprehensive product mix that complicate things. A prominent example is the 1998 merger between Citicorp and Travelers, led by two prominent Wall Street figures, Sanford "Sandy" Weil (Travelers) and John Reed (Citicorp); this merger created Citigroup, the world's largest financial institution at the time that was aimed at creating a one-stop shop offering banking, investment banking, and insurance services. Lots of enthusiasm accompanied this merger: Citicorp's stock zoomed 26% on the news (announced on April 6, 1998). Throughout the merger excitement, however, a "small detail" was overlooked: the merger was illegal. It violated the 1933 Glass–Steagall Act, which prohibited commercial banks (Citicorp) from engaging in insurance, securities trading, and investment banking activities (among Travelers' many businesses). This inconvenience was removed in November 1999 by the Graham–Leach–Bliley Act, which allowed the mixing of commercial banking with investment banking and insurance.

But then came the real challenge: attracting customers to the "financial supermarket" – a one-stop shop for traditional banking, insurance, investment services, and investment banking, among others – which was the vision of Sandy Weil, the moving force behind the merger. So, here was a case of pre-merger unrelated businesses (e.g., commercial banking and insurance) that were aggregated by the merger into a unified product mix (financial services). It was a classic case of unifying "potentially related" offerings.

Alas, it turned out that, despite mighty advertising and public relations efforts, customers rejected the one-stop banking shop idea. They actually liked banking in branches, buying insurance from brokers, and getting M&A services from investment bankers, instead of doing all these businesses at Citigroup offices. Consequently, the Citicorp-Travelers integration famously failed, and the Travelers insurance business was spun off in 2002, thereby abandoning the one-stop financial services idea. Thus, Citigroup's integration failed because customers rejected the "supermarket" vision of the merger architects, which so often looks great on paper or from the promoters' mouths.

Fast-forward 20 years to another "visionary" merger aimed at offering "potentially related" products: the AT&T–Time Warner union. AT&T's growth lagged that of archrival Verizon, leading its CEO, Randall Stephenson, to repeat the already failed idea (AOL–Time Warner merger) of creating an integrated empire of "content" (Time Warner, with brands, like CNN and HBO) and "distribution" (AT&T), delivering through cable and wireless screens the content of Time Warner. Regulators objected to the deal on antitrust grounds but lost a prolonged legal battle, and AT&T and Time Warner officially merged in 2018. In the meantime, the business environment changed, and content and streaming specialists, like Netflix and Disney, managed to successfully provide much of customers' demand, rendering the combination of AT&T and Time Warner dated and largely irrelevant. Finally, in 2022, after wasting massive amounts of investors' money and executives' time, AT&T's CEO got the message and spun off all of its media assets, combining them with Discovery to create another content giant. Once more, customers rejected the merger idea of combining different but "potentially related" businesses to provide a unified product.

So, our second integration risk factor is a merger vision of combining *potentially related* products or services, a move that is often rejected by customers. No quantity of resources and effort will succeed in convincing people to buy what they don't want and to shop where they don't wish to. Note, however, that not all "potentially related" mergers fail. For example, people grew to like eating and shopping in gas stations, or getting medical aid and drugs in pharmacies, but much of the integration effort in these cases went to changing customers' buying habits – a very daunting task.

As we argued in Chapter 4, an alternative to acquiring businesses for the purpose of creating an integrated "provider of everything" is to develop the additional businesses internally – carefully and gradually. This path, however, is rarely considered, due to concerns about the long process of internal development and the high uncertainty facing its success. But in the case of "potentially related" products, the slower development process may be a blessing. Apple, for example, has succeeded repeatedly with its patient and persistent internal development of iPhone-integrated services. Apple's offerings in entertainment (Apple Music and Apple TV+), news (Apple News+), and financial services (Apple Pay, Apple Card, and Savings Accounts) are successful businesses, growing faster than Apple's devices and earning double the gross margin of Apple's device business.[3] So it's definitely possible to sell related products that were developed internally. Integration in this case is much easier and smoother than when the products are separately acquired.

8.3.3   The Integration of a Tech Company by a Nontech Enterprise

Late in 2019, Prudential, a big insurer, bought for $2.3B Assurance IQ, an online insurance agency promoted by its founders as a *data-science enterprise* using, what else? cloud and AI technologies (once more, the "tyranny of the cloud"). Assurance's acquisition was aimed at enhancing Prudential's pedestrian tech and online marketing capabilities, using Assurance's advanced technology and marketing experience. For this, Prudential clearly overpaid. For Assurance's annual revenues of around $300M, Prudential paid $2.3B – a very hefty eightfold sales multiple (recall Chapter 2's Figure 2.4 showing an average sales multiple of 1.65 in 2019). But, hey, Assurance was a "new-age" tech company with alleged artificial intelligence (AI) and cloud capabilities. A cloud company definitely deserves a valuation "in the clouds."

The integration of Prudential and Assurance went badly from the get-go. The target, according to the *Wall Street Journal*, ". . . was supposed to hit $1.0 billion annual revenue by 2021, but clocked in at only $558 million."[4] It turns out that rather than modernizing and technologically advancing Prudential's capabilities, Assurance was struggling to maintain its own business – essentially a standard online insurance agency – dealing with

---

[3] According to Apple's 10-K filings and annual reports, the gross margin of Apple's services was 71.7%, 69.7%, and 66.0% in 2022, 2021, and 2020, respectively, compared to the gross margins of 36.3%, 35.3%, and 31.5%, respectively, for its products (devices). For 2022, the sales growth rate of Apple's services was 14.2%, compared to 6.3% for its products.

[4] Scism, L., 2022, "How Prudential's big tech bet went sour," *Wall Street Journal*, April 29.

mounting competition and nagging customers' complaints. Moreover, rather than being on the cusp of technology, Assurance IQ was in fact a regular online insurance agency, which was lucky to be bought at an exorbitant price. And what about Assurance's enticing AI and the cloud? None of it. "Assurance's key technology was the headsets provided by the agents themselves, to use in pushing older people to buy funeral-expense insurance policies (an original "growth industry"). And it [was] revealed that not all of the startup's leads came from advanced data science. Some, in fact, came from Publishers Clearing House" (*Wall Street Journal*, April 29, 2022). This sorry affair of a botched due diligence and integration reminds us of HP's acquisition of Autonomy (Chapter 1).

So, rather than integrating Assurance's (nonexistent) advanced technologies into its own products and marketing efforts, Prudential had to deal with mounting customer complaints, complex regulatory issues, and a commercially struggling target. Prudential finally gave up the integration efforts and, in 2022, wrote off (declared a loss on) the second half of its investment in Assurance, having already written off the first half of the investment a year earlier. The failure in this case was both in the acquisition stage – believing that the target (Assurance IQ) was an advanced tech entity – and in the integration process: combining the target's online insurance activities with Prudential's own, traditional ones. The exorbitant acquisition price paid didn't help, either.

Our third integration risk factor is thus a *complex target*, particularly a tech or healthcare enterprise acquired by a traditional business (like insurance). The buyers generally don't have the knowledge and expertise to thoroughly grasp the target's technological capabilities, conduct a thorough due diligence, and integrate the target's capabilities with their own. They become enamored of the technology glitz (autonomous driving, AI, machine learning), vastly overpay for the target, fail to conduct a thorough due diligence, and struggle to integrate the target. Combining tech and nontech businesses, executives, and employees is like mixing oil with water. Accordingly, beware the complex target.

8.3.4 The Target's Entrepreneurs Managing It After Acquisition

The large yet somewhat staid toy company Mattel saw an opportunity in 1998 to get into the burgeoning high-tech toy and software game businesses by spending $4.2B to acquire the Learning Company, maker of widely used high-tech toys and games. The Learning Company's chairman and CEO, Michael Perik, and its president, Kevin O'Leary, both founders of the company, went along for the ride and joined Mattel's management, looking after the integration and development of the Learning Company within Mattel.

Integration problems appeared from the start. The Learning Company didn't develop the expected "killer products" under Mattel; rather, it sustained serious losses and massive product returns. The two Learning Company founders, not unexpectedly, blamed Mattel's bureaucracy for impeding their "vision" and innovation efforts, and in an act that didn't enhance confidence, the founders sold much of the Mattel stock they received in the acquisition. After a while, Mattel decided it had enough of those "innovators," and after a year or so of changing executives and strategies, Mattel sold the Learning Company at a significant loss. Having the *original founders* manage the target at the buyer evidently didn't work out.

Want another example? In 2005, the large online auction site eBay paid $2.6B for Skype, which offered Voice over Internet Protocol (VoIP) calls and low-cost connectivity, with the idea of enhancing eBay's commerce by improving communication between buyers and sellers. It was a compelling idea with one minor flaw: eBay's customers didn't want it. They were perfectly happy with just communicating via email or texts and were reluctant to move to voice telephony. Obviously, this created an intricate integration problem of convincing eBay's customers to change their behavior. To make things worse, Skype's Nordic founders, who joined eBay, were mostly interested in spreading Internet communication worldwide rather than changing the habits of eBay's customers. Their connections were primarily in Europe, while eBay's business was mainly in the United States. With the integration – not unexpectedly – limping along, Skype's founders were ultimately replaced, but to no avail. eBay soon wrote off $1.43B of Skype's investment (55%) and later sold it off. Skype's entrepreneurs–managers obviously failed to contribute to the integration of the merger partners.

While there is generally a benefit in retaining the target's key executives after acquisition, certain types of target executives, particularly founders with no managerial experience of working within large organizations, often have a detrimental effect on the integration and the subsequent business development of the target. Founders, particularly those coming from a different culture, as in Skype, add to the problem. The solution lies in putting a top, experienced executive of the buying company in charge of the integration and using the target's executives primarily as technical advisors. Expressing considerable sensitivity and tolerance of the target's executives, and fully recognizing their past contributions, doesn't hurt, either. But, as a general rule, tech entrepreneurs don't blossom in a large, corporate hierarchy, particularly when cross-cultural factors are added to the mix.[5]

8.3.5 Desperately Seeking Synergies

Frontier and Spirit airlines merged in 2022, promising that customers would save $20 per seat, on average and, in addition, that the combined airline would realize annual operating synergies of $500M, once full integration was completed. Similarly, managers of Anheuser–Busch and InBev, upon merging in 2015, projected synergies of $1.5B within three years of the deal's completion; and in 2021, Thermo Fisher Scientific, a producer of scientific instruments, purchased clinical research services provider PPD for $17.4B and promised $125M cost savings over three years. Our Google search revealed that the term *synergies* is the most frequently mentioned merger-related word in public acquisition announcements. Practically every acquisition announcement includes an enticing synergy promise.[6] Eye-popping cost savings, large revenue increases, or new product developments populate acquisition announcements. Yet studies have shown that, by and large, these promises are overly optimistic, sometimes by wide margins.

So, when synergy promises abound and can subsequently be validated by investors, there is pressure during the integration phase to start realizing them by laying off employees, closing shops or branches, merging service centers, etc. Recall the earlier Sprint–Nextel case where customers' service centers were closed en masse during the failing integration phase.

When the promises of synergies are realistic, they can and should be achieved, of course, as early as possible; but when, as is often the case, these promises are overly optimistic, attempts to demonstrate them early on

---

[5] This general rule seems reflected in the acquisition choice of Germany's Merck KGaA. While recognizing the opportunities of using AI tools to advance new drug research and development, Merck KGaA has chosen partnering with AI companies to access AI tools instead of outright acquisition of businesses specializing in AI technology. Merck believes it is better "to leave those [AI] companies in their own ecosystem so they can continue to evolve" (Amolak, H. and S. Haxel, 2024, "Germany's Merck bets on AI drug-design partnerships, rules out acquisitions – Interview." *Wall Street Journal*, June 7).

[6] In addition, our search revealed that the term "synergy" was used more frequently in the announcements of larger mergers (more than $500M) and that the usage frequency of "synergy" in merger announcements has more than tripled from the early 2000s to the 2010s. Apparently, investors keep falling for the "synergy promises."

seriously harm the integration process. Key employees are laid off (thereby degrading the workforce), research and development (R&D) and advertising budgets are cut (harming innovation), important maintenance work is delayed or skipped altogether, and development plans are curtailed. Consequently, the integration phase is hampered because the integrators must desperately seek savings to fulfill irresponsible promises of synergies aimed at allaying acquisition concerns of investors. Overly optimistic acquisition promises are thus a serious integration risk factor.

8.3.6   Hubris: "Get It on the Cheap and Fix It"

What is common to the following five acquisitions? Google acquiring Motorola Mobility in 2012 for $12.5B; Microsoft purchasing Nokia in 2013 for $7.2B; Kmart buying Sears Roebuck in 2005 for $11B; Bank of America acquiring Countrywide in 2008 for $4.1B; and Alcatel buying Lucent in 2006 for $13.4B? A hint: look at the target's pre-acquisition performance. They were all failing businesses. Has-beens. Common to these acquisitions is the fact that they all went horribly bad, causing the buyers' shareholders multiple billions of dollars in losses – about $35B loss, for example, in the case of Bank of America–Countrywide alone. But why did they all falter? Mainly because the *targets* of these acquisitions were seriously failing enterprises pre-acquisition. Losers par excellence. Motorola Mobility, once the worldwide leader of telecommunication and wireless telephony, was a lagging company by the time it was acquired by Google, with negligible market share and revenues. Similarly, Nokia was almost an empty shell when it was purchased by Microsoft. Sears Roebuck, once the leading U.S. retailer, was a shadow of itself, struggling and failing to be competitive when Kmart acquired it, reputedly for Sears' extensive real estate. Countrywide was mired with nonperforming loans and plagued by fraud allegations when Bank of America snatched it up; and Lucent, a product of the breakup of AT&T in 1996, was greatly reduced from a leading, innovative telecommunication equipment company to a failing, laggard business that was coping with accounting issues and allegations of financial reporting fraud. A charming bunch of targets.

What drove the managements of leading enterprises, like Google and Microsoft, to buy such corporate corpses for hefty prices? Hubris, we say. Erstwhile successful executives believed that they could once more find "Rembrandts in the attic" – certain hidden, unexploited sources of substantial value, like patents, knowhow, salvageable loans, or real estate, that they could revive and develop into corporate value drivers. Alas, apparently all the available Rembrandts are hanging on museum or collectors' walls, rather than lying dormant within corporate ruins. Our large-scale model, with more than 40 acquisition success–failure drivers, confirms this observation: the target's pre-acquisition operating performance – lagging sales and falling earnings growth, for example – detracts, on average, from the acquisition's success.

CEOs, ever the optimists and overconfident in their abilities to turn around faltering businesses, sometimes look for failing enterprises and often overpay for them. But the integration of failing enterprises with successful ones is usually messy. Precious time and resources are lost in endless reorganizations and managerial turnovers, often leading to the inevitable accounting write-offs and sale of what remains of the target at a substantial loss. Very few failing targets are successfully revived and integrated with well-operating buyers. A failing target is thus another integration risk factor.

8.3.7 Successful Integrations Don't Come Cheap

A successful integration can't be done as a side job. Key employees need to be fully dedicated to the integration, often for considerable periods: information technology (IT) and other managerial systems of the buyer have to be revamped and consolidated with the target's; buyers' sales personnel require effective training to sell the target's products and become informed of the attributes that they will have to promote; and legal, tax, and accounting experts have to be fully deployed. All of these activities entail considerable time and money. Frequently, unexpected obstacles to a smooth integration occur that require more executives' time and money. Integration can't be shortcutted.

That's what underpins our finding that the likelihood of successful integration increases with profitable, talent-deep, and cash-rich buyers, compared to poorly performing buyers peopled with mediocre employees (the two are, of course, correlated). Alas, many buyers are poorly performing (after all, that's their reason to acquire a business in the first place) and fund-starved (recall the discussion in Chapter 2, Section 2), trying to resurrect lagging growth with acquisitions. Such buyers should be particularly wary of large acquisitions whose integration is particularly resource-intensive and challenging.

8.3.8 Target Size – A Major Challenge

Last, but definitely not least, the target's size relative to the buyer's is a major integration challenge. Small targets can easily be assimilated by an existing buyer's unit or department. A large target, like Nextel in the opening example, poses significant challenges in terms of personnel, technology, intellectual capital, and – notably – executive ego. Large targets also require continued involvement of the buyer's C-level executives during the integration process.

TAKEAWAYS

Summarizing, we have identified and discussed the following eight major challenges to successful integrations:

1. The target is a foreign entity (a cross-border acquisition).
2. The target's products are "potentially related" to the buyer.
3. A nontech company acquires a tech company.
4. The target founders continue to manage it after acquisition.
5. Overly optimistic, pre-acquisition promises of "synergy" are made.
6. The target has been poorly performing with outdated technology.
7. A successful integration is expensive and time-consuming.
8. Large targets pose significant integration challenges.

If the acquisition you are considering is characterized by one or more of these risk factors, be prepared for a prolonged and challenging integration. You will have to devote senior executives and considerable resources to the task. If the acquisition is characterized by two, three, or more risk factors, reconsider the entire acquisition; it will most probably fail.

Note that our eight integration risk factors are rooted in evidence, confirmed by our multivariate statistical model. This is a far cry from the generally vague and hard-to-identify integration challenges you will find in books with merger advice and articles on M&As, which tend to feature discussions of serious cultural differences of the merger partners or matters of environmental issues. Our risk factors, in contrast, are specific, straightforward, and easy to identify.

Finally, integration isn't an independent phase of the acquisition. Most of our risk challenges, like the acquisition of a foreign target or hyped synergy promises, are rooted in the early stages of the acquisition process. So, when you contemplate a specific acquisition, carefully consider the effects of your choices and pronouncements on the down-the-road integration stage. For example, while talking to investors and promising exciting synergies, think of the integration difficulties you are creating by demanding the early realization of efficiencies. Our main message here is this: don't treat target integration as a distant afterthought; you'll soon have to face it.

CHAPTER 9

Accounting Matters

Don't skip this chapter. This is not the debits-and-credits nightmare you recall from college, but instead we discuss several acquisitions-related accounting topics germane to executives and investors. Corporate financial reports – quarterly and annual, as well as internal financial statements used by managers – are jolted in the year/ quarter of an acquisition as a result of consolidating (combining) the accounts (assets, liabilities, revenues, expenses, etc.) of the buyer with those of the target company. Almost every item changes, new ones are added, and the comparability with previous reports is seriously distorted. New accounts with strange names and attributes – like goodwill and in-process research and development (IPR&D) – show up in the reports, and new valuation issues are encountered after consolidation. Both managers and investors should, therefore, be familiar with the impact of corporate acquisitions on the buyers' financial reports, because the acquisition-driven changes affect major managerial and investors' decisions. In this chapter, we will briefly present the essence of the accounting for merger and acquisitions (M&A) consolidations and focus on important inferences that can be drawn from the consolidated (post-merger) financial reports.

"[Accounting] is among the finest inventions of the human mind."
—Johann Wolfgang von Goethe

9.1   THE ACCOUNTING FOR ACQUISITIONS

Despite valiant efforts by accountants to complicate consolidation (buyer's with target's) accounting, its basic principles are straightforward. In essence, at acquisition, all the identifiable assets,[1] tangible as well as intangible, and liabilities of the target company must be newly valued by the buyer at the effective date of acquisition, at their *current (fair) values*, namely, the amounts required to replace them. The previous values of these assets and liabilities presented on the books of the target company become irrelevant. Consider, as an example, the AMD case below.

TABLE 9.1   AMD's Allocation of the Purchase Price of Xilinx as of December 31, 2022, along with the (Pre-acquisition) Values of These Assets and Liabilities Presented by Xilinx on January 1, 2022 (in $ Millions), and Related Information

	Fair Values (Consolidated)	Book Values (at Xilinx)
Cash and short-term investments	$3,948	$3,702
Accounts receivable	299	439
Inventories and prepaid expenses	600	388
Property, equipment and leases	753	328
Acquisition-related intangibles	27,308	788
Other noncurrent assets	433	699
Total assets	$33,341	$6,344
Current liabilities	935	684
Long-term debt	1,519	1,494
Deferred tax and other liabilities	4,878	493
Total liabilities	$7,332	$2,671
Fair value of net assets acquired	$26,009	NA
Goodwill	$22,784	NA
Total purchase consideration (price)	$48,793	NA

Source: Adapted from AMD's 10-K report for the fiscal year ended December 31, 2022, and Xilinx's 10-Q report for the quarter ended January 1, 2022.

---

[1] Identifiable assets are those that can be separately recognized (recorded) and valued, like acquired patents, and are owned by and under the control of the buyer.

Let's delve into consolidation accounting with the AMD example. On February 14, 2022, the leading semiconductor manufacturer Advanced Micro Devices (AMD) acquired Xilinx (adaptive computing solutions) for $48.8B. In its 2022 annual report, AMD (the buyer) listed the assets and liabilities acquired from the target Xilinx (Table 9.1), at fair values, comparing them with the pre-acquisition book values of these assets and liabilities, which had been presented on Xilinx's (the target) quarterly financial report (10-Q) on January 1, 2022, just six weeks before the completion of the acquisition (right column of Table 9.1).

Thus, the total value of the assets acquired by AMD, per its statement, was $33.3B, at fair value, while its pre-acquisition book value on Xilinx's balance sheet was only $6.3B. How did the value of Xilinx's assets zoom to $33.3B in just six weeks, from January 1 to February 14, 2022, when AMD completed its acquisition?[2] That's the magic of "acquisition (fair value) accounting." As shown in Table 9.1, the main increase in Xilinx's assets was in the form of "acquisition-related intangibles": rising from $788M to $27.3B. And what are those acquisition-related intangibles? AMD details them, along with the related amortization rates (remaining years of service), in Table 9.2 (values in $ millions).

Thus, according to AMD's fair value estimates, Xilinx had under its hood $12.3B of developed technology (embedded in its internally developed products, now on the market) and $12.3B value of customer relationships

TABLE 9.2 Breakdown of "Acquisition-related Intangibles" for AMD's Acquisition of Xilinx

	Value (in $ millions)	Remaining Useful Life
Developed technology	$12,295	16 years
Customer relationships	12,290	14 years
Customer backlog	793	1 year
Corporate trade name	65	1 year
Product trademarks	895	12 years
In-process R&D	970	Indefinite
Total	$27,308	

Source: Adapted from AMD's 10-K report for the fiscal year ended December 31, 2022.

---

[2] For comparison, Xilinx's total assets was valued at $5.5B, as of April 1, 2021. Thus, Xilinx's assets grew from $5.5B to $6.3B, approximately $800M, between April 3, 2021, and January 1, 2022 – a period of nine months, implying an average growth of $133M only in six weeks.

(the value of long-term Xilinx's customers) that Xilinx itself didn't disclose on its January 2022 (pre-acquisition) balance sheet.[3] Did Xilinx hide those riches from its own shareholders? Not really. This is just a reflection of the absurdity of the so-called generally accepted accounting principles (GAAP) for intangible assets, as explained thus. (*Generally* accepted by whom? we might ask.)

9.2   THE ACCOUNTING FOR INTANGIBLE ASSETS

Accounting rules in the United States mandate the immediate expensing – that is, being treated as expenses in the income statement, like interest and salaries – of all the costs incurred in the creation of intangible assets, such as patents, brands, customers, etc. So, all of Xilinx's R&D, information technology (IT), employee training, and salesperson compensation that created the $24.7B of technology and customer relations assets (Table 9.2) were buried (expensed) over the years in Xilinx's income statements and therefore absent from its balance sheet. At acquisition, accounting rules require the buyer to value all the acquired assets, whether recorded or not on the target's balance sheet, and that's how the $24.7B value resurfaced.

Just think of the biased profitability indicators of Xilinx (return on equity and return on assets), missing almost $25B from their denominators, because of the expensing of intangible investments. Upon the acquisition of Xilinx, these assets were "resurrected" by AMD and valued at $24.7B in

---

[3] It is not unusual for buyers to allocate large portions of the purchase consideration (acquisition price) to purchased intangibles and goodwill. In its fiscal 2021 annual report, Cisco Systems, Inc. disclosed that for its acquisition of Acacia Communications, Inc. (a fabless semiconductor company specializing in high-speed coherent optical interconnected products), costing $4.983B and completed on March 1, 2021, the company allocated $2.2B and $2.4B to purchased intangible assets and goodwill, respectively. Cisco also disclosed that the purchased intangible assets from the Acacia acquisition consisted of (i) technology, valued at $1.3B with 4.0 years of weighted average useful life, (ii) customer relationships, valued at $490M with weighted useful life of 4.0 years, (iii) in-process R&D, valued at $345M with indefinite life, and (iv) "other assets" valued at $35M with weighted average useful life of 3.1 years. As of July 31, 2021, Cisco's total purchased intangible assets (net of accumulated amortization) with finite lives on its balance sheet included technology ($2.2B), customer relationships ($864M), and "other assets" ($58M). The company also reported $505M of in-process R&D with indefinite life. In Figure 9.1 (this chapter), we portray a similar pattern of large amounts of acquisition-related intangibles and goodwill included in the acquisition price paid by the buyers of the 500 largest acquisitions during 2003–2022.

terms of their current (fair) values. So, the post-acquisition consolidated balance sheet of AMD (the buyer) reflects all the identified assets and liabilities obtained from the Xilinx acquisition at current values, along with AMD's own assets and liabilities, mostly valued at *original costs*. AMD's balance sheet is thus a hodgepodge of asset values – not a particularly meaningful statement of corporate assets. Xilinx's *liabilities* are presented in the consolidated balance sheet combined with AMD's liabilities.

AMD's consolidated income statement just combines AMD's own revenues and expenses with those of Xilinx's, from the effective date of acquisition, eliminating any intercompany (between AMD and Xilinx) revenues and expenses. So, post-acquisition, the buyer's financial reports present, in fact, the combined values of the buyer's and target's specific items (inventories, sales), where the target's assets and liabilities are presented at their current, rather than historical, values.

9.3 HOW USEFUL ARE THE POST-ACQUISITION REPORTS TO INVESTORS?

You should realize that most of the fair value numbers representing the target's assets and liabilities are, in fact, based on the buyer managers' *estimates*, which are sometimes sheer guesses. For example, the values of Xilinx's $27.3B acquired intangibles (Table 9.1) *aren't factual*; they were not observed in any market indicators, like stock prices. They are based on the buyer's subjective estimates, often derived from the present values of the predicted future cash flows of the acquired assets, like patents and customers. These estimated asset values are, therefore, subject to errors and possible biases and manipulations. This is not just our bleak opinion of "fair values." Consider what AMD's own managers say about these "fair values" presented in their 2022 financial report:

> The preparation of consolidated financial statements . . . required management to make estimates and assumptions that affect the reported amounts of assets and liabilities . . . and the reported amounts of revenues and expenses during the reporting periods. *Actual results are likely to differ from those estimates*, and such differences may be material to the financial statements. (Italics ours.)

Accordingly, it's highly questionable to what extent investors can rely on such post-acquisition financial numbers and what is the validity of popular profitability ratios, like return on equity (ROE) or return on assets

(ROA), whose denominators include these estimated items. Later, we will empirically assess the relevance of these asset values.

The consolidated (post-acquisitions) income and cash flows statements, combining the revenues, expenses, and cash flows of the merged entities, provide more relevant information to investors because they rely less on managerial estimates, but they still reflect accounting's major shortcoming: the immediate expensing of intangible investments, such as R&D and IT.[4]

9.4   GOODWILL

Look once more at Table 9.1. The line next to the bottom reads: "Goodwill $22,784 million." What is this hefty sum constituting 68% of the total assets acquired? *Webster's* dictionary defines goodwill as "A kindly feeling of approval and support: benevolent interest or concern." And people say accountants are cold-blooded bean counters. Don't they express via goodwill managers' "kindly feelings, and benevolent interest and concern"? Who knew?

Not really. The $22.8B of Xilinx's goodwill has, of course, nothing to do with benevolence and kind feelings. Worse yet, it has nothing to do with anything of real or practical value. No one will pay a penny for Xilinx's goodwill upon attempted sale. Goodwill is just a plug number: the difference between the total price AMD paid for Xilinx, $48.8B, and the net (of liabilities) Xilinx's acquired assets at fair value, $26B. Accountants misnamed this number *goodwill* because it sounds better than "a plug number." And this very large number appears on the buyer's balance sheet as an asset because there is nowhere else to put it – it's definitely not a liability.[5]

What does goodwill represent? Frankly, we don't know. It may be the reflection of an *overpayment* for Xilinx in excess of the real value of its assets. After all, assessing the value of an acquired business entity – particularly one rich with intangibles – is a highly inaccurate activity, prone to mistakes. Such overpayments are frequent when there are multiple bidders for the target (a contested acquisition) where the bidding process tends to

---

[4] For elaboration on the increasing irrelevance of information in the financial reports of business entities, see B. Lev and F. Gu, *The End of Accounting and the Path Forward for Investors and Managers* (Wiley, 2016).

[5] There are rare cases of "negative goodwill," resulting from a bargain purchase, where the price paid for the target is *lower* than the fair value of its net assets acquired. Negative goodwill is presented as a subtraction from assets on the buyer's balance sheet. This sometimes happened in a government bailout of failing financial institutions where a solid bank was urged to buy a failing one at a bargain price.

drive target prices up. But the fact that practically every corporate acquisition generates goodwill suggests that it may reflect more than just an overpayment. Goodwill may also represent managers' assessment of additional revenues (from new products or a new market penetration), or cost savings that are expected from the merger, but that are not included in the values of the specific identifiable assets – that is, hidden assets or synergies beyond the values of the reported acquired assets. Thus, accounting goodwill remains to a large extent a mystery, similar to its popular meaning as a "benevolent concern."

The problem with goodwill is that it is often large, typically amounting to 50–55% of the acquired companies' total assets.[6] So, it's hard to ignore, but nevertheless it is often dismissed by lenders and financial analysts, because it has no independent sales value, and its sources are shrouded in mystery. Accordingly, many investors just ignore goodwill (subtract it from total assets and book value) for valuation purposes.

Finally, goodwill isn't amortized like most other assets, simply because no one knows at what rate to amortize it. It just stays there on the buyer's balance sheet until a "triggering event" occurs. That is, when it becomes crystal clear that the acquired business that created the goodwill in the first place is underperforming and its value has substantially diminished. In this case goodwill is said to be "impaired," and its value on the balance sheet is partially or fully reduced (written off), and an equivalent expense is charged against income. That was the case, for example, of eBay, which wrote off, in October 2007, $1.4B of the goodwill created by the acquisition of Skype.

Goodwill impairment is thus a managerial public admission of an acquisition failure and, as such, often triggers a stock price decline.[7] For example, Kroll Inc., a risk and financial advisory firm, reported in March 2022 that "Total goodwill impairments recorded by U.S. public companies more than doubled in 2020, from $71B in 2019 to $142B in 2020, but still fell short of the level observed in 2008 ($188.4B) at the onset of the global financial crisis of 2008–2009."[8] So, now you know all about acquisition goodwill. Its real importance lies in its demise: the write-off, which signals to investors that the underlying acquisition has gone bad.

---

[6] Since most identifiable intangibles must be amortized, thereby reducing reported earnings, there is an incentive for buyers' managers to understate the value of the identified assets, thereby inflating the non-amortized goodwill value.

[7] Such public admission of a merger failure and investors' negative reaction motivate managers to postpone the impairment of goodwill as much as they can, as was shown by K. Li and R. Sloan, "Has Goodwill Accounting Gone Bad?" *Review of Accounting Studies* 22 (2017): 964–1003.

[8] Kroll Inc., "2021 U.S. goodwill impairment study," March 2022. These high goodwill impairments in 2020 were, at least partially, caused by the COVID pandemic.

9.5   DETERMINING ORGANIC GROWTH

The periodic (annual, quarterly) growth of revenues and earnings (or of book value – Warren Buffett's favorite growth measure) is an important indicator of operational success of businesses. But, in the year of acquisition, when the target's income statement is consolidated with that of the buyer's, the latter's growth is mechanically enhanced by the combination of two income streams, rendering meaningless attempts to evaluate the rate of growth through comparisons with the buyer's previous sales and earnings. The solution is "organic growth," which is the buyer's growth from the previous to the current year *without* the acquisition's impact. Returning to AMD's acquisition of Xilinx, Table 9.3 shows AMD's revenue and operating income, as reported in its 2022 financial statement (which included Xilinx), with additional comparative information.

TABLE 9.3 AMD's Organic Growth vs. Reported Growth in the Year of Xilinx's Acquisition

	Net Revenue ($ million)		Operating Income ($ million)	
	December 31, 2022	December 31, 2021	December 31, 2022	December 31, 2021
Total (reported) amounts	23,601	16,434	5,464[a]	3,648
Amounts attributable to Xilinx	4,612	–	2,247	–
AMD net of Xilinx (organic)	18,989	16,434	3,217	3,648
Total growth	43.6%	–	49.8%	–
Organic growth	15.5%	–	(11.8%)	–

[a]According to AMD's 10-K (annual) report, reported operating income for the fiscal year ended on December 31, 2022, was $1,264M, reflecting the deduction of $4.2B Xilinx's acquisition-related costs (amortization of acquisition-related intangibles, employee stock-based compensation expense, and other acquisition-related costs). Therefore, operating income including Xilinx's acquisition-related costs was $5,464M ($1,264M + $4,200M).

Source: Adapted from AMD's 10-K report for the fiscal year ended December 31, 2022.

Thus, AMD's reported 2022 revenue growth was an unrealistic 43.6% (23,601/16,434 minus one), reflecting the additional $4,612M of Xilinx's revenues. The organic (net of acquisition) revenue growth, however, was a reasonable 15.5% (18,989/16,434 minus one). Regarding operating income, the 2022 reported growth rate was, once more, unrealistic – 49.8% (5,464/3,648 minus one) – whereas the organic growth rate was in fact negative: −11.8% (3,217/3,648 minus one).

If you wonder where we got Xilinx's additions to AMD's revenues and operating income (second line of Table 9.3, $4,612 and $2,247M), they were reported in a footnote to AMD's 2022 10-K report. Don't thank AMD's chief financial officer (CFO) for this valuable information: accounting rules require U.S. public companies to report the impact of acquisitions on the buyer's consolidated financial report *in the year of acquisition completion.*

9.6 IN-PROCESS R&D

Yet another uncommon feature of acquisition accounting is the item "in-process R&D" (IPR&D), appearing as the last item in Table 9.2, which details the acquisition-related intangibles:

> In-process R&D $970M.

AMD explains in a footnote that:

> IPR&D consists of projects that have not yet reached technological feasibility as of the acquisition date. Accordingly, the Company recorded an indefinite-lived intangible asset of $970 million for the fair value of these projects, which will initially not be amortized. Instead, these projects are tested for impairment annually and whenever events or changes in circumstances indicate that these projects may be impaired. Once the project reaches technological feasibility, the Company will begin to amortize the intangible assets over their estimated useful life.

Stripped of accounting jargon, in-process R&D is the buyer's estimate, generally using the present value of future cash flow projections, of the value of the target's projects *under development* that have not yet passed tests of operating technologically, like a beta test for software, at the acquisition date. In-process R&D is definitely an asset, although its stated value is based on highly uncertain estimates by managers. This is yet another acquisition-related asset lacking market (or liquidation) value. It's like any other R&D, but it is not immediately expensed because it is part of an acquisition.

9.7   WHAT DOES ALL THIS MEAN?

For many buyers of technology companies, accounting rules for post-acquisition consolidation create two rather large assets: acquisition-related intangibles and goodwill, that would not have existed without the merger. These two assets combined generally represent the lion's share of the total acquisition price. Xilinx's *tangible assets*, such as cash and short-term investments, accounts receivable, inventories, and property, plant, and equipment (PPE), which constituted virtually all of Xilinx's reported pre-acquisition assets on its balance sheet, amounted to a paltry 18% of the total value of the assets acquired and 12% of the total Xilinx's purchase price.

The staggering sizes of intangibles and goodwill created by AMD's acquisition of Xilinx is not an aberration; rather, it is common for large acquisitions, particularly tech ones. For the largest 25 acquisitions in each year, 2003–2022 (500 acquisitions over 20 years), Figure 9.1 portrays the median values of acquisition-related intangibles as a percentage of total assets acquired (at current values) along with goodwill as a percentage of the total target's purchase price. While the amount of goodwill was relatively stable over time, hovering around 55% of the total purchase price, the

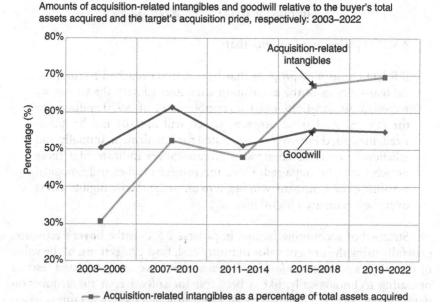

Amounts of acquisition-related intangibles and goodwill relative to the buyer's total assets acquired and the target's acquisition price, respectively: 2003–2022

FIGURE 9.1   The Median Amounts of Acquisition-Related Intangibles and Goodwill for the Largest Acquisitions During 2003–2022

acquisition-related intangibles rose sharply from 30% of total assets acquired in 2003–2006 to 70% in 2019–2022. This demonstrates the increasing *intangibility* of recent acquisitions. The intangibles missing from the target's financial statements pre-acquisition, such as developed technologies and customer relationships, have become the most valuable assets recorded by buyers post-acquisitions. In fact, most acquisitions of the recent two decades or so were made primarily for the targets' intangible assets. Tangible assets are mostly commodities these days.

But do these newly recognized assets actually contribute to the acquisition's success and the buyer's performance? This is an important question for investors and managers, as typically the bulk (more than 80%) of buyers' payment for the targets ends up in these highly uncertain and subjectively valued assets. If, for example, the majority of goodwill reflects overpayment for targets, possibly as a result of buyers' overly optimistic view of the acquisition's synergies, then this "asset" won't contribute to the buyer's future performance. The same is true for misstated amounts of "acquisition-related intangibles."

Figure 9.2 verifies these suspicions by displaying the *success rate* of our sample acquisitions, which were classified by the amounts of acquisition-related intangibles and goodwill (relative to the buyer's total assets before the acquisition). Specifically, we classify the sample acquisitions in each year and in each industry into three groups: low, medium, and high acquisition-related intangibles and goodwill (relative to the buyer's total assets), separately and jointly. Figure 9.2 presents separate results for all acquisitions and for acquisitions made by technology buyers, where large amounts of acquisition-related intangibles and goodwill are more prevalent.

What is striking in Figure 9.2 is that for all configurations – groups of three bars – the order of acquisition success (height of bars) is the same: highest success rates for acquisitions with *relatively low amounts* of goodwill and acquisition-related intangibles, and lowest success rate for acquisitions with *high amounts* of goodwill and acquisition-related intangibles. Thus, acquisitions with high amounts of acquired intangibles and goodwill are less successful than those with low values of these assets. These differences are accentuated for tech buyers (right side of Figure 9.2). For example, acquisitions made by tech buyers with the *lowest* amounts of both intangibles and goodwill (three right bars in Figure 9.2) have a success rate of 53%, which is twice the success rate of acquisitions with the *highest* amounts of intangibles and goodwill, 26%.[9]

---

[9] We further confirm the negative effects of acquisition-related intangibles and goodwill on acquisition success rate by including these variables in our comprehensive statistical model, which we describe in detail in the appendix.

The success rate of acquisitions with low, medium, and high values of acquired intangibles and goodwill, relative to the buyer's total assets

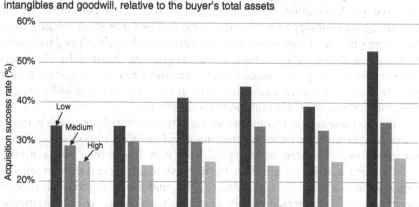

FIGURE 8.2 The Success Rate of Acquisitions Made by Companies with High, Medium, and Low Acquisition-Related Intangibles and Goodwill

This is a highly counterintuitive finding. How can it be that the two balance sheet assets reported under acquisition accounting that are typically the largest – goodwill and acquisition-related intangibles – are *negatively related* to the acquisition's success and the buyer's performance? Obviously, it is *not* that intangibles (e.g., patents, brands, customer relations) do not contribute to acquisitions' success. They definitely do, since they are the major value-creators of businesses. But, we suspect that a big chunk of these subjectively valued assets (goodwill and technology) may reflect the buyer's overpayment for the target, along with the high uncertainty (error) and managerial subjectivity underlying the estimated values of these items. Stated differently, our evidence indicates that high values of these "assets" do not necessarily indicate the existence of value-creating assets, rather the results of overpayment and estimation errors. Most investors take our findings to extremes: they often ignore these assets altogether in their valuations, particularly goodwill.

TAKEAWAYS

The post-acquisition consolidation accounting process described in this chapter provides a mixed bag of information. Some items are highly useful, like the acquisition's impact on revenue and operating income, which enable the calculation of the buyer's organic growth. Other balance sheet items, like goodwill and some acquired intangibles, aren't very useful to investors. The dividing line runs along the subjective – and sometimes biased – value estimates that managers assign: the contribution of the target to the buyer's revenues is a fact, while the value of goodwill is an estimate, sometimes a delusion.

Importantly, what is acutely missing from buyers' post-acquisition financial reports is any systematic information on the *progress of acquisitions*. Recall, for example (Chapter 1), that Google declined for years to provide any meaningful information on the operations of YouTube (like its contributions to Google's revenues and earnings, the additions to YouTube's users, etc.). And YouTube was an exceptionally successful acquisition. In cases where the acquisitions struggle, companies are even more tight-lipped than Google. So, investors are in the dark regarding the success of acquisitions, until managers choose to write off goodwill and/or other acquired assets. This may be years down the road, particularly given the evidence that managers delay reporting the write-off bad news as long as possible. This is unfortunate. Investors should be able to assess the acquisition's success from the start and not be surprised when a failure is finally admitted by management.[10] Particularly for acquisitions that are kept as separate businesses, like YouTube, there should be systematic disclosure of several key performance indicators (like revenue growth, additional users, etc.) in the years following the acquisition. Such transparency will have the added advantage of keeping executives on their toes regarding the integration and performance of the acquisitions, knowing that they are continuously monitored by investors.

---

[10] We know that investors are kept in the dark and surprised by the goodwill write-off because of the negative stock price reaction to most write-off announcements.

CHAPTER 10

Killer Acquisitions

We mention frequently the alarming failure rate of corporate acquisitions – 70–75% – and the consequent substantial losses sustained by the shareholders of acquiring companies. This is bad enough, but it's only money. Can it get worse? Indeed it can, like in "killer acquisitions." Relax, not that kind of killing, which is prohibited by the Ten Commandments. *Killer acquisitions* is the term used for an acquisition aimed at "killing the target," namely, acquiring a business and intentionally terminating its operations to avoid competition with the buyer's products. It is hard to believe, but this happens. The main concern here is antitrust: the target's demise limits competition and innovation in the sector of the deceased. This can be serious: limiting innovation in healthcare, biotech, pharmaceutics, and chemistry, among others, may seriously harm people's health and welfare. While we aren't dwelling in this book on legal and antitrust issues – this aspect of mergers and acquisitions (M&As) is extensively covered in the legal literature – the killer acquisition syndrome raises several interesting managerial and economic issues that warrant its brief discussion here.

"Killing is not so easy as the innocent believe."

—J. K. Rowling

10.1   VISA IS OUT TO KILL PLAID

This case deals with Visa's *debit* (not credit) card business. Visa had a remarkably dominant position in this sector: 70% of the U.S. market, followed by MasterCard with 25% market share. Visa has locked its dominant position by having a network of millions of customers who attract thousands of merchants. It also has long-term contracts with all the major banks, constraining them from issuing debit cards of competitors, thereby leading to an impregnable dominant position. Enter Plaid Inc. This relatively young company is different from the many fintech firms that provide complementary niche services that can be easily integrated into Visa or MasterCard's offerings. Plaid, in contrast, is a potential competitor to Visa and other card issuers due to its *disruptive technology*, and it has already gained a significant presence in the market. According to the U.S. Department of Justice (DOJ) complaint against Visa's attempt to acquire Plaid:[1]

> Plaid powers some of today's most innovative financial technology apps, such as Venmo, Acorns, and Betterment. Plaid's technology allows fintechs to plug into consumers' financial accounts, with consumers' permission, to aggregate spending data, look up balances, and verify other personal financial information. Plaid has already built connections to 11,000 U.S. financial institutions and more than 200 million consumer bank accounts in the U.S., and growing. These established connections position Plaid to overcome the entry barriers that others face in attempting to provide online debit services. (p. 3)

Plaid has thus positioned itself to become the hub of an ecosystem that competes with Visa and MasterCard, and potentially replaces them, though Visa currently outsizes Plaid by many orders of magnitude.

Plaid's unique innovation, according to the DOJ, lies in its "pay-by-bank" system:

> Pay-by-bank is a form of online debit that uses a consumer's online bank account credentials (i.e., a consumer's online banking username and password) – rather than debit card credentials – to identify and verify the user, bank account number and balance, and facilitate payments to merchants directly from the consumer's bank account. (p. 10)

Plaid's system could have lowered customers' fees by a remarkable 95% compared with Visa. Plaid with its unique technology could, therefore, be a real disruptor in the debit card market.

---

[1] *United States of America vs. Visa Inc. and Plaid Inc.*, Case 3:20-cv – 7810, Document 1, Filed 11/05/20.

Not surprisingly, continues the DOJ,

This prompted Visa's CEO to conclude that Plaid was "clearly on their own, or owned by a competitor, going to create some threat to our important U.S. debit business" and to tell his CFO that purchasing Plaid would be an "insurance policy to protect our debit biz in the U.S." (p. 5)

Since Plaid's technology is an effective *substitute* (disruptor) to Visa's, the giant buyer, surprisingly, made clear its intention to "acquire and kill" Plaid:

Indeed, Visa's CEO has already acknowledged that Visa "has no intention of introducing Plaid's pay-by-bank debit service for consumer payments to merchants in the U.S." (Complaint, p. 19)

Thus, what differentiates a killer acquisition from a regular merger is the buyer's intent in the former case to terminate and remove the target from the market. As the Plaid case shows, killer acquisitions clearly suppress innovation, restrict competition, and thereby harm consumers. Fortunately, Plaid's demise was avoided. Visa's intention to kill Plaid was apparently so egregious and the harm to competition and innovation so serious – as made clear in the DOJ's complaint against Visa – that in January 2021, merely two months after the filing of the DOJ's complaint (November 5, 2020), Visa announced the termination of its attempt to acquire Plaid. The prey escaped unscathed.[2]

10.2   HOW FREQUENT ARE KILLER ACQUISITIONS?

It is hard to say. Killer acquisitions are difficult to identify, since after the completion of an acquisition, acquirers rarely disclose the targets' scale of operations and financial results. We can hardly expect a rational chief executive officer (CEO) to publicly announce that "we have completed the acquisition of XYZ and proceed to terminate it." The Visa case was an exception, where its CEO, according to the DOJ complaint, apparently declared his intention to terminate Plaid. Special research methods must, therefore, be applied to identify killer acquisitions.

---

[2] Find more detail on the Visa–Plaid affair and the killer acquisition phenomenon in Marty, F. and T. Warin, 2020, "Visa acquiring Plaid: A tartan over a killer acquisition?" *Cirano*, working paper. The information in this section draws on this study.

Cunningham et al. (2021) did just that.[3] They focused on the innovation-intensive pharmaceutical industry and tracked the development of no fewer than 16,000 drug development projects conducted by 4,637 companies between 1989 and 2010. They focused on the drugs developed by acquired companies and followed them during the pre- and post-acquisition periods. The researchers specifically examined acquired drugs that overlapped with the buyer's drug portfolio, namely, drugs that matched the same therapeutic market (e.g., cholesterol reducing), and used the same mechanism of action as those of the buyers. This matching was required by the researchers, since such drug overlap obviously creates a threat to the buyer and the strongest incentive to kill the target.[4] The indication of a killer acquisition was then a "decreased likelihood of the development of overlapping [drug] projects [by the acquiring company] after acquisition" (p. 652).

At the end of this laborious process, the researchers concluded:

> ... acquirers conducting killer acquisitions are much more likely to undertake acquisition deals that do not trigger FTC [Federal Trade Commission] notification requirements for pre-merger review and thereby avoid antitrust scrutiny. Acquisitions of overlapping targets bunch just below the FTC acquisition transaction value threshold. ... Our conservative estimates indicate that between 5.3% and 7.4% of all acquisitions in our sample (or about 46–63 pharmaceutical acquisitions per year) are killer acquisitions. Eliminating the adverse effect on drug project development from killer acquisitions would raise the pharmaceutical industry's aggregate drug project development rate by more than 4%. (pp. 653–654)

Thus, the researchers estimate that 5.3–7.4% of all pharma acquisitions are "killer acquisitions." It's not a huge number, but it is definitely large enough to harm pharma innovation and competition. The finding that many competitive acquisitions "bunch just below the Federal Trade Commission (FTC) acquisition transaction value threshold" corroborates the intent to kill the targets. Losing 4% of drug development efforts from killing acquisitions isn't insignificant either. A life-saving drug or two may have been

---

[3] C. Cunningham, F. Ederer, and S. Ma, "Killer Acquisitions," *Journal of Political Economy* 129 no. 3 (2018): 649–702.
[4] This seems overly restrictive. Even an acquired drug in the same therapeutic market of the buyer, but not having the same mechanism (similar to Plaid and Visa), would pose a competitive threat to the buyer.

included in those 4%. For that reason, we decided to briefly discuss the killer acquisition phenomenon in this book. The relatively few recorded cases of killer acquisitions is likely a substantial understatement – the tip of the iceberg – given the significant difficulties of identifying killer acquisitions (is a failed acquisition the result of poor integration or an intentional kill?) and buyers' obvious attempts to disguise them.

10.3 IMPLICATIONS

Killer acquisitions are a serious matter. They raise important legal and ethical concerns that will embroil the buyer in extended and costly challenges. The legal issues raised by killer acquisitions were clearly demonstrated by the Visa–Plaid affair, discussed at the opening of this chapter, and ultimately drove Visa to abandon the acquisition. To avoid the limelight, you may decide to acquire the dangerous prey at an early developmental stage, thereby avoiding the FTC or EU reporting requirements. (In other words, "kill them young.") But even killing them early will likely cause a backlash. If you terminate (kill) a promising development project, particularly with health or social implications (pharma, biotech, healthcare, chemical, or artificial intelligence projects), people are likely to find out about it from laid-off target employees or whistleblowers. In the current environment of intense public scrutiny of business enterprises, killing a promising acquisition with adverse social implications will be clearly regarded as harming the "public good" and raise unwanted media and nongovernmental organization (NGO) concerns. You will likely pay a serious reputational price for such action.

Better to acquire the potential competitor, if the FTC will allow it – a big if – and integrate it into your offerings of other products. If the new product seriously cannibalizes your current offerings, perhaps it's time to refresh and redesign them. But even if the new acquisition seriously harms your current products, the acquisition is still yours. Kill your old, noncompetitive products instead. Thou shalt not kill applies to acquisitions too.

CHAPTER 11

Holding onto Losers

Every successful investor knows that as much thought and care as was given to the acquisition of a security should also be given to its disposition. You sometimes hear the following from star investors: "I gained more from selling securities on time than from buying them." However, human nature – or accounting disclosure rules – often drive people in the opposite direction: holding on to losers for too long. The influential behaviorists Amos Tversky and Daniel Kahneman concluded their famous Prospect Theory article with the dictum "Losses loom larger than gains." Therefore, the reluctance to admit to a loss is a major reason why people stick with losers for too long. Evidence shows that corporate acquirers also tend to procrastinate and hold on for too long to failing acquisitions and waste substantial resources and human capital in vain attempts to revitalize them. We will discuss in this chapter the evidence of keeping acquisition losers for too long, clarify the reasons for this, and suggest effective ways to avoid hemorrhaging resources in this way.

"We didn't commit enough to it for it to be an epic fail"[1]
—*Wall Street Journal*

11.1   FAILED ACQUISITIONS ARE KEPT FOR TOO LONG

Ideally, an acquisition should be integrated quickly, depending, of course, on the complexity of the situation (Chapter 8). And, if the integration falters – target customers are bailing out, its employees abandon ship, or the expected

---

[1] Opinion, Pepper . . . and Salt, 2024, *Wall Street Journal*, January 25.

synergies fail to materialize – the target, or what remains of it, should be sold (or spun off), or in extreme cases abandoned. When the integration's failure becomes evident or when the target's performance disappoints without a clear path to recovery, holding on to it is very costly. It drains the buyer's resources, human and financial, and increasingly reduces the salvage value of the target. Optimally, a quick integration process should be followed by a decision whether to keep or dispose of the target, and then the buyer should move on. But that's not what usually happens. Integrations often linger on for an extended period, the target's key employees and executives keep being replaced in efforts to find a winning managerial team, and new remedial strategies are tried, all in a desperate effort to resuscitate the failing acquisition, while almost everyone around has realized it's a limping horse being flogged. Amazon's acquisition of Twitch (videogame broadcasting) in 2014 seems a typical example of holding on to losers for too long. The *Wall Street Journal* (July 29, 2024) title of a thorough article on Twitch says it all: "Amazon Paid Almost $1 Billion for Twitch in 2014. It's Still Losing Money." How do we know that holding on to failed acquisitions is often the case? Analyzing empirical evidence, of course.

11.2   DELAYED GOODWILL WRITE-OFF

Practically every business acquisition creates a goodwill item on the buyers' balance sheet.[2] Goodwill is the difference between the price paid for the target and the "fair (current) value" of the acquired assets, tangible as well as intangible, net of liabilities. You can't miss goodwill; it's a substantial amount, typically reaching 45–55% of the acquisition price. If the acquisition falters, namely, despite all efforts, the present value of its expected cash flows (revenues, efficiencies) drops below its balance sheet value (including goodwill), or in simpler terms: when the target's real value shrinks below what was paid for it, the goodwill value on the buyer's balance sheet should be written off – reduced, partially or fully – and an equivalent expense charged to the income statement (goodwill impairment). This often triggers a substantial drop of the buyer's share price, as investors process the acquisition's failure.

A substantial goodwill write-off, which is, in fact, management's public admission that the acquisition failed to live up to expectations, is often a sign that the failed acquisition was kept for too long. Ideally, those in charge of the target's integration should have realized earlier that the integration floundered and sell off, carve out, or spin off the target, before it's publicly

---

[2] On the accounting attributes of goodwill, see Chapter 9.

tainted by a goodwill write-off. Writing off acquisition goodwill, or part of it, and still holding on to the target rarely ends up with its resurrection. So, generally buyers don't want to reach the stage of holding on to the acquisition while being forced to gradually write its value off – a corporate form of death by thousand cuts. And yet, this is a rather frequent phenomenon. Li and Sloan (2017)[3] report that of the companies having goodwill on their balance sheets (namely, most acquirers), 13%, on average, *per year*, have reported goodwill write-offs (value impairment), and the average write-off was almost 50% of the stated (balance sheet) amount of goodwill – that is, a substantial loss has incurred of the value of the target.[4] In 21% of these write-offs, the entire goodwill was declared a loss, indicating that the acquisition totally failed, often leaving no salvage value. And all these losses are reported as the target's assets are still kept by the buyer while its liquidation value vanishes.

11.3 POSTPONING THE INEVITABLE

Li and Sloan's main finding, however, is that many goodwill write-offs are publicly reported by managers with a *considerable delay*, that is, long after the actual loss of the target's value has occurred. Stated differently, many buyers are holding on to their targets even after they became an unsalvageable corpse. So, instead of expeditiously integrating the target, or, in case of failure disposing of, selling it, or spinning it off, they let the hopeless integration process linger on, further reducing the target's salvage value and wasting company resources in the process.

This is a surprising and damning (to buyers' managements) finding, and it's therefore instructive to briefly describe how the researchers established it. Li and Sloan (2017) examined a major indicator of investors' growth expectations, the "market-to-book ratio" (total stock market value of the buyer divided by its book value – balance sheet total assets minus liabilities). When this indicator falls *below 1*, investors, in fact, expect that the present value of the company's future cash flows to be generated by its assets will fall short of the value of these assets stated on the buyer's balance sheet. Such companies obviously shouldn't have any goodwill amount on their balance sheet, since goodwill indicates the existence of "extra yielding assets," beyond those reported on the balance sheet, having extra earnings power.

---

[3] K. Li and R. Sloan, "Has Goodwill Accounting Gone Bad?" *Review of Accounting Studies* 22 (2017): 964–1003.

[4] Since goodwill is about 50% of the target's acquisition price, on average, a 50% goodwill write-off (loss) is roughly 25% of the target's value (acquisition price).

Thus, the existence of goodwill on the balance sheet is inconsistent with a market-to-book value below 1. Yet, Li and Sloan identified many companies with goodwill that had a market-to-book ratio below 1. Accordingly, argue the researchers, these companies should have long ago written off (erased) their goodwill, and possibly the acquisition's value itself (declaring that the acquisition actually failed). Even so, those companies still held on to the failed acquisition and the related goodwill because their managers delay the write-offs and the associated income-reducing expense.[5]

Thus, Li and Sloan (and their followers) indicate that many "dead targets" are still parked on buyers' balance sheets and are obviously under the acquirers' control, long after they should have been sold or terminated. This obviously supports our claim in this chapter that buyers frequently tend to hold onto failing targets for too long.

11.4 WHY PROCRASTINATE WITH FAILED TARGETS?

The inescapable research conclusion is that the integration of many acquisitions takes far too long, draining company resources in the process. Investors often perceive the integration difficulties, as evident from the falling share prices of the buyers, sometimes even below book value. But why would managers of acquiring companies fall into the trap of holding onto failing acquisitions for too long? What's the fascination with keeping losers around?[6] There are two major explanations to this managerial malaise – sunk costs and loss disclosure – and it's important to understand both of them in order to avoid them.

11.4.1 Sunk Costs

Several years ago, one of us advised the IT department of a large international insurance company. The issue under consideration dealt with the proposed replacement of a key software security system. Proponents of the new system argued that its capabilities are substantially superior to those of the current one – an argument that wasn't in dispute – and that its quarterly

---

[5] In addition to the market-to-book ratio, Li and Sloan use other measures of profitability and value, such as the return-on-asset (ROA), to indicate a delayed goodwill write-off.

[6] There is a similar phenomenon in securities investments: investors tend to hold onto losing securities for too long, see H. Shefrin and M. Statman, "The Disposition to Sell Winners Too Early and Ride Losers Too Long: Theory and Evidence," *Journal of Finance* 40, no. 3 (1985): 777–790.

rentals are about the same as the costs of maintaining and updating the current security system. A win–win replacement situation. Nevertheless, proponents of the new system ran into a heavy headwind: "We have spent, not long ago, $3.5 M on developing and installing the current security system, along with countless hours of IT support personnel. We can't just let all this investment go down the drain, particularly after we convinced the board of the superiority of this system," argued the dissenters of the replacement. Most participants in the meeting were involved in acquiring and installing the current system and nodded their heads in assent. This was a classic case of the "sunk cost" fallacy, as defined by Wikipedia (July 2023):

> In economics and business decision-making, a sunk cost (also known as retrospective cost) is a cost that has already been incurred and cannot be recovered. Sunk costs are contrasted with prospective costs, which are future costs that may be avoided if action isn't taken. . . . [O]nly prospective (future) costs are relevant to a rational decision. . . . Any costs incurred prior to making the decision [the $3.5 M of the current security system in the preceding example] have already been incurred no matter what decision is made. They may be described as "water under the bridge". . . . In other words, people should not let sunk cost influence their decisions; sunk costs are irrelevant to rational decisions. . . . [Yet] Sunk costs often influence people's decisions, with people believing that past investments (i.e., sunk costs) *justify further expenditures*. People demonstrate "a greater tendency to continue an endeavor once an investment in money, effort, or time has been made." This is the sunk cost fallacy, and such behavior may be described as "throwing good money after bad," while refusing to succumb to what may be described as "cutting one's losses." (emphasis ours)

Continued efforts to fix a failing target, throwing more money under the bridge, when objective evaluation clearly indicates that the future revenue growth or cost synergies expected from the target will fall short of expectation, is a classic case of the sunk cost fallacy. One often hears managers saying "We have invested so much in this acquisition that we can't just abandon it." But, when the integration fails, that's exactly what they should do. Let bygones be bygones no matter what the sunk (acquisition) costs were.

General Electric's November 2015 acquisition of the French power company Alstom, for $13.5 B, was very expensive and complex. The acquisition had to receive regulatory approval in more than 20 countries, and, furthermore, GE had to yield to the French government, letting it retain 20% of Alstom and keeping its headquarters in France. GE also committed that no Alstom employees would be fired and, moreover, that it would add to Alstom 1,000 jobs by the end of 2018. Clearly, these were unprecedented, crippling conditions and costly restrictions. But according to GE's executives, it was all worth it, given the large expected benefits from the acquisition, including $1.2 B synergy by year 5.

This GE acquisition went astray almost from the get-go. The worldwide power market softened considerably subsequent to the Alstom acquisition, and the widely publicized synergies didn't materialize, as so often happens. Yet GE, while firing 12,000 employees from its power division (none from Alstom), kept plowing money into Alstom and ramped up its production in failed attempts to resurrect divisional growth. Instead, inventory just piled up at Alstom, in a softening natural gas market where Alstom mainly operated.[7] In October 2018, GE wrote off the staggering amount of $23 B from the value of its Power Division, of which Alstom was a key part.[8] The large investment in Alstom's acquisition – an obvious sunk cost – most likely contributed to the decision to hold on to it for so long. Sunk cost is indeed a powerful fixation.

So, sunk cost is our first explanation for companies' tendency to hold onto failing acquisitions for too long. The second explanation relates to accounting and investors.

11.4.2   Avoid the Loss Disclosure

The sunk cost argument, though clearly valid in some acquisition cases, is based on a behavioral–emotional motive. People feel committed to make good on their past decisions. The *loss disclosure argument*, discussed next, is of a different nature. Once managers sell, or abandon, an asset, they have to write off (eliminate) its value from the balance sheet and charge the loss to the income statement for everyone to see. Investors aren't forgiving to such public admission of a considerable waste of their investment; some will demand explanations from management of what went wrong, and taking responsibility for it, while others will just dump the stock, causing share prices to fall.[9]

---

[7] Reflecting this adverse trend, the annual revenues of GE's Power segment declined by 24% from $35.84 B in 2016 to $27.30 B in 2018.

[8] The write-off primarily reflected goodwill impairment, in the amount of $21.2 B, in the Power Division. GE disclosed in its 10-K filing of 2018 that "The majority of the goodwill in our Power segment was recognized as a result of the Alstom acquisition."

[9] A recent example: *Wall Street Journal* (February 21, 2024) reported that one day earlier HSBC bank, one of the world's largest, wrote off $3 B of its investment in the Chinese lender Bank of Communications. This large write-off turned HSBC's quarterly profit to a loss of $153 M. Investors' retribution for the write-off was harsh: HSBC's stock price lost 8.4% on the write-off announcement.

Research on buyers' stock price reaction to goodwill write-off announcements reports share price drops of 2–5%, depending on the time periods examined, size of write-offs, etc.[10] But this negative investor reaction to write-offs is just the tip of the iceberg. Recall our earlier discussion that many companies postpone the day of reckoning and write off goodwill and other acquired assets long after investors realize and react negatively to indications that the acquisition went astray. Accordingly, the total investors' negative reaction to a failed acquisition is likely on the order of 10–15%. This will obviously raise many questions from investors and directors about the justification and necessity of the acquisition and its failed integration. Managers responsible for failed acquisitions would naturally like to avoid addressing such embarrassing questions and, in extreme cases, pay the ultimate price for a failed acquisition – being fired (recall that the chief executive officers [CEOs] of both HP and Teva Pharmaceutical were fired soon after their botched acquisitions; see Chapter 1). They will therefore do whatever they can to try to salvage the target – even when it's clearly beyond salvageability – and hold on to it just to postpone its termination and the consequent write-off disclosure. So, the accounting requirement to publicly record a loss, often a substantial one, upon the sale or abandonment of an acquisition is a strong incentive to hold onto it for too long, to the detriment of shareholders and the company.[11]

11.5   AND NOW, TO OUR PROOF

Our explanations of sunk costs and the avoidance of loss disclosure for holding onto failed acquisitions far too long are corroborated by our sample data. If our explanations hold, then larger failed acquisitions, which have higher sunk costs and trigger more serious loss disclosure consequences, will lead managers to postpone the write-off of goodwill (and keep the target) *longer* than smaller acquisitions whose write-offs often go

---

[10] See, for example, L. Sherrill and R. Stretcher, "Abnormal Returns Following Goodwill Impairment Write-Offs," *Journal of Finance and Accountancy* 28 (2020): 1–22.
[11] There is a particularly pernicious trick some managers are resorting to in recording large losses from goodwill and acquisitions. It's called the "big bath." That is, delaying the public recognition of acquisition or goodwill loss to a period when very large other losses are reported, like a restructuring loss. The idea is that investors won't distinguish between, say, a loss of \$3 B and \$3.5 B (a restructuring loss with or without the acquisition write-off). It's all a "big bath."

unnoticed by investors. This prediction is clearly borne out by Figure 11.1, which portrays the number of years (time span) from the initial acquisition of a target to the subsequent disclosure of its goodwill impairment. The figure shows the percentage of firms reporting goodwill impairment in each year during a five-year period *after* the initial acquisition.[12] It contrasts large goodwill impairments (more than $5 B) – for which our sunk cost and loss recognition explanations are particularly relevant – with relatively small impairments (less than $300 M).[13]

Figure 11.1 clearly shows that for small goodwill impairments, or write-offs (downward-sloping line), the losses are recognized early on after acquisition, whereas the recognition of large write-offs (upward-sloping line) is considerably delayed by management. Specifically, almost 30% of small

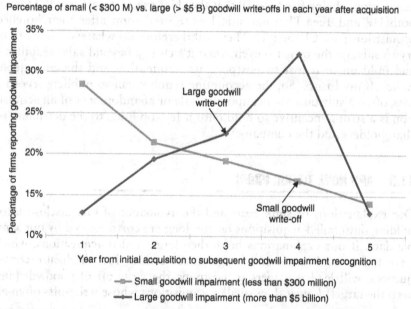

Percentage of small (< $300 M) vs. large (> $5 B) goodwill write-offs in each year after acquisition

FIGURE 11.1 The Time Span Between Acquisition and the Subsequent Goodwill Write-Off

[12] We ignore the period after the fifth year because other factors, such as new management or acquisitions, may affect the timing of goodwill impairment disclosure.
[13] This analysis covers the period after 2003. To ensure our results are not driven by the extremely high concentration of goodwill impairments under severe market and industry downturns, we excluded from this figure the years of the financial crisis (2007–2009) and COVID-19 (2020).

write-offs are recognized in the *first year* after acquisition, followed by 21 and 19% in the second and third year, respectively. That is, by the end of the third year after acquisition, close to 70% of small failed targets have been written-off by management. In contrast, the percentage write-off of large failed acquisitions (upward-sloping line) in the first year is very low – just 13% – increasing slowly with time subsequent to acquisition. Three years post-acquisition, slightly more than half (55%) of large goodwill write-offs have been recognized – considerably less than the 70% of small write-offs. Figure 11.1 is thus consistent with our explanations for the protracted termination of failed acquisitions.

11.6   HOW TO OVERCOME THE ADVERSE EFFECTS OF SUNK COSTS AND LOSS DISCLOSURE?

Successful management of acquisitions requires giving the same level of care and scrutiny to the *back end* of acquisitions (the integration process, and – if failed – the decision to sell or terminate the target) as is usually given to the front end of the acquisition (making the decision to acquire, selecting the target, conducting due diligence). A failing target should not be allowed to linger and waste, in the process, financial and human resources. But how to overcome the powerful obstacles of sunk costs and loss disclosure?

An effective way to do it is by instituting strong corporate discipline and oversight over the integration process. Allowing for some flexibility, of course, at the time of acquisition the buyer's executives should determine the duration given to the integration of the target, based on past experience and the particular circumstances of the case. If by the end of the assigned integration period, say, a year, the integration isn't completed and will require substantially more time and resources, the team in charge of the integration should be replaced by a new team that was *not involved in the acquisition*. This important substitution of integration management eliminates both the sunk cost and loss disclosure obstacles, since the new team will have no emotional attachment to the acquired target and will not be held responsible for its failure. The new integration team will thus cool-headedly and objectively decide whether it is cost-effective to continue the integration attempt for a while longer or terminate it and sell or abandon the target. Failing sports teams are known to quickly change managers; the same should pertain to failing or procrastinating acquisition integration teams. Bygones are bygones.

CHAPTER 12

Means of Acquisition Payment: Cash, Stocks, or Mix?

Does It Matter?

Some acquisitions are paid for in cash, others in the buyer's stock, and the rest in a mix of stocks and cash (and sometimes other means). Most observers don't pay much attention to the means of acquisition payment, focusing instead on the essentials of the deal: the type of business acquired, the purchase price, and the promised benefits. But do the means of acquisition payment matter? Research strongly suggests they do because there is a *message* in the means of payment to both investors and target shareholders. Accordingly, we discuss in this chapter the considerations that should underlie the choice of the means of payment and the messages they convey.

"It's money. I remember it from when I was single [pre-merger]."
—Billy Crystal

12.1 VARIOUS INTERESTING TRENDS

Figure 12.1 portrays the percentage of acquisitions paid for in cash, stock, or a combination of the two, of all acquisitions made during the past 40-some years. The figure conveys a somewhat confusing picture of ups and

Percentage of payment methods: stock, cash, and mixed payment of all acquisitions

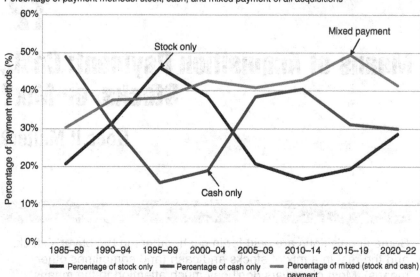

FIGURE 12.1   The Weighted Average (by Deal Size) Percentage of Stock, Cash, and Mixed Payments of All Acquisitions

downs, with lines crossing each other.[1] But, as you will shortly see, there is a method to this madness.

First, let's deal with the easy part. The percentage of mixed payments (top line) has risen slowly from 30 to 40% of all acquisitions. The remaining 60% of payments convey a different story. Consider first the percentage of acquisitions paid for by *stocks*. It started with 20% and rose sharply in the 1980s and 1990s to 45%, mainly reflecting the large increase in the number of high-tech and science-based companies getting involved in acquisitions during that period. These enterprises need all the cash available to them for research and development (R&D) and the creation of other intangibles (brands, trademarks) and therefore pay for acquisitions with their stocks. Furthermore, these companies usually encounter considerable difficulties obtaining bank loans for acquisitions, due to the intangibility (nonmarketability) of their main assets (R&D, patents, brands), which banks often

---

[1] To provide a more economically coherent message, we calculated the percentages in Figure 12.1 by weighing the individual acquisitions by the size (value) of the deal. Thus, for example, a $1.0B acquisition gets double the weight of a $500M acquisition in the percentage calculation. This weighting accounts for the low economic impact of very small acquisitions and the high impact of large ones.

don't consider as collateral. Accordingly, high-tech and science-based companies mostly use their stock for acquisitions, creating the sharp rise of the stock-based payment line in the 1980s and 1990s. Moving on to the early 2000s, we observe a sharp and protracted decline in stock payments for acquisitions, mainly driven by the 2000 stock price collapse, particularly of tech companies, due to the burst of the tech bubble. Buyers' stock prices were so low at that time that they couldn't be used to finance acquisitions, except for in special cases. That's the reason for the long drop in the percentage of stock payments, to 17%, until the post–financial crisis period (2008–2009), when stock prices gradually recovered and the use of stocks for acquisitions increased.

One more thing: in the 1970–1990s, accounting standards allowed the use of the so-called "pooling method" to account for corporate acquisitions. In pooling, the acquired assets aren't revalued at the time of acquisition to their current values – as is currently required by the "purchase method" (see Chapter 9). Rather, the acquirer just combined the acquired assets and liabilities, *at their original values on the target's books*, with its own assets and liabilities. Consequently, under the pooling method, there was no revaluation (usually upward) of the acquired assets, and, notably, there was no goodwill associated with the acquisition (for elaboration on goodwill, see Chapter 9). Buyers' managers obviously favored this accounting method, since it eliminated the increased asset depreciation charges, due to the revaluation of acquired assets, and, in particular, it avoided goodwill amortization (required until 2001). Both of these were drags on reported earnings. But pooling was allowed only for acquisitions paid for in stocks, and the demise of pooling as an accepted accounting rule in June 2001 contributed to the sharp decline in the use of stock for acquisitions, starting in the early 2000s.[2]

By construction, when the percentage of stock payments increased, those of cash payments, presented in Figure 12.1, decreased, and vice versa. Interestingly, during the past decade, the percentage of stock payments reversed its long decline and has inched up steadily; it is now roughly equal to the percentage of cash payments for acquisitions (30% each).

High-tech and science-based companies (Internet, pharma, biotech) – leading sectors in developed economies – are voracious acquirers, usually exchanging their shares with those of target shareholders. Figure 12.2 presents the patterns in the means of payment of tech companies. In comparison

---

[2] Also in the early 2000s, in the wake of the tech bubble burst, interest rates *decreased* significantly, thereby increasing the attraction of taking loans and paying with cash for acquisitions, which was another factor contributing to the declining use of stock in paying for acquisitions, post 2000.

Percentage of payment methods: stock, cash, and mixed payment for technology buyers

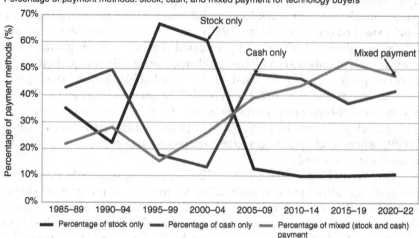

FIGURE 12.2 Technology Buyers: The Weighted Average Percentage of Stock, Cash, and Mixed Payments of All Tech Acquisitions

with all buyers (Figure 12.1), the fall in stock payments for acquisitions by tech companies in the early 2000s was more dramatic: from almost 66 to 10%. And in contrast to nontech buyers, this low level of stock-financed transactions essentially persists to the present. The reason: most tech buyers are presently large and very successful companies (Amazon, Google, and Facebook), which are flush with cash and can afford to use it to acquire businesses without diluting their current shareholders. That's why we see the high percentage (more than 40%) of cash-financed transactions by tech companies in Figure 12.2. These, then, were the long, cyclical trends – and their drivers – regarding the means of payment for acquisitions. But, when considering a specific acquisition, buyers' managers have the freedom to choose the means of payment. What are the considerations underlying these choices? On this, next.

12.2   BUT WHAT DETERMINES THE MEANS OF PAYMENT?

Google bought YouTube in October 2006 for $1.65B, paying for it with its own stock, while Oracle bought Cerner in December 2021 for $28.3B and paid for it in cash, and Facebook acquired WhatsApp in February 2014 for $19B, paid for in a combination of $4B in cash and the remaining $15B with its stocks (using both Facebook Class A shares and restricted stocks, given to WhatsApp's employees). Teva Pharmaceutical went further and raised $35B of debt to acquire Allergan Generics (Actavis) for cash in 2016 (recall from Chapter 1 how well this acquisition went).

Is there a method in the variety of means of payment for acquisition? Or is it just a matter of convenience – the availability of sufficient cash calls for its use to finance the acquisition, and when cash isn't available, stocks are used? Are target shareholders, and investors in general, reacting differently to the various means of payment? And, most importantly, does the specific means of payment affect the consequences of the acquisition? In short, is the means of acquisition payment more than just a financial matter? These are weighty questions we address in the following sections based, as always, on the available evidence.

12.2.1   Hypothesis 1: Buyers Know Better

Researchers have reported an intriguing yet consistent finding: investors' reaction to acquisitions paid for in stock is often *negative* (the buyer's stock price decreases) around the first public acquisition announcement, whereas the reaction to acquisitions paid in cash is, on average, *positive* (or less negative than for stock acquisitions).[3] This clearly indicates that the means of payment for acquisitions conveys different messages to investors. But what are these messages?

Myers and Majluf (1984),[4] among others, argued that buyers' managers obviously cater to their current shareholders, so that when managers believe that their shares are *overvalued*, relative to their true, intrinsic value (for example, when investors aren't yet aware that the company's sales growth has tapered off recently), they will finance acquisitions with stocks to exploit their inflated value, namely, pay for acquisitions with "cheap currency." Conversely, when managers believe that their shares are *undervalued*, they will finance acquisitions with cash to avoid the dilution of the shares held by current shareholders. Investors, in turn, learn over time of managers' underlying motives, so when they see stocks being used to finance an acquisition, they infer that the buyer's shares are overvalued, soon to drop in price, and react negatively by selling the buyer's shares. Hence, the stock price declines for acquisitions paid for by stock (investors inferring that the buyer's shares are overvalued), and the share price increases for acquisitions financed with

---

[3] See, for example, Chattergee, R. and A. Kuenzi, 2001, "Mergers and acquisitions: The influence of methods of payment on bidder's share prices," published by the University of Cambridge.

[4] S. Myers and N. Majluf, "Corporate Financing and Investment Decisions When Firms Have Information that Investors Do Not Have," *Journal of Financial Economics* 13, no. 2 (1984): 187–221.

cash, indicating managers' belief that their shares are undervalued. Thus, according to these scholars, the means of payment for acquisitions reflect buyers' managers perceptions of the valuation of their shares – overvalued or undervalued.

The obvious weakness of this explanation of investors' different reactions to how a buyer pays for an acquisition is that in most real-life cases it is very difficult to know, in advance, even for the company's managers, whether their company's shares are overvalued or undervalued. Even when adverse internal events are unknown to investors, causing share overvaluation, such events must be quickly reported to the public through corporate quarterly reports or special Securities and Exchange Commission (SEC) filings. So, it's doubtful whether an important event, like the means of payment, which is generally determined well ahead of the acquisition's execution, can be explained by a temporary and largely uncertain event, like the over- or undervaluation of buyer's shares. It is time for more convincing explanations for the choice of a buyer's means of payment.

12.2.2 Hypothesis 2: Confidence in the Acquisition's Success

The merger success, namely, the realization of the expected sales growth or cost efficiencies generated by it, is, of course, uncertain at acquisition. But if the buyer's managers have a high degree of confidence in the acquisition's success (e.g., target's products under development are close to completion or new favorable regulations are close to enactment), they will tend to pay for it with cash, thereby securing for their current shareholders all the acquisition's benefits. If, however, the buyer's managers are largely uncertain about the realization of the expected benefits of the acquisition, they will pay for it with stock, thereby *sharing the acquisition's risk of failure* with the shareholders of the target, who obtain the buyer's stock in exchange for theirs. In a sense, the high degree of risk concerning the acquisition's success is shared between the buyer's and the target's shareholders by financing the acquisition with stock. Under this explanation, the main motivation for the choice of payment is the degree of confidence of buyers' managers in the success of the acquisition (Hansen, 1987).[5]

This, then, explains the evidence of investors' reaction to the acquisition's means of payment: investors know that if managers pay for an acquisition with cash, then they are highly confident about the acquisition's success, and therefore investors react positively to the acquisition announcement. In contrast, when the acquisition is paid for in stock, investors infer

---

[5] R. Hansen, "A Theory for the Choice of Exchange Medium in Mergers and Acquisitions," *Journal of Business* 60, no. 1 (1987): 75–95.

that acquirers' managers are largely uncertain about the acquisition's outcome and hence investors have a negative reaction to the acquisition announcement.

This explanation for investors' reaction to the acquisition's means of payment makes more sense to us than the overvaluation/undervaluation explanation outlined earlier. Note that this explanation applies also to mixed acquisition payments: partly stock and partly cash. The relative shares of cash and stock are motivated by the degree of managers' confidence in the acquisition's success.

TAKEAWAYS

If executives and directors of acquiring companies are pretty certain about the acquisition's success – the realization of its expected benefits – they should pay for the target in cash, or in a mixed payment consisting mostly of cash, thereby securing the acquisition's benefits for their current shareholders and avoiding the dilution of their shares. Buyers will also likely benefit from the bump in their stock price, given that investors favor cash-based acquisitions. But managers should do this only when they have enough cash available or need to supplement it with only a modest loan. They shouldn't materially change their company's capital structure (debt-to-equity ratio) by taking large loans to finance acquisitions. We have seen repeatedly in this book that large loans often doom – or at least seriously harm – the acquisition (Teva Pharmaceutical, for example, in Chapter 1). The higher leverage also increases the buyer's financial risk and raises its future financial costs (interest).

If these conditions don't apply, namely, if the acquisition's consequences are substantially uncertain, or free cash is unavailable, and the buyer is still hell-bent on conducting this acquisition, then its stock should be used to finance it. At least this will share the consequences of the acquisition with the target's shareholders, and the buyer won't have to worry about servicing large loans. But in this case, managers should reconsider the acquisition: with highly uncertain acquisition outcomes and no cash to buffer its uncertainty, such as unexpectedly large integration expenses (Chapter 8), perhaps managers should pass on this acquisition altogether (remember, they likely won't lose much, since most acquisitions fail anyway).

CHAPTER 13

But What If Executives Are Irrational or Self-centered?

So far in the book we have assumed that executives making acquisition decisions are capable, rational (unbiased) persons who cater to the best interests of their shareholders. But this idyllic premise flies in the face of so many failed acquisitions (70–75%). How can all this carnage be "in the best interest of shareholders"? There must be something other than shareholders' welfare that motivates many of the acquiring executives. Something that goes beyond economic rationality and shareholders' value maximization. In this chapter, we expose the disturbing evidence on managers' self-serving acquisition motives, as well as on various behavioral biases that lead many executives to believe that they are, in Buffett's words, "a beautiful princess soon to kiss a toad" yet leave in their wake masses of "unresponsive toads" (as per the Preamble). Enter executives' irrationality and self-centeredness.

"It's unfortunate we can't buy executives for what they are worth and sell them for what they think they are worth."

—Malcolm Forbes

Investors, the media, and researchers usually don't question even consequential managerial investment decisions, like major capital expenditures or expensive research and development (R&D) projects. Such decisions are assumed to be the prerogative of managers (made under their "business judgment") and overseen by the board. Mergers and acquisitions (M&As) are a different matter. Large acquisitions, in particular, are often hotly debated in the boardroom, criticized by the media, and examined carefully by financial analysts. The need for a specific acquisition, the suitability of the target chosen, and the reasonableness of the price offered are frequently questioned and castigated by investors and pundits. This was, for example, the case in AT&T's acquisition of Time Warner (2018), where the underlying logic of the acquisition – combining distribution (AT&T) with content production (Time Warner) – was widely questioned by analysts and major investors, particularly because AT&T's archrival, Verizon, avoided this expansion route (Chapter 8). Difficulties in merging the different employee cultures were predicted, and many gasped at the price of the deal – more than $100B (including Time Warner's debt) – and the consequent large increase in AT&T's outstanding debt. That all these questions were warranted became clear just three years later (2021) when AT&T gave up on the acquisition and spun Time Warner off. It was a very expensive (to AT&T's shareholders) and futile exercise.

So, why is it that of all managerial investment decisions, M&A deals are so closely scrutinized by investors and the public? The size of deals (often in the multibillion dollars) has, of course, something to do with it, but we believe that the dismal record of corporate acquisitions is the major driver of the "natives' unrest" to acquisition announcements. With such a poor record, no wonder that investors' general reaction to acquisition announcements is often negative (buyer's stock price decreases) and most acquisition deals are closely analyzed and often publicly criticized. This dismal record of acquisitions also motivated many researchers and M&A observers to look for special *managerial acquisition motives*, which may explain the continuously increasing "urge to merge" in the face of likely failure. It is crucial for anyone involved in or affected by M&A decisions to fully understand these managerial motives that lie beyond shareholders' interests. That's what we'll talk about in this chapter.

13.1 HAVE YOU HEARD ABOUT "AGENCY COSTS"?

Classical economic theory paid little attention to corporate managers. They were assumed to be (i) *capable*, carefully weighing the expected costs and benefits of their decisions; (ii) *rational*, that is, making the right decisions while being generally unaffected by emotional or psychological biases; and (iii) *shareholders' wealth maximizers*, making decisions that result in the highest returns to the owners of the enterprise. Thus, classical economists did not suppose corporate managers to be lax or lazy or to be strongly affected by emotions, like extreme risk aversion or overconfidence, and most important, managers were assumed to be trusted *agents* of the capital entrusted to them by their *principals* (owners, shareholders), and perhaps other stakeholders too, without inserting their own preferences (empire building, higher salaries) into their business decisions. In short, corporate managers were assumed to be angels.

However, observing real-life chief executive officers (CEOs), it quickly becomes obvious that there are very few angels among them. Some managers make colossal mistakes, like Sprint's acquisition of Nextel (Chapter 8); many are overconfident and reckless without the supporting record of achievements; and some even lead their shareholders astray with misinformation (financial reporting fraud). And, most damaging, managers often pursue policies and take actions that obviously aren't in the best interest of their shareholders, like contributing substantial corporate funds to self-serving causes or overpaying themselves (through a friendly board).[1] With the "age of innocence" over, many researchers turned their attention to systematic real-life deviations from managers' rationality and selflessness, namely, to managers pursuing their own goals to the detriment of shareholders (owners). This came to be known as *agency cost*.[2]

Agency costs, in essence, are the cost to the *principal* (shareholders and perhaps other stakeholders) of the *agent* (manager) pursuing their own interests. Thus, for example, a CEO who engages in acquisitions, such as conglomerate ones (see Chapter 5), which benefit the CEO but not shareholders, is creating agency costs. The same is true for acquisition-derived boosts to executives' compensation and improper corporate acquisitions, which create serious agency costs, as explained thus.

13.1.1 Conflict (I): M&As Boost Executives' Compensation

Practically every empirical study reports that most M&A deals trigger substantial bonuses and other compensation increases for executives, particularly for the CEOs of both the buyer and target companies. This, perhaps, would have been tolerable, except that these bonuses are rarely conditioned on the long-term success of the acquisition. They are automatic

---

[1] A particularly egregious and widespread way of cheating shareholders was the *backdating of stock options*. This scheme came to light in the early 2000s, when a researcher found that many companies (led by their CEOs and directors) chose a date during the past year with a particularly low share price to declare it as the option's grant date, thereby substantially increasing managers' gains from exercising stock options, at the expense of other shareholders. See E. Lie, "On the Timing of CEO's Stock Option Awards," *Management Science* 51 (2005): 802–812.

[2] For the original and very comprehensive treatment of agency costs, see M. C. Jensen and W. H. Meckling, "Theory of the Firm: Managerial Behavior, Agency Costs and Ownership Structure," *Journal of Financial Economics* 3, no. 4 (1976): 305–360.

for *conducting M&As.* This obviously creates a strong incentive among corporate executives to acquire businesses even in cases where the expected benefits aren't clear-cut. And when the acquisitions fail, the costs are fully borne by buyers' owners and often target employees, and the CEO's bonuses are rarely "clawed back." A rigorous study on this issue concluded:[3]

> We find that 39% of acquiring firms in our sample cite the comple-
> tion of the deal as a reason for rewarding their CEOs. In almost all
> of the cases, the payment is given in the form of a cash bonus. . . .
> [B]onuses are larger when the deals are larger, ... Measures of
> managerial power [over the board] add significantly to the explana-
> tory power of the variation in the bonus. . . . [W]e find that the most
> frequent [public] motivation for the M&A bonus is the resulting
> increase in firm size and revenues. . . . *Only 22 firms argue that*
> *value enhancement [acquisition success] is a reason for the bonus.*
> *Furthermore, compensation does not appear to increase with deal*
> *performance.* (emphasis ours)

So, this study concludes that buyers' CEOs generally get hefty bonuses for completing acquisitions; that the size of the bonus is often affected by the CEO's power or influence over the board (often substantial); and that most damaging from the agency costs perspective is that the CEO bonuses are rarely affected by the success of the acquisition. Heads I win, tails you lose. The latter finding reveals a major misalignment of CEO and corporate shareholder interests.

A more recent meta study (2020) surveying the findings of 42 research projects on mergers and buyers' CEOs concludes:[4]

> As to the studies that concern CEO's incentives, *all of them* found
> that CEO compensation increases after the acquisition. . . . Over-
> confident and narcissistic CEOs decrease the value of acquisition.
> (Emphasis ours.)

Particularly intriguing from owners–managers' conflicts is the follow-ing research finding, relating to the *target company's* CEOs: "Our multivari-ate baseline tests show that in deals where the target CEO gets a merger bonus, targets get premiums [acquisition price over target's market price of

---

[3] Y. Grinstein and P. Hribar, "CEO Compensation and Incentives – Evidence from M&A Bonuses," *Journal of Financial Economics* 73, no, 1 (2004): 119–143.
[4] A. Węglarz, "Do CEO Incentives and Characteristics Influence M&A? A Systematic Literature Review," *Management Studies* 10 (2020): 79–94.

shares] about four percentage points lower."[5] That's pretty damning: by paying an M&A bonus to target CEOs, buyers manage to pay, on average, 4% less to target shareholders (the bonus presumably leads targets' executives to resist the acquisition less than they might have otherwise). Who would have believed?

The positive effect of acquisition on buyers' CEO pay is twofold. First, buyers' CEOs (and sometimes other top executives, too) often receive direct bonuses for completing the acquisition. Second, the ongoing compensation of buyers' CEO also increases because of the larger post-acquisition size of the buying company after absorbing the target. Empirical evidence is unanimous that company size is the major determinant of managers' compensation.

Summarizing, we *don't believe* that acquisition bonuses and higher post-acquisition compensation cause many CEOs to acquire businesses that seriously detract from shareholder value. But the large, acquisition-related increases to CEO compensation may clearly tip the scales of the many acquisitions whose consequences and uncertainties are borderline. Rather than erring on the side of caution, managers, tempted by large bonuses, may decide to go for it.

13.1.2 Conflict (II): Conglomerate Acquisitions to Ameliorate Executives' Risk Exposure

Consider the case of conglomerate (unrelated) acquisitions. As we discussed in Chapter 5, most conglomerate mergers lack economic justification and therefore fail. The risk diversification achieved by such mergers – when one corporate unit falters, another unit will generally prosper, thereby stabilizing corporate operations and cash flows – can easily and more efficiently be achieved by individual shareholders directly owning stock in the individual companies doing the business of the conglomerate's units. Furthermore, the synergies of such unrelated mergers are minimal to nonexistent, as in the case of Amazon acquiring Whole Foods, or the Chinese real estate developer Evergrande launching an electrical vehicle unit in 2013 (both Chinese units are on the verge of bankruptcy currently). So why are conglomerate mergers still conducted? you ask. To further the interests of managers (the agents), at the expense of shareholders, is our answer.

Specifically, a typical top executive isn't *diversified* like most investors are. Much of the CEO's investments are in the form of their companies' restricted stocks and stock options, and their human capital (reputation,

---

[5] E. Fich, E. Rice, and A. Tran, "Contractual Revisions in Compensation: Evidence from Merger Bonuses to Target CEOs," *Journal of Accounting and Economics* 61 (2016): 338–368.

future earnings power) is closely tied to the fortunes of the company they manage. Executives, therefore, bear substantially higher risk than their shareholders, who are typically well diversified across many investments. Enter conglomerate mergers – while not benefiting shareholders, they do wonders for managers in terms of risk diversification. A traditional oil and gas company acquiring a large alternative energy (solar, wind) business will stabilize its operations over the foreseeable future. Or, a volatile hedge fund owning an insurance company with stable cash flows over the cycle will be able to smoothly ride the ups and downs of the market. Managers' reputation for stable performance, not to mention their annual compensation, will obviously benefit considerably from such intra-company risk diversification.

In Chapter 5, we provided empirical evidence to support our claim that conglomerate acquisitions are mainly driven by managers' self-interested motives. The high costs associated with conglomerate acquisitions – sometimes amounting even to total failure of the investment – are another prime example of agency costs borne by shareholders (on top of the acquisition bonuses discussed earlier). Corporate acquisitions are thus tainted by cases where buyers' managers insert their self-interested motives to the detriment of shareholders, and possibly other stakeholders.

From acquisitions that create conflicts between managers and owners, we move to a case of unethical and short-sighted behavior by managers.

13.2 UNETHICAL BEHAVIOR: BUYING WITH INFLATED SHARES – A PACT WITH THE DEVIL

This case of acquisitions that ultimately harm shareholders involves "inflated (overvalued) shares." Occasionally, managers may suspect that their company's shares are *overvalued*, at least temporarily. These are generally the cases where managers are privy to negative inside information not yet known to investors, like a recent slowdown of sales, setbacks in the development of new products and services (like failure of drugs' clinical tests), or impending resignation of key employees. The public disclosure of these events, in due time, will, of course, knock down share prices, but in the meantime these prices don't reflect the negative events and are, therefore, overvalued. Share overvaluation can sometimes be an industry-wide or market-wide event, like the highly inflated shares of the dotcoms during the late 1990s bubble. In such cases, for a while at least, the company shares are inflated, relative to their true, intrinsic value.

A key question for managers is whether they should exploit such share overvaluations by taking one or all the following actions: (i) acquire a business with the inflated shares (paying with "cheap money"), (ii) issue new stocks, and/or (iii) exercise their stock options and gain from the immediate sale of the exercised stocks at inflated prices.[6] We believe that all three actions are both morally repugnant and bad for business (short-sighted). A pact with the devil. Why? Because, as Michael Jensen said, "The price of inflated shares, *by definition*, will sooner or later collapse, since if they don't, the shares weren't inflated in the first place." Hence, if managers *knew* that their share prices are inflated and bound to fall – because they currently don't reflect the negative news *known to managers* – and use these shares to issue stock to unaware investors or acquire a business by paying target shareholders with "cheap currency" – they in fact cheat the new, unsuspecting shareholders. The fact that current shareholders may benefit at the expense of new ones doesn't justify the deception. Managers aren't supposed to be Robin Hood, moving funds from one group of people to another. Target shareholders, along with their executives and employees, aren't going to forget being conned and will ultimately cause the acquisition to fail.

The classic case of acquiring a large company with inflated shares is, of course, Time Warner's acquisition by America Online (AOL) in January 2000. AOL's share price was obviously highly inflated at the time of the acquisition, since the combined company's shares lost about two-thirds of its value in the first years post-merger.[7] The consequent hard feelings of the target's shareholders and managers – the recipients of AOL's inflated shares – were aptly described by the *Wall Street Journal* (October 3, 2002),[8] thus:

---

[6] Such actions are often recommended to managers by advisors and economists. For example, Shleifer and Vishny (2003) seem to approve that when a company's shares are overvalued, managers should acquire other companies with stock: "(3) bidders in stock acquisitions are likely to exhibit signs of overvaluation, such as earnings manipulation and insider trading" (Introduction). A. Shleifer and R. Vishny, "Stock market driven acquisitions," *Journal of Financial Economics* 70 (2003): 295–311. Or, ". . . if investors sometimes overestimate and sometimes underestimate the value of the firm, a rational manager who maximizes value to existing shareholders should concentrate equity issues to occur during periods of positive sentiments" (p. 56), U. Malmendier and G. Tate, "Behavioral CEOs: The Role of Managerial Overconfidence," *Journal of Economic Perspectives* 29 (2015): 37–60.
[7] We are not suggesting that Steve Case, AOL's CEO and the main architect of the merger, *knew* at the time of acquisition that AOL's share price was highly overvalued. We just focus in this example on the fate of an acquisition with overvalued shares.
[8] Perkins, A., 2002, "The case for AOL merger is clear under examination," *Wall Street Journal*, October 3.

Time Warner shareholders and employees now feel he [Steve Case] duped their company into an unfair merger. . . . I remarked at the time that Mr. Case's most significant stroke of genius was that he bought Time Warner when AOL's market value was at its over-valued peak.

The dire consequences of this "stroke of genius" were years of heavy losses and massive goodwill write-offs at the merged company, CEOs' departures, key employee desertion, and all-around ill-will, which ultimately led to the breakup of the merger in 2009. Finally, the coup de grâce to a "stroke of genius" acquisition with inflated shares."[9]

The disastrous AOL–Time Warner merger is a unique case, due to its size and notoriety. But Feng and I (2011) examined the consequences of a large number of acquisitions paid for with inflated shares.[10] We found that acquisitions paid for with overvalued shares were subject to a higher than average rate of goodwill impairment (managerial recognition of acquisition failure) than those of other acquiring firms and that the share-holders of the acquiring overpriced companies expressed their disap-proval of the acquisitions by bidding down substantially (selling) the shares of the buying companies upon the acquisition announcement. All bad consequences.

So, here is a case of a short-sighted and unethical managerial activity – acquiring a company with overvalued shares – that seems on its face like a good idea but doesn't work in reality. Our following cases deal with irra-tional managerial behavior.

13.3   OVERCONFIDENT EXECUTIVES: TOO MUCH OF A GOOD THING

We have mentioned earlier that classical economic theory largely ignored corporate managers' behavioral traits, implicitly treating them like unbi-ased, selfless, and rational persons efficiently processing all relevant data and making the right decisions for their principals. In contrast, the more recent research area of "behavioral economics" focuses on imperfect deci-sion makers, namely, on "real people," having limited ability to process information (often termed *bounded rationality*), and characterized by

---

[9] The AOL–Time Warner union is sometimes considered the "worst merger of all time" (see McGrath, R., 2015, "15 years later, lessons from the failed AOL–Time Warner merger," *Fortune*, January 10).

[10] F. Gu and B. Lev, "Overpriced Shares, Ill-Advised Acquisitions, and Goodwill Impairment," *The Accounting Review* 86, no. 6 (2011): 1995–2022.

various biases and psychological traits that affect their decisions.[11] In the area of corporate acquisitions, recent research focuses on the actions of *overconfident managers* (see Malmendier and Tate, 2015, ibid).

Frankly, the term *overconfident*, or *overly optimistic*, is a loose one, because the underlying term *confident managers* is also ill-defined. With a 70–75% acquisition failure rate, aren't all acquiring executives overconfident in their ability to succeed in such a "suicide mission"? Apparently, by the term *overconfident* researchers generally refer to a subset of the generally optimistic, confident CEOs, who are significantly over-valuing their ability to turn the acquired company into a success. They constitute the tail of the distribution of generally confident corporate leaders. They truly believe that they are consistently better than others in choosing acquisition targets and integrating them successfully with the company they manage. Why examine the decisions of overconfident CEOs? Because, as you will soon see, they act differently than other managers, particularly regarding acquisitions, and their actions have adverse consequences that you should know about. But first:

13.3.1 How to Identify an Overconfident CEO?

There are some simple (sometimes simpleminded) methods by which researchers identify overconfidence, like comparing managers' earnings forecasts ("guidance") with the subsequently reported actual earnings, and if the forecasts consistently exceed the actuals, the issuing CEO is deemed overconfident. But highly optimistic earnings forecasts can just reflect managerial hype and recklessness, rather than overconfidence. Other researchers asked managers in surveys to predict the best and worst stock prices of their company at the end of next quarter. Suppose the prediction was $26.50–$17.50. If the actual price at the end of the quarter came consistently below the predicted range, say $15.25, the CEO was also deemed overconfident.[12] But what if the CEOs are just poor forecasters? This doesn't make them overconfident. So, we don't give much credence to these schemes of identifying managerial overconfidence.

There is, however, a clever way of identifying CEO overconfidence, which was introduced by Malmendier and Tate (2005) and followed by several other researchers.[13] It requires a brief explanation, but it's worth the effort.

---

[11] For a most enjoyable and thorough book on behavioral economics, see Kahneman, D., 2011, *Thinking, Fast and Slow*, Farrar, Straus and Giroux.

[12] U. Malmendier, and G. Tate, "Behavioral CEOs: The Role of Managerial Overconfidence," *Journal of Economic Perspectives* 29 (2015): 37–60.

[13] U. Malmendier and G. Tate, "CEO Overconfidence and Corporate Investment," *Journal of Finance* 60, no. 6 (2005): 2661–2700.

Top managers, like most rational investors, would like to diversify their investment portfolio, particularly because most managers are loaded with options on the company they manage, which considerably heightens their risk exposure to their company's fortunes. Such risk diversification can be achieved by exercising the stock options (namely, converting the option to a regular share by paying the company the option's strike price) *soon after the options vest* and then selling the shares immediately. That's what most rational managers indeed do. But – and here comes the crux of the identification approach – if the CEO is overconfident (beyond mere rationality) in their ability to lead the company to exceptional growth and success and thereby to substantially higher stock prices, they will hold onto the options and exercise them long after their vesting date and exchange the options for the company's shares when their prices peak. Extremely overconfident CEOs will even wait all the way just prior to the option expiration date and exercise the options before they become worthless (usually 10 years after grant). These "long-holding" CEOs, so confident in their ability to raise the stock prices of their companies, are defined by Malmendier and Tate as overconfident in their ability to manage their companies to greatness and reap the consequent rewards. That's how the researchers identify CEO overconfidence, and they report that between 20 and 40% of CEOs exhibit such overconfidence.

13.3.2 The Actions of Overconfident CEOs

So, how do overconfident CEOs behave? Malmendier and Tate found, not unexpectedly, that these CEOs have a substantially higher tendency or risk tolerance to invest and particularly acquire companies than regular CEOs. They often conduct conglomerate acquisitions, which mostly tend to fail (Chapter 5). Interestingly, investors' reaction to merger announcements by overconfident CEOs is *significantly more negative* than the regular adverse reaction to merger announcements, reflecting investors' mistrust in the acquisitions made by overconfident managers.[14]

Yet, the most important question remains open: how *successful* are the acquisitions made by overconfident CEOs? Perhaps those gung-ho individuals are great acquirers? The answer to this question is critical to the choice of action taken, like should overconfident CEOs be restrained by the board from acquiring companies? So we addressed this question using our acquisitions sample; the results are portrayed in Figure 13.1.

---

[14] On the bright side, overconfident managers innovate more than other managers, per Hirshleifer, Low, and Teoh ("Are Overconfident CEOs Better Innovators?" *Journal of Finance* 67, no. 4 (2012): 1457–1498). Again, that's not entirely surprising: innovation involves considerable risk-taking.

M&A success rate: Average CEOs vs. overconfident CEOs

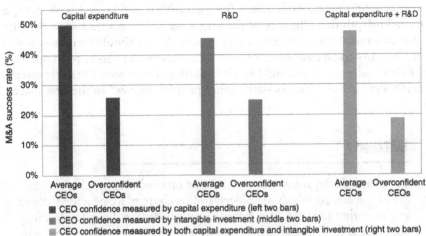

FIGURE 13.1 The Success of Acquisitions Made by Overconfident CEOs

We followed the available research and identified overconfident CEOs as those who invest *more than the industry average* in capital assets and in innovation (R&D). Then we used our measure of acquisition success to determine the success rate of the mergers made by overconfident CEOs versus those made by regular (perhaps just confident) CEOs. The results, shown in Figure 13.1, are instructive: under any measure of CEO overconfidence, the acquisitions made by these CEOs were *inferior*, on average, to those made by regular CEOs. Specifically, for each pair of bars in Figure 13.1 (reflecting different measures of overconfidence: from left to right – excess capital expenditures, excess R&D, and excess capital expenditure plus R&D), the left bar (acquisition success of regular CEOs) is substantially higher than the right bar (acquisition success of overconfident CEOs). In fact, by any measure of overconfidence, the success rates of acquisitions made by overconfident CEOs were below our *sample average* success rate (roughly 30%). So, investors, reacting particularly negatively to acquisition announcements by overconfident CEOs (mentioned earlier), are essentially right: these voracious CEOs destroy shareholder value.

13.3.3   Quo vadis Overconfident CEOs?

So, what to do with such gung-ho managers? We have evidence that they acquire more companies than regular CEOs and, moreover, are poor acquirers. What overconfident CEOs need, we believe, is more than usual directorial oversight, particularly regarding large acquisition proposals.

Much more critical attention should be given to their estimates of acquisition benefits, particularly when the acquisition is financed with debt; a more in-depth due diligence of the target should be made; and in the case of conglomerate acquisitions, a very serious debate should be conducted of the benefits to *shareholders* of such acquisitions. In short, overconfident CEOs require extra oversight by the board and investors. Or alternatively, don't hire such risk-takers with "other people's money" in the first place.

TAKEAWAYS

Economic theory used to treat CEOs as rational and capable caretakers of the company's shareholders. In this chapter, we provided ample evidence that not all CEOs behave in this way. We discussed findings showing that acquisitions by some managers were driven by self-centeredness (conglomerate acquisitions and mergers driven by acquisition bonuses), by short-sightedness (acquisitions paid for with inflated shares), and by self-delusion (acquisitions by overconfident CEOs). Notably, common to all these cases is the acquisition outcome – *below* the already low average of acquisition success rate. Those self-centered or overconfident CEOs definitely contribute to the high rate of M&A failure. Ideally directors and influential investors will rein in those corporate recalcitrants. The acquisition decision, like any other managerial decision, should be made, as far as possible, without being affected by management's behavioral biases and selfish interests, and it should be made for the benefit of corporate owners and other important stakeholders, like employees and customers.

CHAPTER 14

The Human Element

Acquisitions, Executives, and Employees

In Chapter 1 we analyzed two colossal acquisition failures – Teva Pharmaceutical buying Actavis and HP purchasing Autonomy – those failures quickly led to the dismissal of the acquiring chief executive officers (CEOs). Was this quick dismissal an aberration or the normal fate of CEOs who conduct failed acquisitions? In addressing this and related questions, in this chapter we analyze the effects of corporate acquisitions – successful and failed – on CEO tenure and compensation. Other important aspects of the human element of acquisitions are, of course, employees. Accordingly, we also examine the impact of acquisitions on employee headcount and productivity. As often happens in this book, the test results are rather surprising.

"Always look for the fool in the deal. If you don't find one, it's you."
—Mark Cuban

14.1 ACQUISITIONS' EFFECTS ON CEO TENURE AND COMPENSATION

A comprehensive study of corporate acquisitions, as conducted in this book, isn't complete without examining the impact of acquisitions on their major initiators – corporate CEOs. Such assessment goes straight to the heart of the merger dilemma: Are CEOs motivated to acquire businesses solely to advance corporate performance and shareholder value, or are CEOs' *personal motives* affecting their acquisition decisions? We started dealing with this important issue in Chapter 13, where we discussed several topics, like the lavish CEO acquisition bonuses and the many conglomerate mergers in recent years, which benefit CEOs directly, rather than the acquiring enterprise and its owners. We have seen that the personal motives and objectives of CEOs are varied and clearly affect some acquisition decisions, thereby imposing "agency costs" on corporate owners. Accordingly, boards and influential investors have to carefully scrutinize acquisition proposals to clearly identify the personal benefits buyers' and targets' executives obtain from the acquisitions and use this information to determine to what extent such personal gains affect the acquisition decisions of those executives. The outrageously high failure rate of mergers and acquisitions (M&As) could certainly be substantially reduced by avoiding the acquisitions that primarily benefit executives. More effective board and major investors' monitoring of acquisitions is clearly called for.

In what follows, we dig deeper into the issue of personal benefits to executives by considering the impact of acquisitions on CEO *tenure* and *compensation*, the two attributes most important to CEOs. To recap, the overriding objective of this discussion is to determine whether CEOs are unbiased agents of corporate owners and other major stakeholders or whether they have their own axe to grind in conducting corporate acquisitions. This question clearly bears on the dismal performance of corporate acquisitions that vexes us throughout the book. We open the discussion by analyzing the effect of corporate acquisitions on CEO *tenure*. One would expect that only successful acquisitions will lead to tenure extension, but, as you'll soon see, that's not always the case.

14.1.1 Are Acquisitions a CEO's Tenure-Insurance?

Jeff Immelt at GE reportedly acquired 380 businesses, mostly unsuccessful, as evidenced by the company's stagnant stock price during his tenure, yet served almost 20 years at the company's helm.[1] John Chambers, at Cisco, was an underachiever compared with Jeff Immelt: he managed to conduct only 180 acquisitions during his 20 years at the helm of Cisco while the company, still doing well, fell off the ranks of the leading tech enterprises (e.g., "the Magnificent Seven").[2] So, are acquisitions a tenure-insurance policy, no matter their final outcome? If true, this will definitely explain many CEOs' *urge to merge* and the overall dismal record of M&As.

Empirically examining this issue is tricky, though. If one finds a positive correlation between the number of acquisitions made and CEO tenure, like

---

[1] Gara, A., 2017, "For GE's Jeff Immelt, hundreds of deals and $575 billion didn't yield a higher stock price," *Forbes*, June 15.
[2] Nusca, A., 2017, "Cisco's John Chambers: Moving too slow was my biggest CEO mistake," *Fortune*, May 24.

in the Immelt and Chambers cases, the *causality* may run in one of two opposite directions: (i) a large number of acquisitions conducted, even if many fail to resuscitate corporate performance and growth, extends CEO tenure because boards generally reward executives that actively try to change their company's course and give them ample time to make the acquisitions work, or, alternatively (ii) operationally successful CEOs (high sales and earnings growth) naturally have a longer tenure than unsuccessful ones, and therefore have more time to acquire companies. Stated differently, are acquisitions the *reason* for long CEO tenure, or are long CEO tenures the *reason* for conducting many acquisitions? The implications of these two underlying explanations for the positive relation we find between CEO tenure and the number of acquisitions conducted are, of course, very different.

Extracting causation from mere correlations is notoriously hard in empirical work, but we did our best to achieve it, as follows: using our large sample, we compared the tenure of CEOs who conducted few acquisitions (no more than three) with that of CEOs who conducted many acquisitions (four or more) during their tenure. We then examined the voluminous research on the determinants of CEOs' tenure and found that the two main determinants of the length of tenure are the company's *stock price performance* (falling share prices often topple executives), and its *profitability* – the two are, of course, related. To *control* for these primary determinants of CEO tenure, we *matched* (equalized) the two groups of CEOs (those conducting few and many acquisitions), on average, by their companies' ratio of share price-to-book value ("price-to-book") and by their return on assets (ROA), a widely used profitability measure. So, on average, acquisitions aside, the tenure of the two groups of CEOs should be close since they had similar share price and profitability performances.

Yet, as Figure 14.1 shows, this wasn't the case. For our entire sample period 1980–2022 (left two bars in the figure), the CEOs who conducted *more acquisitions* (four or more) served, on average, 13 years (second from left bar), whereas CEOs with fewer acquisitions (one to three) served only nine years (left bar). Thus, we found a substantial four years difference in CEO tenure, mainly related to the number of acquisitions conducted. When we break the sample period into two subperiods (1980s and 1990s versus 2000s) – four right bars – we obtain similar results: CEOs who conducted multiple acquisitions served, on average, three to five years longer than those who made only a few acquisitions (note, however, that in the 2000s, the difference between the two groups narrowed).

The likely reason for this surprising finding is that executives who conduct multiple acquisitions are viewed by their boards and major investors as active managers who try their best to restore their company's growth and enhance its performance and shareholder value, and they should therefore

Acquisitions extend CEO tenure

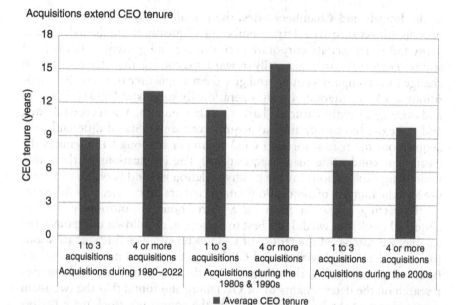

FIGURE 14.1   Acquisition Frequency and CEO Turnover

be given sufficient time to perform these tasks and make sure that the acquisitions they made succeed. However, it is doubtful from these findings whether the heavy price paid by shareholders for the high acquisition failure rate is fully internalized by directors when they extend the tenure of serial corporate buyers. In contrast, CEOs with only a few acquisitions under their belt are apparently just evaluated by their stock and financial performance, having no acquisition pipeline to extend tenure. We thus conclude that corporate acquisitions extend CEO tenure.[3] The crucial question now is whether this reward for acquisitions *distinguishes* between successful and unsuccessful ones. We will address this question later in this section.

---

[3]We aren't suggesting that extending tenure is the only reason for CEOs to acquire companies. Most acquiring executives are probably genuinely interested in improving their company's performance. But the repetition of this activity (acquisitions) necessarily leads to longer tenure, since, once acquisitions are approved, CEOs are often given sufficient time to integrate the target and try to make the acquisition a success. This relation between length of tenure and number of acquisitions made cannot go unnoticed by CEOs.

14.1.2 Acquisitions and CEO Compensation

We have discussed in the preceding chapter the fact that CEOs (and sometimes other executives too) often receive generous bonuses and other types of rewards for *concluding* M&A deals. Note the emphasis on concluding, rather than on *succeeding*. Wouldn't it make more sense to condition the bonuses on the success of acquisitions, namely, on the achievement of the expected synergies and other acquisition benefits promised by executives upon announcing the acquisitions? Of course, it would. But as with so many other aspects of M&As, logic and reality go their own ways.

Acquisition bonuses are one-time rewards, but acquisitions also enhance CEO pay throughout their tenure. Studies have shown that one of the main determinants of CEO pay is the *size of the company* they run. Large companies, it is widely believed, are more difficult to run than smaller ones and require special managerial skills and hence offer higher compensation. Acquisitions, whether successful or not, invariably increase the buyer's size and thereby automatically its CEO's compensation. This provides yet another incentive to acquire businesses.

Figure 14.2 portrays the average *annual increase* of CEO's salary and bonuses over their tenure for chief executives who conducted few acquisitions (one to three), compared with CEOs who made multiple acquisitions

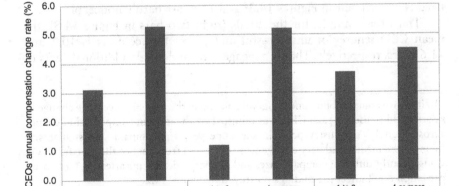

Annual CEO compensation is enhanced by acquisitions

■ Average annual % change of salary and bonuses

FIGURE 14.2 Acquisition Frequency and CEOs' Average Annual Compensation Increase

(four or more).[4] It is clear from the figure that over the entire sample period (1980–2022) – two left bars – as well as for the two subperiods (1980s and 1990s vs. 2000s), the annual percentage increases of salary and bonuses of multiple acquirers were larger than those of CEOs who conducted few acquisitions only. Thus, for example, for the entire sample period (two left bars of Figure 14.2), CEOs who made few acquisitions (left bar) saw their annual compensation increase by 3.1%, on average, compared with 5.3% for CEOs with more acquisitions. While this difference narrowed in the 2000s (right two columns), there is no doubt that acquisitions enhance CEO compensation throughout their tenure.

14.1.3 Key Question: Is Acquisition Success Rewarded?

We have seen that CEOs are generously compensated for conducting acquisitions and serve longer tenures. But, importantly, are they compensated for making *good* acquisitions? Figures 14.3 and 14.4 are similar to the preceding Figures 14.1 and 14.2 – except that Figures 14.3 and 14.4 are classified by successful and unsuccessful acquirers, using our unique measure of acquisition success (see the appendix). The two groups are divided into CEOs who were successful in fewer than 50% of the acquisitions they have conducted over their tenure and those who were successful in more than 50% of their acquisitions (losers versus winners). So, is successful acquisition rewarded? Yes, but what is striking in Figures 14.3 and 14.4 is that the reward for acquisition success is so small. The differences between the bars' heights in each pair in Figures 14.3[5] and 14.4[6] are hardly noticeable.[7]

Thus, for example, for the 2000s (right two bars in Figure 14.3), the mean CEO tenures of unsuccessful and successful acquirers is 10.1 and 11.6 years, respectively. That is a meager one-and-a-half additional years of

---

[4]To improve comparability and economic meaning, the annual percentage change of salary and bonuses of each CEO was adjusted by the median compensation change across the CEO's industry peers in the same year for companies of similar size (namely, the median industry change was subtracted from that of the specific CEO). Consequently, different company sizes and industry-wide events affecting CEO compensation don't affect the findings portrayed by Figure 14.2.

[5]Examining "all years," we stop in 2018 because our merger success indicator requires data on three to four *future years*.

[6]Ibid.

[7]In Figure 14.3 (CEO tenure), the difference between the two bars for each period is statistically significant (nonrandom) at the 0.01 level. In contrast, the difference for each period in Figure 14.4, which focuses on CEO pay increase is statistically insignificant, namely, not reliably different from zero.

The tenure of successful acquirers is slightly higher

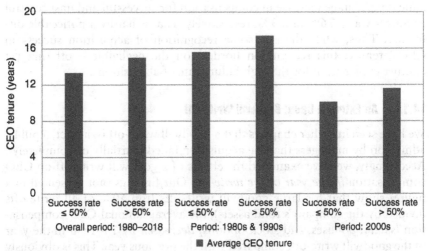

FIGURE 14.3   Acquisition Success Rate and CEO Tenure: 1980–2018

Successful acquisitions hardly raise CEO compensation

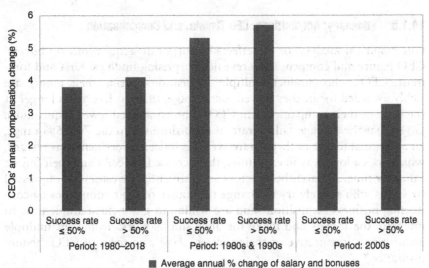

FIGURE 14.4   Acquisition Success and CEO Average Annual Compensation Increases: 1980–2018

tenure for successful acquirers. In Figure 14.4 (during the 2000s), the median annual percentage increase in compensation for successful and unsuccessful acquirers was 3.26% and 3%, respectively. That is hardly a noticeable difference. Thus, while there is some recognition of acquisition success in CEOs' tenure, this recognition borders on the negligible – offering yet another explanation for the high failure rate of acquisitions.

14.1.4   An Extreme Case: Goodwill Write-Off

We have seen in earlier chapters that a goodwill write-off is, in fact, a public admission by managers that the acquisition failed (partially or completely). Accordingly, we have examined the effects of a goodwill write-off on CEO compensation *in the year of the write-off*. Our findings (not presented in a figure) show that for large goodwill write-offs (top 50% of all write-offs divided by the company's total assets), the average annual CEO compensation (salary, bonuses, and stock options) *decreased* by 15–18% in the year of the goodwill write-off, compared with the previous year. This is obviously not an insignificant compensation penalty for publicly admitting acquisition failure, but considering the typical sizes of large goodwill write-offs – generally in the hundreds of millions, or even billions of dollars – and, more importantly, given investors' negative reaction (stock price decreases) to it, such a penalty is expected.

14.1.5   Summary: Acquisitions, CEO Tenure, and Compensation

Our empirical analysis of the effects of corporate acquisitions on buyers' CEO tenure and compensation revealed surprising findings. First and foremost, CEOs who conduct multiple acquisitions during their tenure are richly awarded for it: they served, on average, three to five years longer at the helm of their companies than CEOs who conducted fewer acquisitions. Given that the average failure rate of acquisitions is in the 70–75% range, an additional tenure of three to five years is indeed a very generous reward, which goes a long way in explaining the increase in M&As and their failure rate over time. Apparently, directors and influential investors are impressed by CEOs who actively try to change the course of their companies by conducting business acquisitions and are willing to grant them ample time to integrate the targets and make the acquisitions work. Ironically, multiple acquisitions, irrespective of their success, serve as a form of CEO "tenure insurance."

The reward for multiple acquisitions doesn't end with a longer CEO tenure. Most chief executives conducting acquisitions get a generous bonus for "completing the deal" (as if acquisitions are a highly unusual CEO activity, more demanding than, say, opening new markets for the company's products, or developing successful new products). By increasing the buyer's size, acquisitions also enhance executive long-term compensation. We documented earlier that over their tenure, CEOs with multiple acquisitions receive annual salary and bonus increases that are higher by 2–3% compared with CEOs with fewer acquisitions.

But perhaps, while acquisitions are richly rewarded, failure is heavily penalized? This would have made sense, but that's not what the record shows. The mean tenure difference between CEOs who failed in most of their acquisitions and those who succeeded in the majority of their acquisitions was only *about a year*, and the compensation differences between the two groups were also minuscule. Only when acquisitions end up in total failure and loss, as indicated by a large goodwill write-off, is the compensation penalty more significant (15–18% decrease in the year of the goodwill write-off).

Thus, our evidence points at a major flaw in incentivizing acquiring CEOs: the balance between CEOs' costs and benefits from acquisitions is heavily tilted toward the side of the benefits, thereby creating a misalignment between the acquisition incentives and preferences of owners and managers. When such a misalignment relates to a major corporate activity, like M&A, it obviously creates a major adverse impact on corporate performance and shareholder welfare.

14.2 EMPLOYEES: TURNOVER AND EFFICIENCY

It is time to turn our attention to employees, a major group of stakeholders affected by corporate acquisitions. We do this by focusing on several key aspects of the workforce caught in the changes brought about by mergers. The expected effect of an acquisition on the number of people on the buyers' payroll post-acquisition isn't clear. Successful acquisitions often lead to additional products on the market, wider market penetration, or a higher production rate, all necessitating a boost to employee headcount. On the other hand, some acquisitions involve labor synergies, like closing bank branches, or automating production processes. Such acquisitions, if successful, should reduce the number of buyers' employees. So, our first question, which we will address empirically, is the following:

14.2.1 Do Successful Acquisitions Increase or Decrease the Number of Buyers' Employees?

We used our sample of acquisitions to address this question. We first measured for each acquiring company the change in the number of employees from the end of the year preceding the acquisition announcement to the end of the second year following the year of announcement. This gives sufficient time – 2+ years – for the post-acquisition employee count to settle. We then ranked all the sample companies from the lowest (essentially negative) to the highest (positive) employee percentage change over that period and divided the ranked companies into five equal groups of employee change: lowest change, low-medium, medium, medium-high, and highest employee changes, from pre- to post-acquisitions. Lastly, we measured for each of the five buyers' groups their average acquisition success rate, using our *acquisition success* measure. The findings are presented in Figure 14.5.

Figure 14.5 exhibits a remarkable consistency: as the buyer's post-acquisition employee growth increases (from left to right of the figure), so does the rate of acquisition success (bar's height). Thus, for example, the left bar in Figure 14.5 represents the group (20%) of buyers whose average employee growth rate by the end of the second year after acquisition announcement was the lowest: a 23.4% headcount *decrease* (see percentage on top of bars). The average rate of acquisition success in this group was very low: 15.8% (height of bar and left axis), far lower than the overall success rate (30–35%). In contrast, the right bar in Figure 14.5 includes buyers with the highest average employee growth of 75.1%, on average (note: this represents the combined buyer and target employees); the corresponding

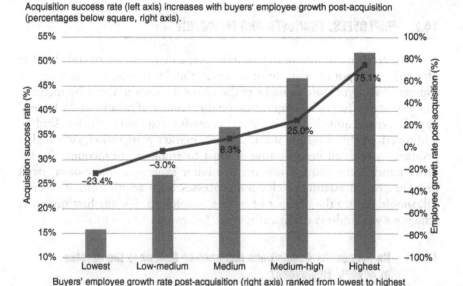

Acquisition success rate (left axis) increases with buyers' employee growth post-acquisition (percentages below square, right axis).

FIGURE 14.5 Buyers' Employee Growth Post-Acquisition and the Related Acquisition Success Rate

acquisition success rate of this group of buyers was over 50% (left axis), well above our sample average. We conclude, therefore, that successful acquisitions lead to a substantial buyer employee growth, both from target employees who continue to work for the buyer and from new employees. Apparently, most successful acquisitions boost the buyers' operations (research, production, sales), which requires increased hiring. These findings, however, relate to the buyers. But an acquisition affects the employees of *both* buyer and target. So, what's the impact of acquisitions on the *sum* of buyers' and targets' jobs?

14.2.2 Acquisitions as Modest Job Killers

Figure 14.6 shows the percentage of employees lost, when the post-acquisition buyer's headcount by the end of the second year after the acquisition announcement is compared with the pre-acquisition *sum* of buyer and target employees. For all acquisitions in our sample (left bar in Figure 14.6), the total loss of employees (relative to the combined employee headcount of both the buyer and target) was 5.14%. A larger loss (7%) was associated with acquisitions involving publicly traded

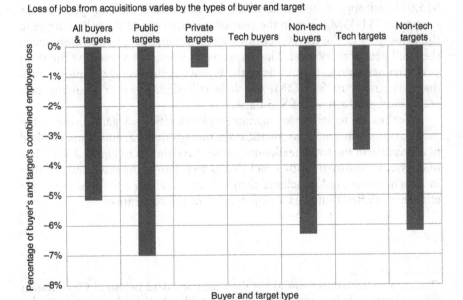

Loss of jobs from acquisitions varies by the types of buyer and target

FIGURE 14.6 Loss of Employee Positions from Acquisition as a Percentage of Buyer and Target Combined Headcount

targets only (second from left bar). Interestingly, for tech buyers (fourth bar from right) and tech targets (second bar from right), the post-acquisition loss of employees was very small: 1.9% and 3.5%, respectively. Apparently, most employees of these companies are talent-rich, and every effort is made to retain them after acquisition. So, overall, acquisitions lead to a 5–7% loss of the total of buyers' and targets' pre-acquisition headcount. That is a rather modest loss of jobs.

Does this combined employee decline reflect the mergers' synergies or its efficiency gains – more products and sales with fewer employees? After all, such efficiencies are often promised by buyers' CEOs in their acquisition announcement to investors. Alas, even that's not the case, as we will see next (as you have realized by now, little good news emerges from acquisitions).

14.2.3   Acquisitions and Employee Efficiency

"Sales per employee" is a commonly used measure of employee efficiency and productivity. We, accordingly, used this measure to examine the effects of corporate acquisitions on employee productivity. Specifically, Figure 14.7 presents the buyers' average, industry-adjusted sales per employee for the year before through three years after the acquisition.[8] Figure 14.7 shows that the average sales per employee in the year before acquisition was $15.08M, dropping down significantly, as expected, in the year of the merger to $11.43M, since in the year of acquisition and the following year, the employees of the merged entities are being integrated and rarely reach their full productivity level. This happens, as the figure shows, by the third year after acquisition (right side of the figure), as the average employee productivity grows to $14.73M, which is still slightly lower than the pre-acquisition productivity of $15.08M.

We thus fail to see the significant employee efficiency gains promised in many acquisition announcements, even though those acquisitions resulted in a decrease in the total headcount, as we have shown in Figure 14.6. This, of course, is consistent with a fact that is well-known by now, namely, that most acquisitions fail to achieve their objectives, where enhanced employee efficiency is often touted as a major target of the acquisition.

---

[8]The industry adjustment was at the three-digit Standard Industrial Classification (SIC) industry code for each individual year. Specifically, the industry median value of sales per employee in a given year was subtracted from the buyer's sales per employee of the same year.

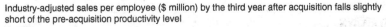

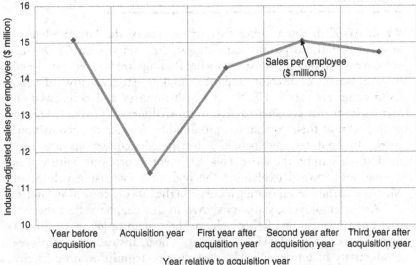

Industry-adjusted sales per employee ($ million) by the third year after acquisition falls slightly short of the pre-acquisition productivity level

FIGURE 14.7 Buyers' Annual, Industry-Adjusted, Sales per Employee Productivity Indicator Before and After Acquisition

Furthermore, we find (but do not present in a figure) that this pattern of acquisitions failing to generate substantial employee efficiency gains existed for both tech and nontech buyers, and across different decades. For tech buyers, for example, employee efficiency in the third year after acquisition was 3% lower than in the pre-acquisition year, and it was even worse for nontech buyers, which experienced a 13% loss of employee efficiency after acquisitions. Acquisitions in the 2000s were associated with employee efficiency loss of 5%, compared with a loss of 3% for the 1980s and 1990s. Corporate acquisitions, accordingly, generally didn't produce the efficiency and productivity gains that buyers' CEOs tout in their acquisition announcements.

TAKEAWAYS

We analyzed in this chapter various aspects of the human element associated with corporate acquisitions: their impact on CEOs and employees. Among the most surprising findings are how generous and tolerant boards of directors and influential investors are toward serial CEO acquirers. These CEOs get lavish bonuses and compensation increases for just *conducting acquisitions*, along with extended terms at the helm of their companies, presumably to make the acquisitions work. In contrast, the penalties for failed acquisitions are very modest – a slap on the wrist. This detrimental corporate culture goes a long way toward explaining the high and increasing volume of M&As and the corresponding increase in the rate of acquisition failure.

As for employees, statistics shown in this chapter reflect the fact that most acquisitions fail to achieve their main target: a significant post-acquisition employee productivity boost. Instead, the employee productivity of buyers falls short of the pre-acquisition productivity by 3–5%. But the total (buyer plus target) employee count loss as a result of mergers is rather modest: 5–7%. Corporate acquisitions aren't major contributors to unemployment. A consolation.

CHAPTER 15

Do It Yourself

Predict an Acquisition's Outcome

Wouldn't it be nice if one could, within 20–30 minutes, predict whether a proposed business acquisition will be successful or not? Of course, it would. So, in this chapter we develop a 10-factor scorecard, enabling you to score a proposed acquisition and receive a reliable indication whether it will turn out to be a success or failure. This scorecard is derived from our 43-variable statistical model, which was estimated using our sample of 40,000 acquisitions made over the past 40 years. So, essentially our predictive scorecard reflects the accumulated attributes and outcomes of 40,000 actual acquisitions. Note, we aren't speaking about the *perfect prediction* of an acquisition's outcome. No prediction will ever be perfect. What our scorecard yields is a forecast of the *likelihood* that the acquisition will succeed. To the best of our knowledge, this hasn't been done before.

"It's difficult to make predictions, especially about the future."
—Niels Bohr, Nobel laureate Danish physicist

15.1 A SYNOPSIS OF OUR SCORECARD

We thought a lot about writing a chapter on the *valuation* of an acquisition target: namely, how to assess the worth of a business to be acquired. We finally decided against it because there are already several useful publications on valuation, like *Damodaran on Valuation*,[1] and reasonably good chapters on business valuation in the leading financial and securities

---

[1] A. Damodaran, *Damodaran on Valuation*, 2nd edition (Wiley, 2016).

analyses textbooks. Most of these publications base their valuations on the "present value of predicted earnings or cash flows" approach, under various scenarios of future economic conditions and expected interest rates. This approach to business valuation makes sense for traditional industries (retail, financial services) and companies with certain financial history to base the cash flow predictions on, say, five to seven years of past earnings, sales, or cash flows. We didn't see how we could substantially improve on these valuation methodologies. Why "kill trees" on this issue?

However, the main challenge in an innovative economy, like the United States, United Kingdom, Japan, and Korea, is to value businesses in *emerging sectors*, such as artificial intelligence (AI) and autonomous driving, currently, without sufficient historical data, and where the size of the product market and the specific technologies that will prove sustainable are shrouded in mystery and uncertainty. Also very challenging, if not impossible, is the reliable valuation of the many enterprises (biotech, software, fintech) that are in the process of developing new products and services whose technological feasibility is yet to be proven and where the size of the potential market is unknown. Currently, such enterprises constitute a large part of the acquisition space, and we aren't familiar with any source or methodology that offers a credible and rigorous valuation approach for these enterprises. The available valuation methodologies, based on cash flows forecasts, are infeasible in these cases for lack of data, and the few published tools we have seen lead, in our opinion, to sheer guesses. Think, for example, about the challenges in predicting the future cash flows of a biotech company with two drugs under development, one in Phase I and the other in Phase II clinical tests, aimed at a new therapeutic area, like treating Alzheimer's disease. "Valuing" such an enterprise is a futile exercise. We didn't see any sense engaging in such guesswork.

So, we chose instead to follow a different approach. Rather than trying to assess the *value* of an acquisition target, we will use our multivariate model (see the appendix) to develop a *scorecard*, which will yield a number indicating the likelihood that an acquisition will be successful. Specifically, we developed a 10-factor scorecard, where the factors represent key attributes of the acquisition and the merger partners, like the price to be paid for the target, whether the target is a foreign entity, and the buyer's recent profitability record. Each factor will be multiplied by a given coefficient (weight), which captures the average effect of this factor on the likelihood of acquisition success using our model on the determinants of acquisition success (see the appendix), and summed up to yield a numerical score, like 0.25. This score will then be evaluated against the scores of our sample acquisitions and their success or failure outcomes to yield the likelihood of success of the proposed acquisition.

Note that our scorecard doesn't require any questionable forecasts of future earnings, cash flows, and interest rates, nor does it call for any assessment of potential markets and surviving technologies. All are highly uncertain in most acquisition cases, and some – even unknowable. In contrast, our scorecard, based on the actual experience of 40,000 acquisitions, is fully evidence-based and provides a very useful decision tool. It informs the user of an acquisition's expected *success likelihood*, based on the average success rates of all acquisitions sharing similar attributes to the one considered. If the estimated success likelihood of the proposed acquisition is, say, well below 30–35%, which is our sample success average, it's best to walk away from this acquisition. If, in contrast, the estimated success likelihood is 65–70%, it's worthwhile to pay the demanded price for this acquisition and make all efforts to integrate it well. We believe that this is what acquisitions' decision-makers really need right now, and the best that can be provided to them, based on rigorous evidence, rather than often-unreliable forecasts and wishful thinking.

15.2 BUILDING THE SCORECARD

We start with our 43-variable model, which identified the main determinants of acquisition success – see the variable list of the model at the end of the appendix. Among the 43 variables are, for example, the following five:

No. 2. *Deal size* – the acquisition's purchase price[2]

No. 4. *Conglomerate acquisition* – enter the value of 1 if this is a conglomerate (business-unrelated acquisition), and 0 otherwise

No. 9. *Deal pressure / competition (#2)* – logarithm of the largest deal value of targets with the same three-digit Standard Industrial Classification (SIC) code that were acquired during the past 12 months

No. 26. *Acquisition premium* – the ratio of deal size to the most recent annual sales of the target

No. 38. *Target's pre-acquisition sales growth* – the target's sales growth over the three years preceding the year of acquisition

---

[2] For statistical efficiency, because the variability of this factor is very large – from a few million dollars to multibillion dollars – we transform this variable to its natural logarithm: Ln(Deal size). Practically, all you have to do for a deal size of, say, $8,000M ($8B) is to Google "natural log 8000" and you'll get 8.987. You will then enter the value of 8.987 for the factor "Deal size" into the scorecard.

TABLE 15.1 Example of Acquisition Factors and Coefficient Estimates of
a Scorecard

Factor	Coefficient	XYZ Acquisition Factor Values[a]	Score
Deal size	−0.094	6.91	−0.649
Conglomerate acquisition	−0.023	1.00	−0.023
Deal pressure / competition (#2)	−0.019	7.69	−0.146
Acquisition premium	−0.011	3.50	−0.039
Target's sales growth	0.127	10%	0.013
Total score			−0.844[b]

[a] These are the factor values for a hypothetical acquisition.
[b] Total score equals the sum of the coefficients times the value of each factor across
the five factors.

When we estimated the full 43-variable model on the acquisitions made
during 2010–2018, we obtained the *estimated coefficients* (left column of
Table 15.1) for the previous five variables.[3]

The example of the five-variable scorecard in Table 15.1, with the factor
values of a hypothetical acquisition, XYZ, yields a score of −0.844. We
structure the recommended 10-factor scorecard in the same way. The resulting scores will be evaluated against the acquisition sample scores to yield a
success prediction, as shown next.

15.3   DO OUR SCORES REALLY INDICATE ACQUISITION SUCCESS?

Does a score like the −0.844 in Table 15.1 really reflect the likelihood of an
acquisition's success? To address this key question, we used all of the 40,000
acquisitions in our sample and computed for each one a score using all of
the 43 variables in our model, in the same manner that the hypothetical five-
variable score was calculated in Table 15.1,[4] this time using real, rather than

---

[3] For the acquisition factors, we assumed: (i) deal size of $1B ($1,000M) having a
natural logarithm of 6.91, (ii) the acquisition was a conglomerate, hence the factor value of 1, (iii) deal pressure value of 7.69 (the natural logarithm of $2,187M
($2.2B), the largest deal value in the industry), (iv) acquisition premium of 3.50, and
(v) target's sales growth rate of 10%.
[4] We observed that for our four-decade sample, 1980–2022, the predictive power of
the 43-variable model improved from decade to decade. We, therefore, decided to
base our recommended scorecard on the most recent decade: 2010–2018. (For our
acquisition success measure, we need four *future years*. That is why we stop in 2018.)

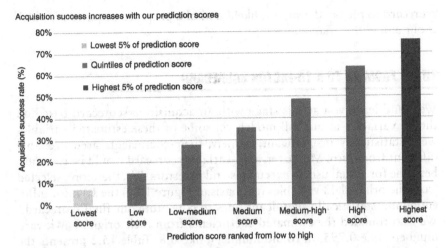

Acquisition success increases with our prediction scores

FIGURE 15.1 The Acquisition Success Rates of Buyers Ranked by Our Prediction Scores, Based on All 43 Variables in Our Model

hypothetical, acquisition values. So, we now have a numerical success score for each acquisition in our sample. We then ranked all of our 2010–2018 acquisitions (close to 10,000 acquisitions) by their *success score*, from lowest to highest, and grouped the acquisitions into five equal-size acquisition groups. Finally, for each of the five groups, we calculated the average acquisition *success rate* (using our unique acquisition success measure; see the appendix) of all the acquisitions in the group. These five average acquisition success rates are portrayed in Figure 15.1 (ignore for the moment the left and right extreme bars).

Figure 15.1 shows a remarkable consistency. As the average group scores increase (left to right), so does the success of the acquisitions. For example, the 20% of acquisitions with the lowest scores (second-from-left bar) had an average acquisition success rate of just 15%, while the 20% of acquisitions with the highest scores (second-from-right bar) had an average success rate of almost 65% (double the average success of acquisitions in the sample overall). The 5% acquisitions with the highest scores (rightmost bar) had a phenomenal success rate of 75%! A dream come true.

We conclude, therefore, that our calculated acquisition score, based on the estimated 43-variable model, is indeed *strongly correlated* with actual corporate acquisition success rate, and accordingly, can be used to build a scorecard to predict the success likelihood of a proposed acquisition, which is our aim in this chapter.[5]

15.4 FROM 43 TO A 10-FACTOR SCORECARD

We could leave you at this stage with an acquisition scorecard based on the 43 variables in our full model, yet some of these estimated variables were statistically insignificant; namely, their coefficients aren't reliably different from zero. Moreover, a 43-variable scorecard would be too cumbersome for actual use by executives and investors. We, therefore, selected from the original 43 variables (the basis of Figure 15.1) the 10 most influential and statistically significant ones to constitute our final scorecard.[6] We also rounded the estimated coefficients from their original awkward numbers, like 0.795, to round numbers, like 0.8. Table 15.2 presents the list of the 10 factors constituting our proposed scorecard, the coefficient of each factor, and an illustration of the use of the scorecard for a specific acquisition.

---

[5] For the statistically inclined, to more rigorously assess the predictive power of our model and scorecard, we compute the area under the receiver operating characteristic (ROC) curve (AUC) of our model. AUC is a commonly used approach for evaluating the performance of models designed for predicting future outcomes, such as the success or failure of businesses. Specifically, we randomly split our sample in each year into the training sample for estimating the coefficients of the model and the testing sample for validating the prediction of the model (this random assignment is repeated many times to yield an average result). This test evaluates the *out-of-sample* performance of our model in predicting acquisition success/failure and informs on the usefulness of our model in correctly classifying successful vs. unsuccessful acquisitions, using the coefficient estimates of the model. We find that the AUC in the test sample, ranging between 70 and 75%, is substantially higher than the 50–50 chance of a random guess, a common benchmark for determining the predictive usefulness of statistical models. We also found that the predictive power of our model measured by the AUC value has increased over the sample's decades.

[6] To facilitate the implementation and interpretation of this scorecard, we further simplified the definition of one of the factors in the scorecard: *stock percentage in acquisition payment,* by converting it into an indicator variable based on a threshold level (i.e., the indicator for stock percentage in acquisition payment takes the value of 1 for acquisitions paid for with more than 80% of the buyer's stock, and 0 otherwise).

TABLE 15.2 The Proposed 10-Factor Scorecard

Scorecard Factor	Coefficient[a]	Factor Values for an Acquisition Example[b]	Score
1. Deal size (natural logarithm of acquisition price in $ millions)	−0.10	6.75	−0.675
2. Buyer's goodwill growth (0 for less than 5% of buyer's total assets)	−0.50	0.00	0.00
3. Conglomerate merger (0 for same industry acquisition, 1 for conglomerate)	−0.25	0.00	0.00
4. High stock percentage in acquisition payment (1 for over 80% stock payment)	−0.50	0.00	0.00
5. Foreign targets (0 for domestic targets, 1 for foreign targets)	−0.50	0.00	0.00
6. Buyer's long-term debt growth	−0.25	0.11	−0.028
7. Change in buyers' profitability (ROA) over the three years pre-acquisition	1.00	0.03	0.03
8. Buyers' market-to-book ratio preceding the acquisition	0.05	3.64	0.18
9. S&P 500 return (change) during the year before acquisition	−1.00	−0.07	0.07
10. Number of buyer's acquisitions during the five years pre-acquisition	0.04	2.00	0.08
Total score			−0.34[c]

[a] A negative coefficient means that as the factor's value increases the success likelihood of the acquisition *decreases*, and vice versa for a positive coefficient.

[b] The acquisition illustrated in Table 15.2 has a deal size of $850M, and goodwill growth of less than 5% of the buyer's total assets. The buyer is in the same industry of the target (no conglomerate), has stock payment percentage less than 80%, and acquires a domestic target. The buyer has a long-term debt growth of 11% after acquisition, and its change in profitability (ROA) before acquisition was 3%. The buyer's market-to-book ratio at the time of the acquisition was 3.64. The S&P 500 return during the 12-month before the acquisition was −7%, and the buyer had two acquisitions during the prior five years.

[c] Total score equals the sum of the coefficients times the value of each factor across the 10 factors.

The following are the details of the 10 factors in the acquisition score-card, presented in Table 15.2, with (rounded) estimated coefficients and a hypothetical example:

1. *Deal size*. The price paid for the target, transformed into natural log (see footnote 2). The price paid for this hypothetical target was $850M, and the natural log of 850 is 6.75, recorded in the table. The estimated coefficient of this factor is −0.10 (rounded), so the score of this factor is −0.10 × 6.75 = −0.675 (see right column of Table 15.2).

2. *Goodwill growth*. The effect of the acquisition on the growth of the buyer's goodwill (divided by total assets) at the end of the year of acquisition completion. This factor gets the value of 1 if the goodwill growth is more than 5% and 0 otherwise. The estimated coefficient of this factor is −0.50. In the example, the goodwill (over total assets) growth in the year of acquisition was *less* than 5%, so its factor value is 0.00, which is this factor's score.

3. *Conglomerate acquisition*. This factor, with an estimated coefficient of −0.25, gets the value of 1 if the target is conglomerate, namely, business-unrelated to the buyer, and 0 for related targets (horizontal or vertical mergers). In the Table 15.2 example, the acquisition was horizontal (related), namely, not a conglomerate, and therefore the factor value is 0, which is the factor score.

4. *High stock payment*. If the acquisition price is paid by 80% or more with the buyer's stock, the factor value is 1, and 0 if less than 80% of the deal price is paid with stock. In the example, 60% of the deal value was paid by stock, so the factor value is 0, which is its score.

5. *Foreign target*. If the target is a foreign entity, its factor value is 1, and 0 for domestic targets. In the table's example the target was domestic, so the factor value is 0.

6. *Long-term debt growth*. This is the growth in the buyer's long-term debt in the year of acquisition. In the example, the buyer's debt growth was 11%, so the factor's score is −0.25 × 0.11 = −0.0275 (−0.028 rounded).

7. *Change in buyer's pre-acquisition profitability*. This factor reflects the change in the buyer's ROA during the three years before the year of acquisition. In the example, the change was 3%, so the factor's score is 1 × 0.03 = 0.03.

8. *Market-to-book ratio*. The buyer's ratio of total market value (number of shares outstanding times share price at year-end) to the balance sheet book value (assets minus liabilities) at the end of the year before acquisition. In the example, this ratio was 3.64, so the factor score is 0.05 × 3.64 = 0.182.

9. *S&P 500 change (return)*. This is the change in the S&P 500 index during the year before acquisition. In the example, the index went down by 7%, so the factor score is −1.00 × −0.07 = 0.07.
10. *Acquisition experience: number of buyer's prior (five years before the acquisition year) mergers*. In the example, this buyer had two acquisitions in the prior five years, so the factor's score is 0.04 × 2 = 0.08.

Summing the 10 individual factor scores yields a total score for this hypothetical acquisition of −0.34.

15.5 THE ACTUAL PERFORMANCE OF THE 10-FACTOR SCORECARD

Once the score for a specific acquisition is determined by following our scorecard instructions illustrated in Table 15.2, it can then be used to classify acquisitions to those with high/positive scores versus those with low/negative scores. By using our scorecard, acquisitions with greater and more positive scores are expected to have a higher likelihood of success, whereas lower success rates are expected for acquisitions with lower and more negative scores.

We demonstrate the use of our scorecard in Figure 15.2, which is based on the sample acquisitions made during 2010–2018. The figure portrays the

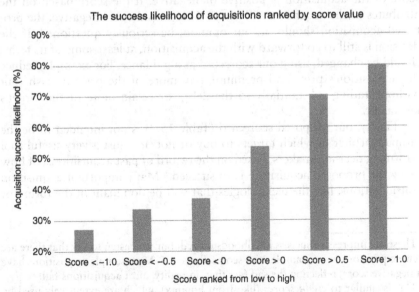

FIGURE 15.2 The Acquisition Success Likelihoods for the 10-Factor Scorecard: Scores with Negative vs. Positive Values

average acquisition success likelihood of acquisitions whose scores are above the 0 threshold, like 0.5 and 1.0, or below the 0 threshold: −0.5 and −1.0. Figure 15.2 also shows the success likelihood for acquisitions scoring just above and below 0 (score > 0 and score < 0), an intuitive threshold value. Thus, the success likelihood of acquisitions with positive scores (> 0) is almost 55%, whereas the success likelihood of acquisitions with negative scores (< 0) is 38%.

Figure 15.2 is similar to 15.1, except that it is based on the 10-factor scorecard, rather than on the 43-variable one (15.1), and provides a breakdown of acquisition success likelihoods for negative and positive scores. The data underlying Figure 15.2 are the scores derived from the 10-factor scorecard, computed for all of the 2010–2018 acquisitions in our sample. Figure 15.2 shows that for acquisitions whose scores are in the positive domain, with values such as 0.5 and 1.0, the likelihood that an acquisition will succeed is substantially higher than 2010–2018 average of 30%. The likelihoods of acquisition success are 70% for scores between 0.5 and 1.0, and 80% for scores above 1.0.[7] The likelihoods of success, however, are lower than the average when the score is negative. For example, Figure 15.2 shows that the average likelihood of success is only 37% for an acquisition scoring below 0, and 27% for those scoring below −1.

Accordingly, the first step of using our scorecard to evaluate the prospect of a proposed acquisition should focus on determining whether the score of the acquisition is positive or negative. If the score based on the attributes of the acquisition (Table 15.2) is considerably negative, the proposed acquisition should, in our opinion, be seriously questioned. If the decision is still to go forward with the acquisition, at least some of its terms should be changed, using our scorecard as a guidance. For example, reduce the acquisition's price and premium, pay more of the price in cash (but without adding substantially to the debt), or retain more of the target's key talent.

Finally, our proposed scorecard (Table 15.2) is not intended to be the ultimate arbiter of which targets to buy or not. It is just a very useful tool informing decision-makers, based on the record of past acquisitions, of how likely the proposed acquisition is to succeed.[8] Many important acquisition considerations, like the technologies that will be dominant in the future or

---

[7] These are impressive success likelihoods indeed. But we hasten to say that there are few acquisitions in our sample with scores above 0.5. Most sample acquisitions have a negative score, reflecting the sad fact that, in reality, most acquisitions fail.

[8] This is similar to *credit scores* (like from Equifax), which are extensively used by lenders, but rarely as the only determinant of the lending decision.

the urgency of plugging holes in the buyer's product mix, are not reflected by our scorecard and will have to be considered along with our suggested score.[9] In short, we provide here hitherto unavailable important information that should be considered along with other relevant factors by acquisition decision-makers.

15.6   SCORECARD DEMONSTRATIONS

We demonstrate in this section the proposed scorecard for two prominent acquisitions: Sprint's acquisition of Nextel Communications Inc. for $35B in 2004–2005, which was discussed in Chapter 8, and Microsoft's acquisition of Nuance Communications Inc. for $18.8B in 2021–2022. The former – a widely known failure, whereas the latter is likely a success. The factor values used in these demonstrations are real-life numbers.

The scorecard for Sprint's acquisition of Nextel, a deal involving two wireless providers featured in the Preamble of this book and in Chapter 8, is illustrated in Table 15.3 (the values of the 10 factors of the scorecard are included in parentheses). This acquisition was announced in December 2004 and completed in 2005. Subsequent to the acquisition, Sprint substantially underperformed its industry peers: its three-year sales and gross profit growth post-acquisition (2006–2008) were 2.75% and −6.9%, respectively, versus an industry average of 30.2% and 26.5%. In 2007, two years after completing the acquisition, Sprint reported a massive $29.7B goodwill impairment write-off related to the acquisition of Nextel.[10] Sprint's three-year (2005–2007) stock return post-acquisition was a negative −40.8%. By any measure, Sprint's acquisition of Nextel was clearly a failure.

The score of this acquisition, illustrated in Table 15.3, is very negative, −1.69, mostly driven by the large size of the deal ($35B), its large goodwill growth (10% of the buyer's total assets), and the high percentage of the purchase price paid in the form of stock (98.8%). The extensive acquisition experience of the buyer – 11 prior acquisitions – didn't help in the

---

[9]The buyer's valuation of the target's technologies under development and their roles in the merged business (e.g., creating new products and services leading to new revenues), however, is directly reflected in the acquisition price and its components, such as goodwill and acquisition-related intangibles (see Chapter 9). Our scorecard illustrated in Table 5.2 considers both the total acquisition price for the target and the growth of the buyer's goodwill after the acquisition.

[10]Sprint's 10-K for the year ended on December 31, 2007 (filed on February 21, 2008).

TABLE 15.3 The Acquisition Scorecard of Sprint's Purchase of Nextel Communications Inc. in 2004–2005 (Each Variable/Factor Is Presented in Parentheses)

Scorecard Factor	Coefficient	Factor Value	Score
1. Deal size ($35B)	−0.10	10.46	−1.046
2. Goodwill growth (1, as the growth was 10% of total assets)	−0.50	1.00	−0.500
3. Conglomerate merger (0 for same industry merger)	−0.25	0.00	0.000
4. High stock percentage in acquisition payment (98.8% stock)	−0.50	1.00	−0.500
5. Foreign targets (0 for domestic target)	−0.50	0.00	0.000
6. Long-term debt growth (32%)	−0.25	0.32	−0.080
7. Change in buyers' profitability before acquisition (−2.6%)	1.00	−0.026	−0.026
8. Buyers' market-to-book ratio (2.66)	0.05	2.66	0.133
9. S&P 500 return during the year before acquisition (10.9%)	−1.00	0.109	−0.109
10. Number of buyer's acquisitions during the prior five years (11)	0.04	11.00	0.440
Total score			−1.69

unfortunate choice of Nextel. Figure 15.2 indicates that the expected chance of success of an acquisition with a score below −1.0 is 26–27% – extremely low. Note that this highly negative score is based on information that was available before or at the time of the acquisition completion, well ahead of the disastrous completion of the actual acquisition. Given its highly negative score, the failure of this acquisition by Sprint is hardly surprising: among all acquisitions made during 2004–2005, the success likelihood of acquisitions with scores around −1.69 was no more than 20%. If only Sprint's CEO and board members had access to our scorecard at the time.

Table 15.4 demonstrates the acquisition scorecard for Microsoft's acquisition of Nuance Communications Inc., a U.S. company specializing in conversational AI and ambient intelligence in healthcare, financial services, and telecommunications (the acquisition was announced in April 2021 and completed a year later). As Microsoft has significantly increased its involvement in AI in recent years, this is obviously a same-industry acquisition (not a conglomerate).

Table 15.4 shows that this acquisition avoided most of the factors identified in this book as detractors of acquisition success. The acquisition was

TABLE 15.4 The Scorecard of Microsoft's Acquisition of Nuance Communications Inc. in 2021–2022 (Each Variable/Factor Is Presented in Parentheses)

Scorecard Factor	Coefficient	Factor Value	Score
1. Deal size ($18.88B)	−0.10	9.85	−0.985
2. Goodwill growth (0 as goodwill grew by 3.62% of total assets only)	−0.50	0.00	0.000
3. Conglomerate merger (0 for target from same industry)	−0.25	0.00	0.000
4. High stock percentage in acquisition payment (0 for all-cash deal)	−0.50	0.00	0.000
5. Foreign targets (0 for domestic target)	−0.50	0.00	0.000
6. Long-term debt growth (−5%)	−0.25	−0.05	0.013
7. Change in buyers' profitability before acquisition (12.67%)	1.00	0.127	0.127
8. Buyers' market-to-book ratio (14.35)	0.05	14.35	0.717
9. S&P 500 return during the year before acquisition (29.0%)	−1.00	0.29	−0.290
10. Number of buyer's acquisitions during the prior five years (12)	0.04	12.00	0.480
Total score			0.062

associated with only a slight increase in the buyer's goodwill (3.62% of total assets), the target was from the same industry (an AI-focused enterprise), the buyer didn't use stock in payment (it was an all-cash deal), the target was domestic (Nuance is a U.S. company), and there was no increase in the buyer's long-term debt post-acquisition (Microsoft's long-term debt, in fact, decreased slightly after the completion of this acquisition). Thus, despite its large size ($18.88B) and the unusually high S&P 500 returns during the 12 months before the acquisition announcement (29%), negative factors, the score for this acquisition by Microsoft is positive (0.062), reflecting in part Microsoft's strong profitability growth and its large market-to-book ratio before the acquisition. Figure 15.2 indicates a success likelihood of 54–55% for this acquisition, well above our sample average success rate of 30%.

15.7 CUSTOMIZATION OF THE SCORECARD BY INDUSTRY

A final improvement of the scorecard presented in Table 15.2 is to customize it for individual industries. This seems logical since acquisition success differs across industries, as do the business models and assets used. For example, the most valuable assets of tech firms are intangibles, such as research and development (R&D), patents, brands, and human capital, rather than physical assets, which are key to oil-and-gas companies, among others.

Because industry-specific scorecards are likely to be more predictive than a general one, we modified our general scorecard of Table 15.2 for key industries or industry groups by adjusting the coefficients of some of the 10 factors in the general scorecard, according to the industry-specific estimations of our model. For example, for biotech/pharma and software buyers, we decreased the coefficient on the change in the buyer's profitability (ROA) before acquisition, because these firms' reported earnings (and ROAs) are generally uninformative, due to the mandatory expensing of the large intangible investments in these sectors.[11] For software firms, we increased the size of the negative coefficient on foreign targets (recall the disastrous experience of HP acquiring the UK software firm Autonomy, illustrated in Chapter 1). We also did the same to the coefficient on conglomerate mergers for two science-based industry groups, biotech/pharma and computers/semiconductors/instruments, to reflect the greater challenge of the many cross-industry acquisitions involving these tech firms. The direction and magnitude of these adjustments to the coefficients of our industry-specific scorecards are, again, guided by our general scorecard model applied to each individual industry. Table 15.5 lists the coefficients for each of the six industries chosen for an industry-specific scorecard, including various science-based industries (computers/semiconductors/instruments, biotech/pharma, software), and several nontech industries, such as oil and gas, financial services, and healthcare. For industries not included in Table 15.5, such as manufacturing, retail, telecom, and utilities, the general scorecard presented in Table 15.2 applies.

Figure 15.3 shows the performance of our industry-specific scorecards for a wide variety of industries (e.g., tech, nontech, manufacturing, financial, healthcare, retail and other services, and infrastructure), covering most economic sectors. The three bars for each industry represent the success

---

[11] Recent research, for example, finds that a high percentage of companies reporting losses is driven by dated accounting standards mandating the expensing of internal investments in intangibles. Such companies are, in fact, profitable, and their reported losses are not informative of their operations (see F. Gu, B. Lev, and C. Zhu, "All Losses Are Not Alike: Real versus Accounting-Driven Reported Losses," *Review of Accounting Studies* 28, no. 3 (2023): 1141–1189). See also Chapter 9 of this book for a more in-depth discussion of the accounting issues of intangibles.

TABLE 15.5   Coefficients for Industry-Specific Scorecards

Scorecard Factor	General Scorecard	Coefficients for Industry-Specific Scorecards(A. Computer, semiconductor, and instruments, B. Biotech and pharmaceutical, C. Software, D. Oil and Gas, E. Financial services, and F. Healthcare)					
		A	B	C	D	E	F
1. Deal size	-0.10	0.00	0.005	-0.10	0.05	-0.05	-0.10
2. Goodwill growth	-0.50	-0.50	-0.75	-0.15	-0.75	-0.00	-0.50
3. Conglomerate merger	-0.25	-0.50	-0.85	0.00	-0.50	-0.50	-0.25
4. High stock percentage in acquisition payment	-0.50	-1.50	-1.25	-0.50	-0.50	-0.50	-0.50
5. Foreign targets	-0.50	-0.125	0.00	-0.75	-0.50	-0.50	0.75
6. Long-term debt growth	-0.25	-0.03	-0.03	0.025	-0.10	-0.025	-0.025
7. Change in buyers' profitability before acquisition	1.00	1.00	0.00	0.25	-0.75	1.00	0.50
8. Buyers' market-to-book ratio	0.05	0.05[a]	0.05[b]	0.10	0.05	0.05	0.05
9. S&P 500 return during the year before acquisition	-1.00	-1.50	0.00	-1.50	0.00	-1.00	-1.00
10. Number of buyer's acquisitions during the prior five years	0.04	0.00	-0.07	0.08	-0.04	0.04	-0.04
Total score							

[a] 0.05 if market-to-book ratio is no greater than 6 and 0.15 otherwise.
[b] Ibid.

likelihood of acquisitions associated with – from left to right – acquisition scores below −1.0, scores < 0 (negative), and scores > 0 (positive). The squares on the top horizontal line indicate the difference in acquisition success likelihood between positive and negative scores – the right and middle bars in each triplet of bars (right axis). The first three bars on the left of Figure 15.3 are for the general scorecard presented in Figure 15.2 (we took the bar for scores below −1.0 and the bars for scores below and above 0 from Figure 15.2 to form the first three-bar group). The height of the squares in the top line, which indicates the performance of the scorecard in predicting acquisition success likelihood by distinguishing between positive and negative scores, indicates improvement in the performance of the industry-specific scorecards over the general scorecard. That is, the larger the difference between the success likelihoods of acquisitions associated with positive and negative scores, the better the success prediction of our 10-factor scorecards.

It is clear from the squares in Figure 15.3 that most industry-specific scorecards perform better than the general scorecard (left three bars) in predicting acquisition success likelihoods (namely, the industry-specific squares are higher than that of the three left bars). Thus, for example, for the healthcare scorecard (the rightmost three bars in Figure 15.3), positive scores (right bar) indicate a success likelihood of almost 70%, whereas negative scores (second-from-right bar) indicate a success likelihood of 30% only. This difference is more than twice as high as the difference of 17% (= 54%–37%) under the general scorecard (the leftmost three bars). A comparison of the three bars across industries also shows that industry-specific scorecards generally yield higher acquisition success likelihood for positive scores and lower for negative scores than the general scorecard. Thus, customizing our scorecard for specific industries improves the performance of the scorecard.[12]

---

[12] For example, applying the software industry scorecard in Table 15.5 to Microsoft's acquisition of Nuance Communications Inc., represented in Table 15.4 for the general scorecard, yields a score of 1.005 for the software scorecard, which is substantially higher than the initial score of 0.062 obtained from the general scorecard shown in Table 15.4, further reinforcing the positive prospects of this acquisition.

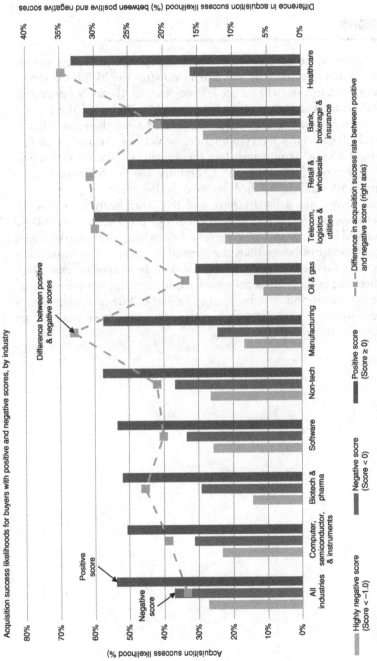

FIGURE 15.3 The Average Acquisition Success Likelihoods of the General Scorecard (Table 15.2), and the Industry- or Industry-group Specific Scorecards (Table 15.5)

TAKEAWAYS

In this chapter, we have developed a unique prediction scorecard for corporate acquisitions. The scorecard estimates the likelihood that a proposed acquisition will succeed. It consists of 10 easily obtainable factors, such as the acquisition price, or the number of the buyer's prior acquisitions. The scorecard was derived from the most influential variables in our 43-variable model, which was estimated on our sample of 40,000 acquisitions (see the appendix). The general scorecard is presented in Table 15.2, and its use is demonstrated in Section 15.5 and is applied to two well-known acquisitions in Section 15.6 – one a total failure and the other likely a success. To further improve the prediction success of our proposed scorecard, we customized it in Section 15.7 to several key industry scorecards, which generally perform better than the general scorecard. The acquisition scorecard proposed here is ready to be used by corporate executives and directors considering a proposed acquisition and by investors voting on an acquisition or considering whether to buy or sell the shares of acquisition partners. Caveat: like any other prediction model, ours may also be subject to error.

Epilogue: How to Spring the M&A Failure Trap

"I am 76 years old, and I have never learned a lesson in my entire life."[1] So said Larry David in the sitcom *Curb Your Enthusiasm*; this seems to characterize well the attitude of many corporate executives and their boards, as well as that of influential investors and fund managers regarding corporate acquisitions. How else can the continued and even worsening failure rate of acquisitions be explained? It seems that none of the major drivers of the destructive 70–75% failure rate of mergers and acquisitions (M&As), highlighted throughout this book, has been internalized, removed, or even significantly improved in recent decades. In fact, some of the failure drivers, like conglomerate (synergyless) acquisitions, which seemed to have vanished from the merger scene decades ago, came back with a vengeance in recent years. Accordingly, without the institution of certain major changes in the process of corporate acquisitions, mergers and acquisitions are doomed to continue their destructive path of failure and loss of corporate value. In an attempt to change the course of acquisitions, this epilogue is devoted to outlining the main changes that have to take place in order to change the current path of M&As in a major way. In a sense, it's what's needed to spring the M&A failure trap.

E.1 CHANGE THE ACQUISITION INCENTIVES OF CORPORATE EXECUTIVES

One doesn't get a major reward for just participating in a golf or tennis tournament, for buying a nonwinning lottery ticket, or for being on the short list of the Pulitzer Prize.[2] The rewards of all such "tournaments" go to the winners. Corporate acquisitions shouldn't be different. They are a major

---

[1] A comment made by Larry David in the final episode of HBO's sitcom *Curb Your Enthusiasm*, April 2024.

[2] Some sport tournaments reward all participants with relatively small amounts of money, essentially to cover their costs, but the "big money" always goes to the winners.

part of the business world's "competitive tournaments" in which companies strive to come out on top of the competition. In these business tournaments there is no place for automatic acquisition bonuses, just as there are no major awards for participation in sports tournaments. Only *successful acquisitions*, those that meet their expectations, be it enhancing corporate growth or refreshing their dated business models, should be rewarded. Rewarding acquisitions irrespective of their outcome – the current practice – gives executives the wrong signal: acquire serially.

In addition to abolishing automatic acquisition bonuses, the boost to managers' compensation from the growth in the company's size brought about by a merger, whether successful or not, should also cease. This compensation practice leads executives, among other things, to hold on to failing acquisitions for too long, as we have shown in Chapter 11. Accordingly, compensation increases should also only reflect successful acquisitions, not merely the growth of company size. The same goes for chief executive officer (CEO) tenure. We have seen (Chapter 14) that CEOs conducting multiple acquisitions are often rewarded with substantially longer tenure than those with few acquisitions, presumably to recognize their continued efforts to resurrect growth and allow the CEOs sufficient time to integrate the acquisition targets. This procedure, too, gives the wrong signal: as long as a chief executive continues acquiring businesses, they will be given ample time to see the acquisitions through.

So, the upshot of this recommendation for corporate boards is to make a clear distinction between successful and unsuccessful acquisitions and reward only the former. The latter – unsuccessful acquisitions – should initiate a thorough post-mortem investigation by a board committee, searching for the reasons of failure, and the corporate changes that have to be instituted to avoid the repetition of acquisition failure, such as improved due diligence of the target, a more successful price negotiation, more attention paid to target integration, etc. Unlike Larry David in the opening of this epilogue, a failed substantial acquisition should be a teachable moment in the enterprise's life.

E.2   CORPORATE ACQUISITIONS SHOULD BE THE LAST RESORT

Business acquisitions resemble an organ transplanted in a sick body, a body suffering from malfunctioning organs, and a collapse of bodily functions. A business enterprise needing a transplant (acquisition) similarly suffers from malfunctions: stagnant growth, loss of market share, a thinning product pipeline, or a dated business model. Physical organ transplants are always used as a last resort. Doctors will try every treatment available before resorting to an organ transplant, given the difficulties of finding the right match and the considerable risk of the receiving body rejecting the transplant. Business acquisitions encounter similar risks. So, acquisitions should never be the first treatment for an operational problem, but rather the last one.

In Chapter 1 ("The Good, the Bad, and the Ugly") we recounted the saga of Teva Pharmaceutical's ("the Bad") disastrous acquisition of Actavis to restore lagging growth and supplement its soon-to-expire patent-protected blockbuster drug Copaxon. It is clear from the extensive news coverage of this acquisition that once Teva's leadership realized its precarious position (far too late), they set their mind on a "big transformative acquisition" to right matters. Teva even hired a new CEO specifically to execute such an acquisition. It also seems clear from news reviews that insufficient attention was given to acquisition alternatives, like joint ventures with other drug developers or developing their own drugs to replace Copaxon. Interestingly, Teva's stock price, after a protracted and severe decline post-acquisition, performed quite well recently (early 2024) due to such joint efforts and drug developments.[3]

We devoted Chapter 4 to discussing the major alternative to acquisition – internal development – and presented empirical evidence showing that internal development (generated by research and development, capital expenditures, etc.) easily surpasses corporate acquisitions in generating future sales and gross profit growth and in stabilizing sales volatility. The main reasons are that internal development is far less expensive than acquisitions (you don't have to pay a hefty premium to target shareholders), it can be terminated on the first sign of development failure, and the integration of internal development projects is much easier and more likely to succeed than the integration of acquisition targets. Of course, internal developments of drugs, say, take time and therefore must be planned well in advance of a crisis and not when patents are soon to expire. But that's what good management is all about.

So, our second recommendation to improve an acquisition's success is to not acquire in the first place. That is, resist the pressure to acquire from investment bankers, consultants, and certain investors, and consider seriously, even try, the available alternatives to acquisitions. Only when all else fails or is infeasible should managers embark on business acquisitions.

---

[3] On April 10, 2024, Yahoo! Finance featured multiple positive reports on Teva Pharmaceutical, like "Teva Confirms Efficacy and Safety of Ajovy for the Prevention of Migraine" and "Teva and mAbxience Announce Strategic Global Licensing Agreement for Oncology Biosimilar Candidates." There are always alternatives to acquisitions.

E.3   THOROUGHLY ASSESS THE RISK THAT THE ACQUISITION WILL FAIL

In Chapter 8, on integration, we developed an "Integration Risk Profile" intended to alert buyers' executives to cases and circumstances when target integration will be particularly challenging, even likely to fail. The same risk profile, with a few additions, should be in front of the acquisition's decision-makers when they discuss the merits of a proposed merger. Rather than primarily dwelling on fantasies of outlandish synergies, of new markets to be conquered or developed, or of a considerably expanded product mix, including new products whose demand has yet to be established, equal time should be devoted to a thorough *risk assessment* of the acquisition's likeli-hood to fail. The following risk profile of acquisition challenges will assist executives and board members to focus on the main risk drivers of acquisi-tion failure. Each of the following risk elements was fully discussed and analyzed in the book (references provided), so we just briefly reiterate them here:

- **Beware of Following the Crowd (Chapter 6)**
  It is widely believed that there are opportune times to acquire businesses, such as when capital markets are "hot" or when one's industry peers are buying (sector frenzy) – like now, in 2024, acquiring artificial intelligence (AI) targets. The merger waves associated with these opportune periods indicate that many executives indeed follow these best-times dictums. However, we have shown (Chapter 6) that following the acquiring crowds ends up with inferior acquisitions, mainly due to the scarcity of suitable targets and the high acquisition premia demanded during buying frenzies.
- **Avoid Paying a High Acquisition Premium (Chapter 7)**
  Paying a high acquisition premium, particularly in contested (multibuyer) acquisitions, likely reflects a substantial overpayment for the target and is a major reason for acquisition failure. High premia rarely indicate the existence of "Rembrandts in the attic."
- **Foreign Targets – Challenging Integration[4]**
  The integration of foreign targets, particularly large ones, is prone to fail because of deep-rooted cultural differences between buyers' and targets' employees, difficulties of relocating target employees to the buyer's home country, a challenging due diligence of foreign targets because of different laws and accounting regulations in the target's

---

[4]This and the following risk elements are all discussed and demonstrated in Chapter 8.

country and the extent of their enforcement, and frequent interference in the merger by the target's government.

■ **The Challenge of Large Targets**

Targets that are large, relative to the buyer, pose serious challenges of merging different corporate cultures and of achieving the expected synergies (often requiring massive employee layoffs, closure of outlets or branches, etc.). Merging the managements (big egos) and operating systems of two large enterprises, and establishing clear lines of control and communications, is particularly difficult when the merger partners are large.

■ **Poorly Performing Targets Often Continue to Perform Poorly**

Overly confident executives (Chapter 13) are often self-assured in their ability to turn around failing targets. But consistently successful "turnaround artists" are rare, and most poorly performing targets continue to underperform and drag down the buyer.

■ **Conglomerate Acquisitions Still Don't Make Sense (Chapter 5)**

Conglomerate (business-unrelated) acquisitions were popular in the 1960s–1980s, then fell into long disrepute, but recently made a comeback, particularly among tech companies.[5] Conglomerate acquisitions often fail because they simply lack business logic. There are generally no synergies from such mergers, either, because the merging units are not related in a business sense, and, while there is some risk diversification from such mergers, this can be easily achieved by shareholders owing stocks in the merged candidates. So, absent business justification, most conglomerate acquisitions are doomed to fail.

Thus, if the proposed acquisition you are considering shares one or more of these risk factors, its likelihood of success is slim. Such proposed acquisitions require a thorough failure risk analysis at the board level, perhaps with the assistance of outside experts, to make sure that this specific acquisition is indeed needed, that the merger candidate is the right one, that the expected benefits were objectively and reliably estimated based on various economic scenarios, and that the buyer's staff is fully capable of successfully and expeditiously integrating the merging units. Acquisitions sharing these risk characteristics require close "adult supervision."

---

[5] One of the main reasons for this comeback is that many tech companies have been flush with cash in recent years, but due to antitrust policy, they are unable to acquire companies in their own line of business. Conglomerate acquisitions enable them to use some of their excess cash in lieu of paying or increasing dividends.

E.4   AVOID HYPING THE PROPOSED ACQUISITION

Corporate executives generally present to investors a rosy picture of their company's financial results (quarterly sales and earnings growth) and its economic condition. Such overly optimistic managerial assessments of past operations are often challenged by analysts in quarterly earnings conference calls and "investors' days" so that investors receive a more balanced operational picture of the company. But in no area are the company's economic prospects more hyped by executives and one-sided than in the public announcements of acquisitions. Such acquisitions are often termed by executives "transformative," the synergies claimed are eye-popping ("accruing from day one"), the expected market share gains are impressive, and, generally, the proposed acquisition is claimed to establish a new dawn for the company. Empirical studies have indeed confirmed that earnings and sales forecasts made on acquisition announcements, along with the synergies promised, are often exaggerated, sometimes wildly so. The reason for all this hype is, of course, to garner shareholder support and vote for the merger.

Buyers' executives should recognize that hyped, unrealistic acquisition promises aren't cost-free. In addition to the (un)ethical issues raised by misleading investors, there is the practical danger of "forecast capture."[6] Once you predict, say, "EPS accretion of 15% by next year" or the "closure of 25 branches in a couple of years," alert investors will verify your forecasts later and raise embarrassing questions when the promises are not met. Accordingly, unrealistic growth or synergy forecasts put adverse pressure on buyers' executives, particularly at the sensitive merger integration phase, to demonstrate the achievement of the promised synergies. And if the forecasts are indeed overly optimistic, then they will not be achieved without seriously harming the integration, and the acquisition along with it.[7] So, to improve the likelihood of the acquisition's success, executives of the merging entities should "curb their enthusiasm" and avoid the announcement of unrealistic merger benefits. There is really nothing to be gained from such hype, which is almost uniform in merger announcements and therefore is heavily discounted by investors anyway. In contrast, announcing realistic acquisition targets, coupled with an assessment of the uncertainty involved in integrating the targets, will considerably enhance executives' reputation as honest, straight-shooters. Not a mean achievement.

---

[6] Occasionally, corporate executives are also sued by harmed investors for predicting misleading benefits of the acquisition.
[7] In Chapter 8, we discussed the failed acquisition of Nextel by Sprint. To demonstrate the promised cost savings, customer service centers were closed or curtailed, just when they were needed most to stem the post-merger customer desertion.

So, we end our book journey, which started with highlighting the M&A failure trap and its seriously adverse consequences on the buying companies and their shareholders' fortunes, with an encapsulation of the multiple lessons and recommendations provided throughout the book, all aimed at improving the acquisitions' likelihood of success. In particular, we propose five major recommendations intended to spring the failure trap:

1. Replace the current pro-acquisition incentives to buyers' executives, irrespective of acquisition success, with incentives conditioned on merger success.
2. Consider corporate acquisition as a last-resort action to improve lagging operations and reshape stagnant business models, rather than the first resort, by seriously considering the array of alternatives to conducting a merger.
3. Seriously assess the failure risks of acquisitions, like following a buying crowd, acquiring a foreign target, or conducting a conglomerate acquisition, which generally harm acquisition success, and reject acquisition proposals when such risk assessment warrants it. Don't succumb to the widespread "urge to merge."
4. Avoid hyping a proposed acquisition in public announcements and, thereby, getting captured by your own over-optimism.
5. Make good and timely use of the acquisition predictive scorecard, which we developed and demonstrated in Chapter 15.

Instituting these five changes to the acquisition process will turn a "failure trap" into a business success.

Appendix: Our Research Methodology

This book is unique among merger and acquisition (M&A) publications (except academic research) by being totally based on evidence and facts. To fully appreciate our book's findings and recommendations, one has to have at least a cursory knowledge of the unique methodologies we used to generate them. In particular, some awareness is recommended regarding our large sample of acquisitions, our comprehensive indicator of acquisition success, and the statistical model we use to identify the various determinants of acquisition success. This appendix provides a brief, painless description of the methodological approach underlying this fact-based book. No special statistical knowledge is required to comprehend this appendix. Please give it a try.

Our approach to the analysis of M&A's attributes and consequences is fully fact-based; that is, it derives from a sample of actual acquisition cases (about 40,000 of them), which extend over the past 40 years, and which is analyzed by advanced statistical models, mainly regression and logit analysis. Occasionally, we also rely on the results of solid, data-driven research done by others. In this appendix, in a nontechnical manner, we briefly discuss the following: (i) our measure of acquisition success, (ii) the sample we use, and (iii) the model designed to identify the factors contributing to acquisition success.

A.1   OUR MEASURE OF ACQUISITION SUCCESS

A major difficulty in drawing useful lessons from the considerable number of existing empirical studies on M&As is the use of different *acquisition success measures* by the various researchers. Some use investors' reaction to the initial acquisition announcement as a success measure (a success is when the stock price of the buyer increases upon the announcement). But as we have seen in Chapter 1, at the time of the initial acquisition announcement investors know next to nothing about the merger details, except for the wildly hyped executives' claims of benefits and synergies, so investors are largely unable to thoroughly assess the acquisition consequences at its announcement date. Other researchers measure acquisition success by the change in the buyer's stock price over two to three, or more, years following the acquisition, as the information about the acquisition success filters out to investors. That's better, yet stock prices over such an extended duration are affected by many factors unrelated to the acquisition. And some researchers measure acquisition success by financial (accounting) measures, like the buyer's sales or earnings growth subsequent to acquisition.

Each of these acquisition success measures has certain merits, so we decided to create a comprehensive success measure that combines the key aspects of merger success. We thus define an acquisition as *successful* if the following three requirements are *all* met:

- *The buyer's sales growth over the three years subsequent to the acquisition year is positive, and/or the three-year change of gross margin (sales minus cost of sales) is positive, relative to the buyer's industry average.* There are acquisitions that are aimed at enhancing a company's sales (revenue), like customer acquisition or buying a company with products on the market, while other acquisitions are aimed at reducing production costs, like acquiring a modern manufacturing facility or an airline with more efficient airplanes. Accordingly, we focus in our success measure on both sales growth and gross margin increase (reflecting the expected decrease in the cost of sales). Note that we require that the buyer's sales or gross margin growth will *exceed* the industry average growth over the examined period. This is quite a demanding requirement, but that's the aim of successful acquisitions.
- *The stock price of the acquiring firm didn't decrease over the three years post the acquisition year.* Most acquisition failures are reflected by sharp decreases in stock prices as investors gradually learn about the failure. The absence of such a price decrease is therefore an indication, from investors' perspective, of the acquisition's success.
- *There was no goodwill write-off during the three post-acquisition years.* A goodwill write-off (impairment), where the value of the acquisition goodwill on the balance sheet is decreased or totally written off as an expense in the income statement (see Chapter 9), is often the first public admission by managers that the acquisition failed. The absence of a goodwill write-off during the three years after the acquisition year is therefore a strong indication, from managers' perspective, that the acquisition was a success.[1]

---

[1] In cases where a company had more than one acquisition in a given year, we apply our success measure to the largest acquisition in that year.

Summarizing, any acquisition in our sample that fulfills the three requirements outlined here is defined as a successful acquisition, whereas all other acquisitions are defined as failures. Over our entire sample period, 1980–2022, the success ratio was 36%, decreasing significantly to 30% in recent years. Thus, according to our measure of acquisition success, 3 in 10 acquisitions succeed, on average. Over all years, the pattern of acquisition success is indicated by Figures 1 and 2 in the Preamble. Our research shows a decline in successful acquisitions over time (with a few brief periods of improvement, like a few years after the 2007–2008 financial crisis), the reasons for which are provided throughout this book.

A.2   OUR SAMPLE AND DATA SOURCES

We obtained our sample of M&A transactions from the Securities Data Company (SDC) Mergers and Acquisitions Database compiled by Thomson Reuters. Our sample includes a subset of all the M&A transactions that were executed during 1980–2022, since we focus on *publicly traded buyers* that had share prices and deal value (acquisition price paid) available in the database. Nonpublic (private) buyers generally have scarce financial information available in the database, and no stock prices, and therefore do not meet the data requirements of our research inquiries. Because the SDC database includes very few transactions prior to 1980, we focus on the period 1980–2022, covering 43 years of data. We placed no restrictions on the geographic location of buyers and targets and therefore include in the sample many cross-border acquisitions, which represent an increasing trend of M&A deals in recent decades (Chapter 3). We have also placed no restrictions on the *acquisition targets*, thereby including in the sample publicly traded targets, private targets, and targets in the form of subsidiaries, and other business entities.

We require each buyer in our sample to have financial data on the Compustat database and stock price data on the Center for Research in Security Prices (CRSP) database in order to derive the financial and stock performance data of the acquirers before and after the transaction. Some private targets had certain financial data (e.g., sales and assets) on the SDC database that we used. We also used the DealStats database provided by the Business Valuation Resources (BVR) to locate the financial data for private targets that are not available in the SDC database. In total, our sample comprises roughly 40,000 M&A transactions, conducted over 43 years (1980–2022).

A.3 OUR STATISTICAL MODEL

Our statistical analysis is mainly based on regression (Logit) models, which are the main workhorse of empirical (data-based) research in the natural and social sciences. In the following section, for the uninitiated, we provide a nontechnical, reader-friendly description of regression analysis, and its structure and uses, so no part of this book will be beyond the grasp of readers. We start with an intuitive description of a regression analysis.

A.3.1 What Affects Our Cholesterol Level?

Suppose that a medical researcher, aware that high levels of "bad cholesterol" (low-density lipoprotein, or LDL) contribute to coronary diseases, wants to find out what factors affect a person's level of cholesterol, a key step in treating sick people. The researcher conjectures (based on prior observations) that cholesterol levels may be affected by a person's age, weight, sex, and parental cholesterol level (heredity). To determine the validity of these conjectures, the researcher uses the medical records of a sample of 10,000 patients who were treated in a large Boston hospital and derives from these records each person's cholesterol level when they were first admitted to the hospital, as well as their age at the time, weight, sex, and whether one of their parents, at least, suffered from a high cholesterol level. This search yields a database of five columns, each having 10,000 numbers and indicators.[2] This database constitutes the raw material and input for the regression analysis. The regression model can be depicted as follows:

$$\boxed{\begin{array}{c}\text{Cholesterol}\\\text{Level}\end{array}} = a \times \boxed{\text{Age}} + b \times \boxed{\text{Weight}} + c \times \boxed{\text{Sex}} + d \times \boxed{\begin{array}{c}\text{Parents'}\\\text{Cholesterol Level}\end{array}}$$

The four factors (boxes) on the right side of the equality sign (called *independent variables*) are assumed to contribute to the variable on the left side (the *dependent variable*), namely, the cholesterol level. The direction (increasing/decreasing cholesterol level), as well as the statistical significance, and the strength of effect of each independent variable (e.g., weight), given the levels of all other variables, will be indicated by the *estimated regression coefficients a, b, c,* and *d*. The regression is then run (estimated) using the dataset of five columns of 10,000 numbers in each, with one of

---

[2]The variable sex is indicated as: female = 1, male = 0.

several statistical software packages available (e.g., SAS). The regression process yields the estimated values of the coefficients *a, b, c, d,* and their significance level (indicating the likelihood that the effect of the variable on the level of cholesterol is different from zero).[3]

Suppose the estimated coefficients of the cholesterol researcher's regression analysis were as follows:

a = 0.63 (statistically significant)

b = 0.20 (statistically significant)

c = 1.10 (statistically significant), and

d = 0.40 (statistically *insignificant*)

The first thing the researcher learns from the coefficient estimates is that coefficients *a, b,* and *c* are statistically significant; namely, the effects of a person's age, weight, and sex on their cholesterol level is real (nonrandom), whereas the impact of the parents' cholesterol level (coefficient *d*) is insignificant, that is, not reliably different from zero. The second inference, derived from the fact that the coefficients *a, b,* and *c* are *positive,* is that the association between age, weight, and sex, on the one hand, and cholesterol level on the other hand, is positive; namely, a higher age, a heavier weight, and being female increase cholesterol levels, on average. By how much do they increase cholesterol level? It depends on the size of the estimated coefficient *times* the mean of the variable over the entire sample.

For example, the estimated coefficient of weight (*b*) is 0.20. If the average weight of the 10,000 individuals included in the study was 150 lb, then the estimated coefficient of weight (0.20) indicates that weight contributes to a person's cholesterol level 30 points (0.20 × 150 = 30), on average. Accordingly, if the average cholesterol level of the people in the study was, say, 200, then 30 points (15%) came from their weight. A person's weight therefore has quite a considerable effect on their cholesterol level. We can even do more than that: we can also measure the contribution of *gaining weight* to a person's cholesterol level. For example, gaining 10 lb would increase the person's cholesterol level by 2 points (0.20 × 10).

So, a regression analysis applied to a large and representative sample of subjects is a very powerful statistical tool for drawing conclusions and recommendations. We therefore used it for our M&A analysis throughout the book.

---

[3]This example of cholesterol level and its determinants is solely for illustrative purposes and is not related to any medical knowledge or actual evidence.

A.3.2   Our M&A Regression Model

Look back at the earlier equation where cholesterol level was set equal to the sum of the variables age, weight, etc., each weighted by their respective regression coefficients. Now replace cholesterol level with our indicator of M&A success presented earlier.[4] Also replace the right-hand variable age with the size of the acquisition target; replace the variable weight with the debt raised for the acquisition; replace sex with whether the target is domestic or foreign; and finally, replace the parents' cholesterol level with whether the merger is conglomerate (unrelated) or not. You now get the following M&A regression model, which is, for demonstration purposes, a highly reduced version of the model we use in this book.

$$\boxed{\text{Acquisition Success}} = a \times \boxed{\text{Target Size}} + b \times \boxed{\text{Debt Raised}} + c \times \boxed{\text{Target Domestic or Foreign}}$$

$$+ \; d \times \boxed{\text{Merger Is Conglomerate or Not}}$$

This model (equation) is similar to the regression model we use in this book, except that rather than the four right-side variables, we have 43 variables representing various factors and attributes that affect acquisition success or failure (see the list of variables, next). And, instead of the hypothetical sample of 10,000 patients in the cholesterol study, we have a sample of roughly 40,000 actual acquisition cases. But the underlying purpose and power of analysis of our M&A regression model is the same as that of the hypothetical cholesterol researcher. That is, we systematically examine the effects of 43 factors on acquisition success. For example, if the coefficient a in the previous equation turns out in our regression estimation process to be negative and statistically significant, it implies that the larger the target size, the lower the success of the acquisition (due, in particular, to a more difficult integration), given the effects of all other variables in the regression. This information is obviously important to managers and directors planning an acquisition and to shareholders asked to vote on the proposed merger.

---

[4]Cholesterol level in the previous example is a *continuous variable*; namely, it can take any positive number (e.g., 185, 200, or 220). In our acquisition model, the left variable is dichotomous: 1 for successful acquisitions and 0 for failed acquisitions. The regression version used for this case is called a *logit analysis*, and that's the one we use for our acquisition model.

Our use of a multivariate (multiple variables) regression model has many advantages. For example, we have recently seen a consultants' report claiming that the correlation between merger success (measured by the buyer's post-acquisition stock returns) and the size of debt raised for the acquisition was negative. On this basis, the report's authors recommended against financing acquisitions with debt. But what if the debt level raised for acquisitions depends, among other things, on the size of the target, which, as we have seen, also detracts from the merger success? So, it may be that it's not the size of the debt raised that reduced merger success but rather the size of the target, which happens to be correlated with debt raised, but apparently was not known to the report's authors. This, in fact, invalidates their recommendation to executives. Some large targets may be paid for in stock (no debt raised), detracting nevertheless from the acquisition success. We, in contrast, include in our regression model *both* the amount of debt raised *and* the size of the target, and the estimated model will indicate which of the two variables (perhaps both) adversely affects the merger success. So, our conclusions and recommendations, based on the *simultaneous consideration* of 43 acquisition success factors, are much more comprehensive and reliable than those of many of the correlation-based merger studies currently available.

A.4 SUMMARY

If you have kept with us so far, and surely all readers did, you will be rewarded by fully understanding the uniqueness of our approach to the study of corporate acquisitions. Like determining statistically the impact of the four factors portrayed in this appendix (target's size, debt raised, target's domestic/foreign origin, and being a conglomerate), we determine in this book the impact of some 40 acquisition factors or attributes on merger success. This is the fact-based foundation of the inferences and recommendations we draw throughout the book. Our regression model also enables us to construct a unique *scorecard of acquisition success* (Chapter 15), allowing executives and investors to *estimate the likelihood of a merger's success*. Like the hypothetical cholesterol researcher in the opening example of this section who guides doctors based on facts, in this book we guide executives, directors, and investors based on the accumulated experience of 40,000 corporate acquisitions conducted throughout the world.

Finally, we provide here the full list of the variables (factors) used in our regression model to determine acquisition success.

The List of Variables (Factors) Included in Our Model for Determining Acquisition Success
(An "indicator variable" means that the variable gets the value of either 0 or 1)

	Variable	Definition and Measurement	Estimated Effect on M&A Success (Positive/Increase, Negative/Decrease)*
(1)	M&A success	An indicator variable for a successful acquisition, defined as an acquisition that achieves (i) above-industry-average sales growth or gross margin growth, (ii) positive stock returns, and (iii) no good-will write-off, all during the three-year period from the year after acquisition	N/A
(2)	Deal size	Logarithm of deal value (acquisition price of target)	Negative**
(3)	Buyer's goodwill growth due to acquisition	An indicator variable for buyers with an increase in goodwill that is more than 5% of the buyer's total assets from the year immediately before acquisition to the end of year of acquisition	Negative**
(4)	Conglomerate acquisition	An indicator variable for conglomerate acquisitions (no industry overlap between the buyer and target)	Negative**
(5)	Buyer's and target's industry relatedness	Percentage of target's industry lines of business shared by the buyer before acquisition (a proxy for the buyer's knowledge about the target's business)	Positive**
(6)	Buyer and target from the same industry	An indicator variable for buyers and targets operating in the same industry (a horizontal merger)	Positive**
(7)	Private target	An indicator variable for the target being a private (not publicly traded) company	Negative**

	Variable	Definition and Measurement	Estimated Effect on M&A Success (Positive/Increase, Negative/Decrease)[*]
(8)	Acquisition means of payment: Percentage of stocks used for acquisition	Percentage of stock in the total payment used for financing an acquisition (from 0 to 100%)	Negative[**]
(9)	Deal pressure/competition, indicator #1	Number of targets with the same 3-digit SIC industry code acquired by the buyer's industry peers during the past 12 months	Negative[**]
(10)	Deal pressure/competition, indicator #2	Logarithm of largest deal value of targets with the same 3-digit SIC code that were acquired by peers during the past 12 months	Negative[**]
(11)	High-tech buyer	An indicator variable for the buyer being a high-tech firm	Negative[**]
(12)	High-tech target	An indicator variable for the target being a high-tech firm	Negative[**]
(13)	Foreign target	An indicator variable for the target being a foreign (non-U.S.) entity	Negative[**]
(14)	Percentage of shares acquired by the buyer	Percentage of target's shares (ownership) acquired by the buyer in current acquisition deal	Positive[**]
(15)	Related deals	An indicator variable for the presence of related deals (e.g., divestitures, competing bids, and defensive transactions)	Positive[**]
(16)	Buyer's restructuring (reorganization)	An indicator variable for an acquisition being part of a buyer's restructuring (reorganization)	Negative[**]
(17)	The pooling method (see Chapter 9)	An indicator variable for an acquisition subject to "pooling of interest" accounting method	Negative
(18)	Advisor financing	An indicator variable for buyers receiving financing from merger advisors	Positive
(19)	Fairness opinion	An indicator variable for buyer's advisors providing fair valuation opinion	Positive

(*Continued*)

(*Continued*)

	Variable	Definition and Measurement	Estimated Effect on M&A Success (Positive/Increase, Negative/Decrease)*
(20)	Other roles of advisors	An indicator variable for buyers' advisors playing other roles in the acquisition (e.g., general advisory, deal manager, or representative of major shareholders)	Negative
(21)	Private equity and hedge fund involvement	An indicator variable for buy-side or sell-side private equity or hedge fund involvement in the acquisition	Negative
(22)	Acquisition during post-recession periods	An indicator variable for acquisitions made during the two-year period following a recession	Positive**
(23)	Voting control	Percentage of buyer's voting control in the target	Positive
(24)	Friendly acquisition	Indicator variable for friendly acquisition (target's board consent)	Negative**
(25)	Prior acquisition history of buyer	Number of acquisitions made by the buyer over the five years before acquisition	Positive**
(26)	Acquisition premium	Acquisition price of target divided by target's recent annual sales	Negative**
(27)	Acquisition by new CEOs	Indicator variable for acquisitions made by buyers' chief executive officers (CEOs) during the first year of their tenure	Negative**
(28)	Acquisition by overconfident CEOs	Indicator variable for acquisitions by overconfident and overly optimistic CEOs, measured by buyers' investment aggressiveness in capital expenditure and research and development	Negative**
(29)	CEOs' managerial ability score	A variable measuring managerial ability, computed by the methodology of Demerjian, Lev, and McVay, "Quantifying managerial ability: A new measure and validity tests," *Management Science*, 2012, 1229–1248	Positive**

	Variable	Definition and Measurement	Estimated Effect on M&A Success (Positive/Increase, Negative/Decrease)*
(30)	Long-term debt growth associated with the acquisition	Percentage change of buyer's long-term debt from the year immediately before acquisition to the year immediately after acquisition	Negative**
(31)	Employee headcount growth	Percentage change of buyer's employee headcount (number) from the year immediately before acquisition to the year immediately after acquisition	Positive**
(32)	Amount of time spent on conducting the acquisition	Time lag between deal announcement date and deal effective date (a proxy for buyer's thoroughness of due diligence)	Positive**
(33)	Long delay in completing acquisition	Indicator variable for buyers spending more than one year to complete the acquisition	Negative**
(34)	Change in buyer's return on assets (ROA) before acquisition	Change in buyer's ROA from three years before acquisition to the year *before* acquisition	Positive**
(35)	Buzzword intensity of buyer's acquisition announcement	Ratio of the number of buzzwords (e.g., *synergy*) included in buyer's statement of acquisition purpose to the total word length of the statement	Negative**
(36)	Target's accounting information availability and transparency	The number of key accounting variables available for the target	Positive**
(37)	Buyer's market-to-book ratio	Buyer's ratio of market value to book value before acquisition	Positive**

(Continued)

(Continued)

Variable	Definition and Measurement	Estimated Effect on M&A Success (Positive/Increase, Negative/Decrease)*
(38) Target's sales growth before acquisition	Target's sales growth rate before acquisition (from three years to one year before acquisition)	Positive**
(39) Deal complexity	The number of words in the synopsis of the acquisition deal	Negative**
(40) Target's intangible assets pre-acquisition	Indicator variable for targets with above-industry-average intangible assets (divided by total assets)	Positive**
(41) Acquisition-related intangible assets	The amount of intangible assets recognized from the acquisition on the buyer's balance sheet (divided by total assets)	Negative**
(42) Investor reaction to acquisition announcement	Three-day cumulative abnormal returns (stock price change) of buyer's stock around the first deal announcement date	Negative**
(43) Stock market conditions prior to acquisition	S&P 500 return (price change) over the 12-month period before acquisition	Negative**

*This column indicates the sign and statistical significance of the regression coefficient estimates. Negative, for example, means that the variable (say, deal size) has a negative (reducing) effect on the acquisition's success.

**Indicates statistical significance at the 0.05 level or higher. The absence of an asterisk means that the effect of this variable on acquisition success is essentially zero.

Index

Page numbers followed by *f* and *t* refer to figures and tables, respectively.